PLACEBOCRACY

AND OTHER AILMENTS

A CLASSICAL LIBERAL TAKE

ON AMERICA TODAY

MARK J. HARTWIG

ISBN: 978-1-59152-260-7

Published by Yucca Ash Press; PO Box 2330, Livingston, MT 59047.

For more information, email Mark Hartwig at hartwig@montana.net;
or mail Yucca Ash Press, PO Box 2330, Livingston, MT 59047.

sweetgrassbooks
an imprint of Farcountry Press

Produced by Sweetgrass Books; PO Box 5630, Helena, MT 59604; (800) 821-3874; www.sweetgrassbooks.com.

Library of Congress Cataloging-in-Publication Data on file.

Produced and printed in the United States of America.

24   23   22   21   20   1   2   3   4

To my father,

who taught me to think

and then, on occasion,

smacked me alongside the head for overdoing it.

Democracy never lasts long.

It soon wastes, exhausts and murders itself.

There never was a Democracy Yet,

that did not commit suicide.

—John Adams

LETTER TO JOHN TAYLOR, DECEMBER 17, 1814

CONTENTS

INTRODUCTION

The United States was founded upon the principles of classical liberalism. These tenets have long been abandoned, mostly because we have forgotten them. And now, we now find ourselves aboard this great ship of democracy, beating through a fog of ignorance through shoals that harbinger its eventual demise. This latter is, by all means, a dramatic statement. Nonetheless, it is true, though not irrevocably so.

America's ailments, much like those of her historical democratic predecessors, originate as a form of internal corruption, not from without. The ultimate fault lies with us, her constituents. And, with those of past decades. Today, many of us point to the election of Donald Trump in 2016, as an indication that the country has come to a turning point, that Trump's election portends the decline of our republic. This misses the reality of what that election actually signals. Trump is neither the cause of our decay or, as some would have it, its cure. Instead, he is a symptom of what has long ailed us, the culmination of our illness, if you will, as are the likes of Bernie Sanders and Alexandria Ocasio-Cortez. Understanding this demands some examination of the core tenets underlying America's foundation, together with their subsequent, progressive erosion.

At its heart, classical liberalism is somewhat akin to libertarianism, though not imbued of the latter's absurd notion that, despite the realpolitik environment of the human condition, there is no meaningful role for government in the affairs of its constituents and global intercourse. Instead, the underlying premise is that individual economic and political liberty interests are natural rights and may not be subjugated by the state. Instead, in the interest of the social contract arrived at by people in establishing a form of governance to their mutual benefit, some of these rights may be ceded to government to manage, with the caveat that they may be taken back, by force of necessary, should such authority abuse the the trust of it constituents. Thus is voluntary acquiescence given to the state for purposes of the common good, such as the implementation of infrastructure, providing for national defense and establishment of such other mechanisms as may be agreed to as being of general public benefit. The common threads among these are that the institutions contemplated by classical liberalism are more readily implemented and managed by an organized, central authority and that they are voluntarily submitted to by the governed.

Conversely, individual self-reliance is not seen as a function to be relinquished. Instead, this is deemed an obligation on the part of constituents. At the time these notions rose to the fore, there was a prevailing sense of responsibility for one's self, family, neighbors and community. Government involvement in such personal matters was simply not contemplated. Proponents also realized that this model of governance, democracy, once instituted, would create immediate tension between the interests of the governed and those of the state. Among these were John Locke, whose philosophical notions formed the pillars of our republic, and John Adams, the only honest intellectual to lead it.

John Adams posited that democracy is both bloody and messy. And while he, together with his founding peers, sought to ameliorate the ever latent dichotomy between state and constituent interests by devising a system of checks and balances, including the separation of powers scheme, the succinct roles of the executive, congressional and judicial branches of government, we now enjoy. Adams recognized the overarching premise that the excesses of state would best be forestalled by an informed and educated populace. He advocated to this end throughout his life. It is of great significance that by education, Adams was not referring to what is taught in schools today. His notion of education, based upon personal experience, was predicated upon learning a vast array of topics and employing that knowledge, together with experience, as the basis for critically analyzing present and foreseeable events and conditions. This was, once upon a time, coined as a classical liberal education. Unfortunately, this approach to education has become obsolete and therein lies the genesis of America's malaise.

The abandonment of critical thinking as an educational mandate has parlayed into a societal incomprehension of the key elements necessary to sustain democracy. Thomas Jefferson once advised his his teenaged nephew, to pursue a regime aimed at learning to think critically by studying history, geography, mathematics, science, philosophy, literature, Latin and at least one additional modern language. Were the boy of a 21st century persuasion, and assuming no dearth of qualified educators, his likely texted response would have been "LOL." Although the entirety of the subject matter proposed his nephew by Jefferson is of import, perhaps the greatest loss to our present academic curricula is the teaching of comprehensive, contextual history.

Instead, history is now presented in a vacuum of context, as a series of random events, connected only by their characterization as crimes perpetrated against the rest of humanity by Europeans. Yet, it is context, not emotional rhetoric, that allows evasion of past foibles and instead fosters an understanding of the circumstances leading to and from specific instances in history. In this light, rather than reviling America's founders and demanding their vestiges be stripped from public notice, we might see ourselves in those times. I would venture that most Americans, other than blacks, if warped back into the contextual surroundings of the 18th century, would have accepted slavery and, indeed, denigrated the likes of John Adams for despising it.

Had John Adams, virulently opposed to slavery, or even Thomas Jefferson who, in spite of his blatantly self-serving practices to the contrary, held principled objections to slavery, sought to abolish slavery in drafting America's founding instruments, in the context of then existent societal mores, the American revolution would simply not taken place. Instead, in crafting those documents, they provided for an organic evolution of the Constitution, assuring it could be amended in concert with societal changes. Had they not done so, the Bill of Rights and all that has subsequently flowed therefrom would never have been possible. This is unique to America. The upshot is that any fool can judge from afar. The truth lies in historical context.

The abandonment of history, as an educational requisite, on grounds that it has been unfair, has offered the rationalization for also discarding any education in civics, the branches of government, their functions, evolution and the rights and obligations of those governed within a democracy or, more specifically, this republic. As a result, we have forgotten that self-sufficiency and responsibility are, in and of themselves, impediments to the encroachments of states. We no longer apply objective reason in the face of emotional political rhetoric. We assail, rather than defend, the equal application of democratic doctrines and no longer keep a weather eye to those human frailties that would debase the continuity of democracy out of self-interest. The direct result of these failings is that America's democracy has become a fiction—a sociopolitical delusion. It has instead devolved into a Placebocracy. And, absent change, this will not be a static condition. We will further decline into some form of techno-totalitarian form of governance.

To understand this, one must accept the reality that, regardless of intentions on the part of politicians, or "pols," government is the natural foe of democracy, just as critical thinking is the inherent enemy of the state. The classical liberals of the past understood this. In essence, it is incumbent upon constituents of democratic regimes to resist government's nascent need for expansion and over-governance. This necessitates a perpetual willingness to question state actions, all the while remaining self-reliant instead of dependent on state largesse.

Unfortunately, where the beneficiaries of democracy forego their obligations, the balance that should be maintained between a democratic government and its constituents is swayed in favor of state encroachments. The hardships of self-sufficiency and education, necessary to keep the state at arm's length, succumb to that most human of conditions—laziness. Ultimately, the threat posed to democracy by the state is realized through a complacent constituency. Conjunctive to this problem, and it is difficult to divine which comes first, are political promises of free cheese.

Elected officials are members of the public who run for office. Some are dynastically endowed, others less so. All hold the requisite objective of garnering more votes than their political opponents. Faced with constituents ever less inclined towards appeals aimed at maintaining the ideals of the democratic republic, candidates, either by taking advantage of this circumstance, or out of commonality with such malaise, have increasingly turned to pledges of bestowing direct economic benefits on their supporters. And so, the devolution begins.

Once elected, pols devise legislation meant to deliver on promises made, always with an eye to re-election, pandering most efficiently to actual supporters and those with a latency for gratitude. This cycle more or less idled along until the 1930s, when Franklin Roosevelt, buttressed by the relatively new income tax and Keynesian notions favoring federal deficit spending and centralized management of the economy, as well as discouraging private sector savings, instituted the New Deal. Touted ideologically as salvation for the little man, the average American enduring the Great Depression, in actuality the scheme endowed the federal government with unprecedented power and centralized control over the US economy. Moreover, it institutionalized the acceptability of economic dependency on the federal government by individuals, agricultural concerns, large corporations and other special interests. Consequentially, under its interpretation of the golden rule—that he who has the gold makes the rules—it also precipitated the ongoing era of "big government" and full-time politicians. The advent of big government gave rise to organized special interest groups and lobbying firms, all clamoring for a piece of the pie, whether in the form of direct subsidies, government contracts, special tax loopholes or captive markets. And, through these influences, career politicians became inexplicably wealthy, shifting government from a laissez faire approach to private sector commerce towards ensuring a level playing field and then, finally, to becoming the arbiter of who would succeed and who would not—predicated, in large part, on the depth of donor pockets and the weight of special interest voting blocs. The only group unprotected from this turn of events was, and remains, the middle class.

It is worth noting that coincidental to the implementation of Keynesian economic principles, commencing with the FDR era, any express mention of "critical thinking" was stricken from the country's lexicon of educational goals. Instead, educational ambitions were redirected towards "making good citizens," to which, of late, has been added the buzz phrase of promoting "excellence in education." The latter is described through multiple euphemistic adages, none of which include critical thinking.

Now, returning to the new economic reality, as a practical matter, when government gives there is an exponentially increasing demand for more. The dictates of political pragmatism, a politic definition of systemic corruption, lead government to sate such demands which, in turn, fuel expansion of the bureaucratic machinery necessary to do so. Presently, it would be safe to surmise, there is not a single branch of government, or subset thereof, remaining untainted by this condition, whether through military spending, granting of foreign aid, the purchase of third-party services or the acquisition of paper clips and toilet paper for government facilities. The net effect of this has been to steer government away from whatever form of efficiency it is capable of, towards the sole, unfettered goal of appeasing demand and ensuring the financial security of elected officials and upper echelon bureaucrats, military and otherwise. Hence, we are now faced with a federal budget, bloated beyond all reasonableness and utterly uninfluenced by any desire for fiscal responsibility or bang for every buck spent.

The ensuant cycle was remarkably predictable. Demands on the State increased. In turn, this precipitated an insatiable appetite to fuel government expansion. To sate these circumstances, federal taxes were increased. Not just on incomes, but on everything that affected American consumers, the bulk of whom were in the middle class. Taxes were imposed on raw materials; manufactured goods; wholesale and retail wares; on all wages at each of these stages; and in form of excise taxes on necessities, such as heating oil, diesel and gas. These "hidden" taxes are, quite naturally, reflected in consumer prices. In addition, Congress authorized increases of the national debt, which now stands in excess of a staggering $22 trillion dollars, and continues to do so, without addressing how this sum will ever be repaid. Government has also discouraged savings, which at present stand at about $400 per person. Federal borrowing was, and is, of course critical to supplementing payment for rising expenditures and the discouragement of savings was meant to stimulate the economy through consumer spending. Middle class incomes did not meet the real rate of inflation created by all of these turns of events. Nor was the economic wherewithal of the class redefined. The class began to shrink and the cycle repeated, as it does to this day, though each iteration carries the the added burden of the freshly economically disenfranchised clamoring for a piece of the action.

Over the course of the last approximately 70 years, each successive cycle has led to a decrease in the federal government's ability to meet the financial demands of its domestic constituents and foreign dependencies. Each such cycle has also culminated in increased centralized control by government and large corporations over the factors of production (land, labor, natural resources or ideas, information and available capital) and a corollary curtailment of individual economic liberty interests.

We arrive now at the present, the institutionalization of the Placebocracy which, as I define it, is the point where government, unable to continue with economic appeasement, devises solutions that appear to solve the problems of its constituents, while actually making things worse. In short, public frustration management has replaced constructive resolutions, and the ailing patient, given false hopes for a cure, will nonetheless die. Realization, albeit on an instinctual level, of the government's inefficacy in prudently managing the economy has crept into the American psyche and the elite, in government and the private sector, have begun to respond. Employing tactics including instilling fear over homeland security, pimping unsettled science regarding the causes of environmental changes and the promotion of racial, ethnic and economic divisiveness, America's leadership has embarked upon a surreptitious path of limiting individual political liberty interests. This, to ensure its control over the populace in the face of a growing inability to manage public frustrations borne of further economic decay. The manifestation of this path is quite evident.

Through the National Security Agency, under the guise of searching out terrorists, the government has accumulated data on all Americans, including every manner of electronic communications. Local police departments have employed, without federal challenge or judicial oversight, the technology (Stingray) to monitor cell phones. The 4th and 14th Amendments to the US Constitution, barring unreasonable searches and guaranteeing the privacy rights of individual Americans, have lost all meaning. The 1st Amendment—ensuring the right to freedom of expression—has also come under assault, though in novel ways. Unthought of even a mere decade ago, pols are actually floating notions of licensing journalists, regulating the dissemination of news through social media, banning targeted news outlets and criminalizing, or subjecting to civil penalties, the dissemination of "false" news. This is beyond frightening.

Certainly of late, media, both mainstream and otherwise, have been guilty of misrepresenting facts and mixing political opinions into representations of fact; however, the mere suggestions that government may put itself in the position of determining what is "fake" news and what is not, should give pause for concern. Augmenting these ideas is the reality that federally funded schools and government agencies have instituted bans against the free voicing of political and other ideas, leaving it to these institutions to define what is an acceptably communicated idea. The differences between these concepts and China's institution of "re-education" camps and creating a social "grading" system, whereby those deemed "subversives," based upon obedience to party doctrine, are denied employment, access to social media and the right to travel, if they fail the "grade," are becoming indistinguishable. Only the methodology differs. China's implementation of these schemes were implemented quickly and arbitrarily, while ours is being devised on an evolutionary basis. Small wonder then, that these recent developments in China have not elicited much protest from American pols, tech firms or large corporate interests. In truth, our elites have abandoned any semblance of ideology, as well as their moral compasses, and are embarked solely on a track to perpetuate the evolved State and preserve themselves, at any cost, save one paid by them. It should be added that the purported differences between political entities in this country are laughable. We are ruled by an elephant's ass; the distinction between Republican and Democrat having become so blurred that an ever growing number of Americans no longer truly believe that a party-line vote will actually make a difference. So we have begun to seek meaningful representation on the fringes of each, which is leading to discord within each of the parties.

The end game strongly suggests a further devolution. Just as our democracy succumbed to the present—a now failing Placebocracy—the latter's demise will, absent a stunning reversal, inevitably cede to the complete emergence of tyranny. This will take the modern form of a techno totalitarian regime which, I believe, may well be realized within our lifetimes.

The specter of this threat will likely not resonate with the present generation or its more recent antecedents. All are comprised of individuals unschooled in contextual history, civics, government, understanding of the Constitution and its relevance, past and present, or political economy. Accordingly, they have no benchmarks within their realm of knowledge against which to measure the sea changes that have and will occur. To those of us of the fading generations, however, the picture is somewhat visible. All of us, regardless of education, have witnessed the transformations of the past several decades and are able, even if only anecdotally, to measure the extent and consequences of these.

The common thread I have found among my generational peers, people I have spoken with at home and around the country, in researching this book, is that their alarms are shrieking and their bullshit detectors are pegged. Most of the people I spoke with are in the economic middle class. Within this group, comprised of Independents, Republicans and Democrats, from all walks of life and deriving their incomes by equally varied means, there appears to be a consensus that we, as a nation, are facing serious problems. There was, however, no such consensus on the question of what these are, in specific terms, except to the extent that almost all felt economically threatened. Nor was there wide agreement with respect to solutions. Some of these people admitted to voting for Trump. Few attested to liking him. And, most agreed that the election of Donald Trump was not tantamount to a mandate.

The common view on Trump appeared to be that he is largely irrelevant, except to himself and his ability, in spite of his apparent discord with the political mainstream, to reap the financial benefits associated with his office, no matter how shortly held. Speculation was raised, for example, how many Trump cohorts or family members have capitalized on short term market reactions generated by "random" Trump tweets on Twitter. In this, I am reminded of Dick Cheney, cheering notions of invading Iraq with the assistance of private contractors, while holding Halliburton shares in a blind trust. Or the Clinton charities soliciting foreign contributions while Madame Secretary "twerked" in office. There does, however, appear to be delight, among a not inconsequential number of people, that the election of Trump sent tremors throughout the mainstream establishment.

The people I spoke with tended to trilateralize fairly evenly with respect to their future political choices if their financial stability continues to erode. Some professed that they would stay home during the next presidential election cycle. Others allowed that they were inclined to give Trump a second chance, if faced with an unpalatable alternative. A final bloc offered the inclination to take leave of the political center for offers of more radical solutions—both on the left and the right. The latter shift did somewhat manifest during the 2018 mid terms. This trilateralization of opinions exemplifies the problem of the middle class as a political force. Although bound by a common threat to its economic well-being, the middle class is incapable of cohesive action because it is constituted of too great a variety of sociocultural subsets. This realization, which in hindsight should have been readily apparent to me, presented problems in crafting this book.

My initial aim was to present the problems facing our country, her ailments, if you will, from a middle class perspective. And, although squarely within the middle class financially, the realization that the middle class is not united in any fashion, save as an economic classification, led further to the understanding that it would be impossible to present a view of America from a uniformly middle class point of view because there is no such thing. As said, the glue that binds the middle class is its delineation as an economic bloc. In this, it moves in unison, seeking political stability when its financial circumstances are secure. This changes, however, in the face of economic uncertainty. In such cases, the class fractures, with each segment seeking solutions on the basis of commonality with others of similar sociocultural backgrounds. Hence, as an example, while an accountant and a carpenter may well unwittingly synchronize their political choices during the good times, they will not necessarily do so when things go to hell in a hand basket. The net result is that a middle class under threat to its economic health will serve to destabilize the country politically. The same dynamic extends in cases where, as now, the middle class shrinks due to the assault of poverty upon its lower earning echelons.

All told, my realization was that, although there are philosophies that encompass the middle class, there is no distinctly middle class philosophy. Absent such unification, attempting to present a view of America from a middle class perspective would be like plotting a course without a starting point or surveying a lot without first establishing a verified corner. It struck me, then, that it would make more sense to examine the problems America faces through the constructs of classical liberalism. In spite of its growing obsolescence, having all but vanished from our lexicon of socioeconomic and political considerations, it nonetheless represents the philosophical roots of our republic. As such, it presents the perfect baseline from which to examine the tree that has grown out of these. Moreover, it is a philosophy I am comfortable and familiar with and have an intimate understanding of, having adopted it some decades ago. At first blush, this notion presented a problem—whether the lens of classical liberalism could be applied to those present conditions its designers were unaware of. During John Adams', Thomas Jefferson's and George Washington's era, for instance, America's economy was agriculturally based, not driven by industry and technology as it is today. Nonetheless, I realized that the underlying tenets of this philosophy are as organically capable of evolutionary application as has proven its progeny, the United States Constitution. This proved relatively easy. however, it did result in a compulsion to craft a new term and devise some new approaches, without forgoing the underlying tenets of classical liberalism I chose to employ. Placebocracy is that term and the analysis of capitalism, as an economic system, presents a somewhat novel perspective, necessitated by the dogmatic terminology devised by Milton Friedman and others during the cold war. Ironically, this approach also allowed me to develop a critical analysis of present middle class conditions from a relatively objective standpoint.

In the foregoing context, the various chapters of this book examine particular ailments of present day America from the following standpoints. First, how that facet of the American condition affects the natural rights of the individual. Secondly, how does it resolve the inherent tensions between individual liberty interests and the interests of the state. Third, to what extent have we, as constituents, caused or exacerbated the problem by abrogating our responsibilities within the framework of democratic principles. And finally, what has been the overall net effect. The final chapter of this book is not directed at our malaise. Instead, it presents an inexhaustive offer of solutions to the problems presented in the chapters preceding it, somewhat akin to skipping a stone over a pond. These are offered, not as conclusive remedies, but as the types of possible responses that might be crafted from a classical liberal perspective. In any event, these are meant to engender discussion, if nothing else.

Each chapter of this book is meant to be somewhat self-contained, yet is designed to present a tile of the mosaic that depicts the full landscape of the problems we face as a country. The subject matter ranges from democracy, politics and economics through media, technology and education. In each instance and to the extent possible, I have striven to provide a contextual background to the issue at hand. Context is of critical importance. Nothing happens in a vacuum. Events are formulated by past and present circumstances. Hence, information, as with other forms of data, is generally meaningless without an objective understanding of the "who, why, what, where, when and how" that give rise to it. Incidentally, these criteria used to be the pillars of journalism. Sadly, this no longer appears to be the case.

Plumbing the depths of contextual understanding also requires the application of critical analysis in order to interpret the impact of the past upon the present. Facts alone are insufficient. Thus, as extrinsic examples, while there is no great challenge in understanding the consequence of American slavery on modern African American culture; the impetus behind Japan's entry into WWII; the events leading to Hitler's empowerment; or similar events of immediate consequence, objectively resolving the broader range of surrounding facts and underlying long term, sociocultural circumstances that triggered these outcomes is a more arduous task. And, it is one that must be undertaken in order to arrive at some understanding of this world we live in. I have endeavored to address that need in this book. The sources I have relied upon are cited within the body of this work. Further, the books written by others, that are not referenced, but which have influenced my thought processes and thereby played a crucial role in the evolution of this work, may be found at its end.

Every book, whether a work of nonfiction or a novel, is certainly imbued with the inherent biases of its author and may almost as surely be further influenced by the cultural mores of its time. Sometimes this is the deliberate intent of the scribe, on other occasions it is mere happenstance. Either way, it is unavoidable. Any writer asserting to the contrary is either naive or has opted for deliberate misdirection. Certainly this book is thusly affected, though not intentionally. The only solution to the dilemma posed by extrinsic influences on the written word is to devour as many books as possible on a single subject. For instance where, as is usual, history is written by the victorious, one would do well to also seek out anti-histories, apply one's accumulated knowledge to the sum and, to the extent possible, divine therefrom some semblance of reality. The same principle applies to the reading of biographies, economics, politics, philosophy, religion and so on. Indeed, it is generally applicable to the realm of all ideas, The net effect of this approach, the epitome of critical thinking, will not result in some epiphanous realization of the truth. There is likely no such animal. It does, however, lend itself to a person's notions landing within the realm of plausibility.

There is one additional, value-added attribute of books. If, as I believe, each of us is the sum of our knowledge and experiences, then it follows that we gain in these by also absorbing the knowledge and experiences of others. There is no better avenue to do this than through books. And so, by reading books, together with that I have accumulated elsewhere, I have mooched and plagiarized the knowledge and experiences of others, synthesized and interpreted these and added them to my own. The result is this book, the foibles in which I take full responsibility for, while ceding full credit for its positive facets to the superior wisdom of others. I hope that you enjoy this examination of the present state of America and that it will serve to broaden the field of debate, not only as to that which ails us, but also in terms of the solutions we must craft. ⁓

There is a cult of ignorance in the United States,
and there always has been.
The strain of anti-intellectualism has been a constant thread
winding its way through our political and cultural life,
nurtured by the false notion that democracy means that
my ignorance is just as good as your knowledge.

—Isaac Asimov

CHAPTER 1

A DEMOCRACY
LEFT UNTENDED . . .

A democracy left untended will mutate into the worst form of tyranny. Attendance to democracy's needs demands, first and foremost, a constituency that understands all of its functions. Absent such ken, there can be no recognition that the rights deemed sacrosanct within a democratic structure is accompanied by a degree of sacrifice that must be made in order to assure the continuity of those rights and the design that is meant to perpetuate them.

In the context of this Republic, we Americans, who are its constituents, have devolved to an extent that can only be described as abject ignorance on subjects relevant to the Constitutional structure of governance and its philosophical basis; the functions of its bodies; the rights and obligations of its citizenry; and, even the most basic understanding of its economic principles. Manifestation of this dilemma has taken countless forms. Germane to the present political clime of increasing polarization, this illiteracy may be partially exemplified by the phenomenon that public dissent—a right embodied in our principles of governance—has veered towards the proposition that opposing views should be squelched legislatively, through social media and even by force. No thought is given to the reality that political changes, such as the remedying of social injustices, are made possible through Constitutionally institutionalized mechanisms. Nor, over the hue and cry that "my rights trump yours," is pause taken to consider that absent those mechanisms, no amendments to the the status quo would be possible within the framework of legality. Of note, and by way of contrast, the mere suggestion of dissent is deemed a crime in a multitude of countries throughout Asia, Africa, Latin America and even parts of Europe.

In lieu of knowledge regarding the American political structure, and its inherent demand for civil discourse as a cornerstone of legislatively recognizing evolving circumstances and social mores, we are left with the distinctly uncivil, emotional rhetoric of the ill-informed. One need only examine the so called "AntiFa," (Anti-Fascist) and "Proud Boys" movements for a sampling of this. Members of both have expressly and publicly committed themselves to violence as a means of silencing anyone who disagrees with their worldview. These threats have been leveled at supporters of various candidates for legitimately exercising their constitutional rights. No such vitriol has targeted totalitarian regimes such as China and Saudi Arabia, or the unconstitutional surveillance excesses of the US National Security Agency (NSA) permitted by Congress and every president, Democrat and Republican, starting with the last Bush to hold that office. AntiFa, in spite of its rhetoric, is actually a pro-fascist movement or, perhaps, it is simply a collective of idiots, none of whom have ever bothered to look up the meaning of "fascism." The Proud Boys suffer no such delusions, at least. They are avowedly fascist. In either event, what is frightening, is that the tone of extremist rhetoric has been taken up by academics and politicians alike. Make no mistake about it, this observation is equally applicable to yet unnamed, emergent extremists, budding terrorists, if you will, on both the left and the right of the political spectrum.

There are of course instances where civil disobedience and even violence are licitly employed as means of protest; however, these must be solely undertaken within constitutional parameters in order to retain legitimacy. Peaceful civil disobedience is an appropriate reaction to the unlawful enforcement of statutes and rules that fall within Constitutional folds, and sensibly should, as is often the case, be accompanied or followed by litigation. Violent protest, or even open revolt, is reserved for those instances where the State has enacted and enforces laws that are Constitutionally infirm and where the processes of law fail to remedy those abuses. Such was the case with the American Revolution, rooted in England's failure to allow parliamentary participation by the colonists, although they were deemed to be British subjects, and an inability by the British parliament and judiciary to reconcile historical and legal precedent with the unique circumstances presented by the British colonies in America. Failing in their considerable and lengthy efforts to seek legal and political redress, the Colonists ultimately relied upon the doctrine of "natural law," invoking the right to relinquish their country of origin and form a new political society. Most significantly, reliance on the British constitution and exhaustion of all legal processes allowed the American Revolution's subsequent characterization as legitimate. As John Adams warned Thomas Jefferson, the fundamental distinction between the American and French Revolutions lay in that the former sprang from legal doctrine, while the latter, supported by Jefferson, took the form of a populist uprising without any basis in law.

History has, of course, proven Adams right. Although the modern French Republic did ultimately rise from the ashes of the French Revolution, initiated in 1789, its populist nature resulted in the slaughter of tens, if not hundreds of thousands and the Republic, as a semblance of modern France, did not arise until 1870. The intervening period was marked by civil upheaval, generally dictatorial governance and wars. Indeed, turmoil also followed establishment of the Third Republic in 1870, and the modern French Republic, also referred to as the Fifth Republic, was not established until 1958 under the leadership of Charles de Gaulle.

Historically, the impetus for violent regime changes, particularly insofar as the garnering of popular support therefore is concerned, has been embedded in socioeconomic injustice. History also evidences, quite unassailably, that success in the immediate utilization of violence as the fundamental means of overthrowing a tyrannical regime is generally short-lived. In essence, the employment of tyranny to overcome tyranny results in a new form of tyranny. The successive system is, more often than not, further oppressive than its predecessor. So too, as the adage goes, do violent revolts tend to eat their young. This reality was most glaringly exemplified by the Russian and Chinese revolutions. Both ended in totalitarian rule and engendered the State's wholesale decimation of its opponents, including erstwhile allies, real and imagined, by the millions.

Converse to the norms associated with revolutionary regime changes, the American Revolution was, and remains, unique. It was, as has been pointed out, predicated upon law. Moreover, its leadership held the institutionalization of a democratic republic as its objective, with the notion in mind, that the excesses of the prior State should not be visited upon the constituents of the newly formed Republic. These ideas did not materialize in a vacuum. Rather, they arose from the seeds of post Renaissance classical liberalism, most particularly, as was espoused by the philosopher John Locke, that specific liberty interests, including the right to self-determination, inure to the individual, not some higher institutional authority. And, in essence, that these rights are loaned to the State for administration, with the right of reversion should the State abuse its powers in so doing. Though loosely fashioning the American Republic on the Roman model, America's revolutionaries, cognizant of its pitfalls, crafted a Constitutional framework of checks and balances designed to avoid these. Woven throughout the fabric of the new republic was a tacit understanding of the individual need for self-sufficiency as a criterion for avoiding governmental intrusion into the affairs of her citizens.

Key to the genesis of the new American Republic was the fact that its revolutionary leaders were classically educated and relatively well armed in their knowledge of history, philosophy, law, sciences, maths and language. And therein lies the contrast to other revolutionaries of the past and, more importantly, the self-styled modern American insurgents of the present.

Americans have simply abrogated all responsibility to be educated in the history and application of the United States Constitution. Elected politicians, law enforcement officials, military personnel and all manner of public servants are sworn to uphold the Constitution. Civilians tout its importance in seeking to invoke their rights over those of others. Tragically, the Constitution, together with its Amendments, has been rendered increasingly fragile by the mere fact that a majority of public servants, nor most Americans, bother to read it, much less understand it. True, there are some who parse it for personal, ulterior purposes. These are akin to an old acquaintance, a former drug smuggler who was caught, became a born again Christian and is now a contractor with a somewhat controversial reputation. In response to his proudly offered proclamation that he studied the Bible on a daily basis, I suggested that he was merely looking for loopholes. He paused, then laughed and allowed that I was probably right, "business being a tricky thing, after all."

Anecdotally, I can attest that over the course of the last decade, I have had a multitude of conversations related to the Constitution and the Bill of Rights and during the course thereof, learned that less than a third of the conversants had read either document. Only a handful were cognizant of its origins. Our schools take great pains to point out the admittedly plentiful historical wrongs that have been perpetrated against minorities and others in this country, but are silent as to the Constitutional implements that have been utilized to provide redress and impose, oftentimes, drastic course changes. Ironically, given today's immigration debacle, the only Americans required to read the US Constitution and offer some evidence of comprehending it are immigrants who become citizens.

Compounding the utter lack of knowledge related to American governance is the growing trend to decry the Constitution as an archaic device contrived by "old white men" to impose injustices upon women, minorities and others; that it should be gotten rid of. Yikes!

Specific assaults on the Constitution have also become increasingly commonplace. Two examples: Politicians, activists, educators, social media providers and even the media have all overtly and expressly sought to dilute the protections of free speech guaranteed under the First Amendment to the Constitution. Each would, if successful, proclaim themselves to be the final arbiter of defining the parameters of permissible speech. Debate would be barred. And, of late, some elected federal legislators have advocated extra-legislative interference with the enforcement of immigration laws by US Immigration and Customs Enforcement (ICE), in spite of the fact that Congress, through Article I of the US Constitution, is charged with formulating the laws ICE is meant to enforce. The chilling thread binding these and other attacks on the rule of law is that violence, as a means of invoking change, has gained acceptability, if not advocacy, from all manner of public figures, from pundits to politicians including, though certainly not limited to commentators from CNN and Newsmax, as well as Maxine Waters and Donald Trump.

And, we have, of course, ongoing institutional efforts to undermine Constitutional protections, exemplified by the shredding of our 4th and 14th Amendment privacy protections by the NSA, FBI and every Podunk police department with access to Stingray or similar technology. Similarly, under the aegis of national security, the omnipotent Patriot Act and its progeny present us with secret judicial proceedings, sans access to evidence or witnesses. All with nary a public whimper, in spite of the Constitutional implications.

Singularly, such onslaughts against the Constitution and the laws within its purview would be, as has been the past case, easily defeated. Even an attack from one quarter or another would be manageable. Continuous attacks on all fronts, mounted from within government and externally, however, present a clear and present danger. Should these efforts prevail it would, in my opinion, signal the demise of the US democratic Republic. Its replacement, call it the Second American Republic, if you will, would be a totalitarian state entirely capable, given the available technologies, of repelling any effort to turn the clock back. The frightening aspect of this would be the likelihood of blind acceptance of such a change by all of those who agreed with the new regime's initial worldview. Subsequent dissent, due to a change in that outlook, would be readily crushed.

The greater tragedy is that the collapse or transformation of America's Republic would likely trigger the erasure of the democratic ideal from the global consciousness. This uniquely western philosophical concept could not re-emerge from the black hole of techno-totalitarianism that is consuming the world exponentially.

The doom and gloom envisioned in the preceding paragraphs is not unimaginable. We have systemically deconstructed educational principles denoted by critical thinking; the development of curriculae that demand a formal knowledge of classical liberal traditions. We no longer teach civics. In sum, we have denuded ourselves of the tools requisite to the application of rational thought in understanding and resolving emerging sociopolitical and economic problems. We have plunged into a form of counter-renaissance devolution, a modern dark age and, as such, are no longer able to plumb the depths of the social contract we live under and develop the scope, both as to rights and obligations, of its egalitarian principles. Unfortunately, the erosion of these principles has become institutionalized. ∾

CHAPTER 2

THE EQUAL PROTECTION CLAUSE ENSURES...

T he Equal Protection Clause ensures the equal right to try, not to succeed. It is one of the most misunderstood and abused protections offered within the US Constitutional scheme. The actual verbiage of the clause is found within Section 1 of the 14th Amendment to the US Constitution and reads as follows:

> *All persons born or naturalized in the United States, and subject to the jurisdiction thereof, are citizens of the United States and of the State wherein they reside. No State shall make or enforce any law which shall abridge the privileges or immunities of citizens of the United States; nor shall any State deprive any person of life, liberty, or property, without due process of law;* **nor deny to any person within its jurisdiction the equal protection of the laws.**

Taken at face value, there being nothing contextually to suggest it should be interpreted otherwise, the Equal Protection Clause sets forth a requirement that every person within the jurisdiction of the United States must be treated equally in the eyes of all laws. In short, it mandates a level playing field. There is not a scintilla of linguistic interpretation suggesting the clause ought to be interpreted in Orwellian terms, that all people are equal, but some people are more equal than others. Yet, this is precisely what has happened. In fact, I would go so far as to say that the clause, as applied, has been translated into the notion that some people have a right to succeed, while others do not. It would also not be untoward to suggest that in the grand scheme of things, inequities among Americans have increased due to a failure to employ the Equal Protection Clause as it should be. That said, it would not do justice to the clause's employment to not first examine its positive consequences.

The purpose of the Clause, adopted in 1866, is to assign recognition, acceptance and implementation of the the notion that "[o]ur Constitution is color blind and neither knows nor tolerates classes among citizens." Although offered in form of a dissent, penned by Justice John Marshall Harlan in <u>Plessy v. Ferguson</u>, a US Supreme Court decision rendered in 1896 that upheld Louisiana's law requiring the segregation of blacks and whites traveling on trains, this interpretation of the Clause ultimately prevailed— albeit through a slow and arduous process. And, indeed, there is more ground to gain, and there will continue to be, as social mores evolve. This is the oft misunderstood aspect of the Equal Protection Clause and the Constitution in general; that the fluidity of social evolution does not require its re-writing, rather, the passage of time merely awaits its application to freshly emerged questions—usually in the wake of considerable societal pressure and flurries of civil rights litigation. Thus, for example, while same sex marriages were not expressly contemplated by the drafters of the Equal Protection Clause, its language allows, or even mandates, its applicability to future, distinguishable groups of people. This was exemplified by the US Supreme Court's 2015 determination in <u>Obergefell v. Hodges</u>, that same sex couples are constitutionally guaranteed the right to marriage. Over time, judicial interpretation of the Equal Protection Clause has institutionalized desegregation; the equal rights of people of all races, colors and nationalities; women's rights and, same sex marriages, as well as other individual liberty interests.

Absent the clause and its constitutional underpinnings, social up-heaval aimed at implementing the rights of existent and emergent minorities, or distinguishable groups, could licitly be ignored or, as is more common in other regions of the world, suppressed through state sanctioned violence. The plights of the Rohingya in Myanmar, women in Saudi Arabia, and Tibetans and Uighurs in China are mere instances in a global sea of oppressive reactionaryism meted out to "distinguish-able" groups of people.

Not content with the "color blind" ambition of the Equal Protection Clause, however, judicial interpretation and institutional implementa-tion of the clause have overstepped the imperative to establish a level playing field by stacking the deck. Post the US Supreme Court's decision in <u>Brown v. Board of Education</u>, rendered in 1954, which eventually culminated in the abolition of school segregation, the Court went on to mandate busing students, oftentimes dozens of miles between their homes and outlying school districts. The objective was to ensure an adequate mixture of black and white students within schools. The program was universally unpopular, in part because little thought had been given to the impact on students forced to spend hours on school buses. Although the Court eventually backed down from this position, the stage was set for affirmative action. The US Supreme Court deci-sions allowing the busing mandate and subsequently diluting its implementation were <u>Swann v. Charlotte-Mecklenburg Board of Education</u>, decided in 1971, and <u>Milliken v. Bradley</u>, a decision rendered in 1974. The subsequent advent of Affirmative Action" engendered a shift towards abject and overt reverse discrimination. In essence, affirmative action espoused the altruistic theory that the realization of equality necessitated no more than awarding persons of color and other minorities a leg up as a means of rectifying the injustices perpe-trated against them in the past. In practice, both in government and federally funded institutions, such as universities, people of a specifically designated group were, and continue to be, given preferential treatment over those not deemed part of the group. This translated into advantages in university admissions, employment opportunities, granting of contracts and other benefits based upon race, gender or other attributes. In some instances, quota systems were instituted, all with little consideration for other factors such as merit or qualifications.

Although the US Supreme Court softened the blow of these practices in several decisions, for instance, barring a system of strict racial quotas in publicly funded universities, workarounds have been devised. Ultimately, these approaches have failed in their promise of delivering any meaningful semblance of equality. Instead, the policies of affirmative action and similar programs have added to the increasing polarization of American society. Moreover, they are demeaning to the very groups they purport to help; the underling assumption being that minorities, whether racial, ethnic or gender based, are simply incapable of prevailing in a landscape where the playing field is level—where there is an equal right to try. And, while much has been undertaken to offer success to those who might avail themselves of programs designed to guarantee some modicum of success, nothing of significance has been accomplished in leveling that playing field.

The greatest impediment to creating an equal opportunity, is the failure to provide young people with a solid K–12 grade school education. Although this is a general truism, it is more succinctly applicable to impoverished areas, regardless of race or ethnicity, though the effect on African Americans and American Hispanics is significantly higher than on other groups because they are more greatly affected by poverty. Moreover, there is a direct and unassailable correlation between poverty and the lack of education. According to the US Census Bureau, in 2016, some 40.6 million Americans were deemed to be living in poverty. Of these, 22.6 million were aged twenty-six and older, 24.8 percent had no high school diploma. Another 13.3 percent had finished high school, but not attended college; 9.4 percent attended college, but did not finish; and 4.5 percent completed college. In general, 9 percent of those living in poverty were white; 22 percent black; 2 percent Asian; and 19 percent were Hispanic. Bear in mind, that poverty, as defined for purposes of the federal government's statistics, means a family of six living on $32,928 per year, ranging down to a single person living on $12,228 per year. Not included are those who live on more money than is defined as poverty level, but is considerably less than is required to cover the cost of living. A family of four, deemed to be living at poverty levels, is assumed to be living on no more than $24,563 a year. Yet, according to the Economic Policy Institute and others, the present average cost to pay for the needs of a family of four is at least $60,000 per annum. It would appear then, that if poverty were to be defined in terms of the present economic realities, the number of Americans living in poverty, or at near poverty levels, would be even more devastating.

The nexus between poverty and a dearth of education of any kind, never mind one of qualitative attributes, is fairly indicative of the circumstance that those who are not properly afforded an education, regardless of race or other distinguishing factors, are a distinguishable group meriting recognition under the Equal Protection Clause. These people are denied access to the level playing field contemplated by the concept of equal protection. They do not have the equal right to try because they are bereft of the tools necessary to do so. This is not happenstance. It is the result of an institutionalized inequitable distribution of educational resources, including funding and curriculae. The US Supreme Court buttressed this conclusion in San Antonio School District v. Rodriguez, ruling in this 1973 decision that the Equal Protection Clause does not require equitable funding of students within a State's public school system. The Court determined that education is not a constitutionally protected right. The Plaintiffs in that case had sought a finding that, as a result of wealth discrimination in funding various school districts, a suspect or distinguishable group requiring protection was formed of the impoverished. The argument that should have prevailed is that while there may be no constitutional right to an education, where the State offers an education, funds it, and mandates attendance at schools, there is a requirement, through the Equal Protection Clause, that this be done equally for all students; that each student must enjoy the same quality of education and funding therefor as any other. Those who do not receive the benefit of equitable distribution of educational resources are, in and of themselves, the distinguishable class. This argument gains further weight in that most public school systems, directly or indirectly, receive the benefit of federal funding. It follows then, that even if the Courts are reluctant to apply the Equal Protection Clause where it is most needed, by minimizing poverty through education, Congress has the power and means to do so.

Now, while it is true that Congress and the Executive Branch of government have paid some lip service to the problem, these have given us inanities such as "No Child Left Behind," a funding initiative that allows lowering of the bar every time correlative public school test scores do not meet the established standards of education, thereby allowing continued federal funding. And, we have lunch programs that offer students meals that nobody wants to eat. The evidence that these and similar programs do not work lies in the statistics gathered by the federal government. These continue to show that the link between poverty and a lack of education is consistent and, further, that the rate of impoverishment is growing. Again, mention must be made of the fact that there has been a failure to update the definition of poverty, which should encompass those of the middle class who are sliding into poverty. This begs the question of why, particularly in light of the premise that the Equal Protection Clause is to create an equality of opportunity, does the problem remain unresolved. The reality is that there is far more to be gained by the establishment in perpetuating the problem and capitalizing on it.

Hell, let's face it, poverty is an industry. The economic underclass has become a matter of design, rather than coincidence or bad luck. Every dollar appropriated for the poor is a catalyst for two outcomes. The first, that it expands, almost exponentially, the bureaucrats charged with administrating social welfare programs and secondly, that it creates a bloc of voters, grateful to whichever political entity devises new means of subsidization. Politically, this has also translated into deliberately carving out segments of the impoverished and uneducated groups, along racial and ethnic lines, and managing the frustrations of these blocs by kindling racial and ethnic tensions in order to garner political support and divert attention away from the underlying problem. Hence, blacks blame Hispanics and Asians for their plight, while Hispanics and Asian blame each other and blacks, while everyone blames whites.

The fact of the matter, I would argue, is that there is no political desire to educate people and thereby reduce poverty. To do so would liberate politically useful groups of Americans, mostly minorities, presently held captive by their circumstances. Were this to happen, it would become more difficult to manage their political choices. This system is beyond racist. It is dehumanizing to an utterly despicable extent.

Utilizing the concepts contemplated by the Equal Protection Clause as they presently are, to foment hatred and promote the disparaging of various groups by others is a short visioned gambit. Were the Clause to be applied in a manner designed to meet the challenges of creating equal opportunities for people to try, by providing the educational tools necessary to do so, some reasonable semblance of a "color blind" society might, with time, be achievable. From a rational perspective, the cost of equally educating all people, would seem to be far less than providing an ever expanding social safety net that leaves so many without hope for an attainable future. In 2015, the average annual per person cost for welfare benefits was about $18,000 (The Federal Safety Net), while expenditure on education, per student during the same year, was about $12,000 (US Department of Education). As an aside, given that poverty and lack of education are widely accepted causes for crime, it is worth noting that during the same year, the average cost of incarcerating a prisoner in federal prison for a year was about $32,000 (US Bureau of Prisons). These numbers suggest a wide margin for improvement in education.

Finally, the notion that the present atmosphere of discord can be managed over the long term is absurd. Public frustration management will succumb to outright chaos when people realize that a diet of placebos is simply inadequate to meet their needs. ᴄ᷒

CHAPTER 3

PLACEBOCRACY IS
DEMOCRACY'S BASTARD . . .

Placebocracy is democracy's bastard stepchild. It is the system our Republic has evolved into and it is failing. To iterate, in additional terms, the definition of Placebocracy offered in the Introduction to this book, it is the political state arrived at when Democracies, no longer able to meet the demands of their constituents, most often economic, contrive ineffective solutions that are held out to resolve the issues, while actually making them worse. Simultaneously, public attention is diverted from serious matters through the creation of straw men meant to redirect public angst or assuage its largely irrelevant, minor demands. Less democratic regimes employ similar tactics, but these are generally laughable in their transparency, though those laughing aloud are dealt with summarily and harshly.

Public frustration management is one of two primary tools of Placebocracies. The dilution of civil liberties, though more nuanced in democratic regimes, is the other.

In the context our present system, this American Placebocracy, the issue of its evolvement demands some examination. At heart, the greatest enemy of any democracy is its constituency. The nature of a democratic regime is such that a balance must be struck, and maintained, between the liberty interests of its constituents and intrusion into those interests by the state. The dictates of common sense and history ordain that when private sector demands are made of government, the state's acquiescence will result in its imposition of responsive conditions. On the most basic level, for instance, a public demand for national security results in the establishment of a military, the costs of which are then taxed to the population. If there is a dearth of volunteers willing to serve in the military, a draft is imposed. And, of equal significance, the state assumes responsibility for defining what constitutes a threat to national security. While this last bit may become problematic, as discussed elsewhere in this book, the general principle underscored by this example is sound. People, quite justifiably, want to go about their business without fear of invasion. Mechanically, similar principles can be extrapolated from public requests for the creation and maintenance of national, or even local, infrastructures— highways, and the like. So far, so good. But, what happens when the population, or a segment thereof, seeks continuous governmental support for additional purposes, culminating in assurances of economic well being for individuals, corporations and all that lies between. Therein lies the rub.

Foiling government's tendencies to foray into the private affairs of citizens requires a physical and philosophical commitment to self-reliance. Such an undertaking requires knowledge of the relationship between states and their constituents, most glaringly because it is an inherent human characteristic to opt for paths of least resistance. The acquisition of this understanding suggests the need for education. This begets the emergence of two conflicts. The first, between education and laziness, and the second between the arduous task of self-sufficiency and laziness. Compounding this is the latent disposition of governments to divert educational regimes from the tenets of critical thinking towards practices that promote relative docility and satiation of predicted demands in the labor market. Critical thinkers are imminently less manageable than constituents who are educationally trained and prepared for specific fields of endeavor. Hence, in place of critical thinking, as of the middle of the last century, we have the statutory expression that the purpose of education is to produce "good citizens." From the State's perspective, quite naturally, this means people ill-inclined to question its practices. This is not a matter of some conspiracy. Instead, as much as people are inclined to forego self sufficiency in favor of reliance upon the state, government's natural inclination is towards expansion of the industry that it is and to entrench the co-dependency of its constituents.

In political terms, the base reality today is such that any politician running on a platform suggesting state growth should be held in abeyance through a renaissance of voter economic independence has not a scintilla of a chance at winning. Rand Paul, though not my favorite pol, was right in espousing the general view expressed in the preceding paragraphs, but failed to make a showing in the 2016 presidential race. Conversely, promises to voters of direct economic benefit of one kind or another tend to carry the day. Recognition of the electoral benefits of campaigning on a "free cheese" platform, by virtue of the fact that this actually works, leads to competition among pols to devise an ever growing array of constituent benefits. These then become classified institutionally and in the psyche of voters as entitlements. This cycle started in earnest with Franklin Roosevelt's New Deal, which was financed from the outset by the relatively recently institutionalized income tax and the embracement of those never ending gifts from John Maynard Keynes—the philosophy embodying a centrally controlled economy, deficit spending, unrestrained borrowing by government and the accumulation of national debt on the grandest of scales. In spite of some brief interludes during which the notion of a balanced budget bloomed amongst pols, this is still the prevailing model.

The unavoidable by-product of feeding at the state trough is the promulgation of statutes and regulations designed first to funnel as much money as possible into state coffers in order to meet a portion of the costs associated with entitlement programs and, ultimately, to assert increasing control over the daily lives of the populace. Again, there is no conspiracy attached to these developments. Instead, this is the natural course of events where an entity that is not inherently endowed with funds is required to provide money to someone it has promised to pay. It must develop the means of obtaining that money from some other bodies that have it. And, in assuming a patriarchal role by giving into the demands of a specific group, it assumes the right to regulate aspects of that group's liberty interests—much as parents do for their children. Where that entity is the state, it simply exercises legislative power to take what it needs, redistribute what it has taken and construct the criteria by which it does so. As the the demand for government largesse increases, the supply to meet that demand decreases, and in its efforts to resolve this dilemma, government further empowers itself—and, it grows. By virtue of that process, the state also must be said to be curtailing the economic liberty interests of those it takes from because it does so by force through taxation of incomes. It further impacts the economic liberty interests of the entire population by taxing, often on multiple levels, all necessities: housing, transportation, food, health care, utilities and fuel among them. As an example, according to the US Energy Information Administration, on January 1, 2018, the average State and Federal tax on a gallon of regular gasoline at the pump is $0.4651 cents. This does not include taxes on production costs, including labor, refinement, transportation and retailing of that gallon of gasoline.

This system might be deemed to function at its genesis, where the state takes from Peter and Mary to pay Paul. However, the system begins to fail when Mary runs out of money and now Peter is required to support Paul and Mary. This brings us to the present.

At first blush, one might assume that Paul and Mary are are metaphorical references to individuals on some form of public assistance. To some extent this is true. As discussed in the preceding chapter, poverty has become institutionalized in this country. Nor has there been any meaningful effort to address poverty. It is representative of a useful class of people who have been trained to vote for political promises —none of which has served to re-instill their dignity by promoting self-sufficiency. Moreover, the number of people encompassed by this economic class is growing in direct proportion to the increasing numbers of people in the middle class who can no longer make ends meet. However, this is not the entire picture. The normalization of reliance upon government largesse for financial success has permeated every aspect of the national economy. Democrats and Republicans alike, in spite of public rhetoric, particularly by Democrats, to the contrary, pandering to corporate constituents in return for campaign contributions, future positions and every other imaginable form of patronage, has led to utterly unjustifiable subsidization of the corporate sector. This has taken a multitude of forms including, though certainly not limited to, direct subsidies; loan guarantees; product acquisition; grants; specifically targeted tax credits; direct tax relief; regulatory protection; the creation of captive markets; and narrowly tailored bid specifications. By way of examples, the US Department of Agriculture reports agricultural subsidies totaled about $24 billion dollars in 2017 and are expected to rise to some $35 billion dollars by 2019. In the meantime, some 1.31 billion pounds of excess cheese and 2.5 billion surplus pounds of various meats, are stored in order to maintain price stability —all at a time when the costs for both have never been higher for the American consumer. And we have Elon Musk, whose companies, according to the *Los Angeles Times,* had received some $4.9 billion dollars in federal and state support by 2015. Some estimates put corporate subsidization at as much as $100 billion dollars per annum, but none of these include government bids that are specifically tailored to allow only one or a few companies to compete for these. I would suggest that these add an additional $200 or $300 billion dollars to the annual cost of political favoritism. Jeff Bezo, owner of the Washington Post, former watchdog over the excesses of government, through Amazon alone, for instance, was recently awarded a $600 million dollar contract with the CIA and is first in line to win a data management contract with the US Department of Defense, valued at some $10 billion.

The trade-offs between government officials, elected and otherwise, and large corporations have permeated every aspect of the public sector economy. Efficiency in the management of our state ship has succumbed to cronyism—a system designed to assure the political survival and economic well-being of public officials, at the expense of corporate welfare. Of note, the corporate sector, in this context, does not include middle class owned small businesses. These are politically irrelevant and therefore are not invited to the feast among vultures.

Returning to metaphors, then, it should be offered that Peter is the middle class. Peter foots the bill. According to the Internal Revenue Service and the St. Louis Federal Reserve, 33 percent of federal tax revenues are generated from individuals earning between $34,000 and $99,000 per year. An additional 25 percent of all tax revenues come from individual yearly earnings ranging from $100,000 to $199,000. Federal tax receipts from individuals total some 47 percent of all taxes taken in. Payroll taxes, half of which are paid by employees, total about 34 percent of all tax revenues. The half payable by employees is largely attributable to those who are earning below $100,000 per year. The self employed pay all of their employment taxes, regardless of income brackets. Three percent of federal taxes are derived from excise taxes, most of which are paid by consumers in the middle class. In fact, in 2014, the US Treasury Department reported that a then scheduled increase in middle class taxes would result in a loss of some $200 billion dollars in consumer spending the following year. Corporations contribute about 9 percent of federal tax revenues. Of note, individuals earning more than $200,000 per year account for just over 42 percent of all tax revenues, but are also able to avail themselves of tax loopholes not generally available to lower income earners. Hence, while their tax rates on adjusted gross income are generally higher, they are offered more latitude in calculating that threshold of income. In addition, the retail prices of consumer goods incorporate the cost of taxes on raw materials; manufactured goods; and wholesale and retail wares, including the payroll taxes levied at each of these stages. Contextually applied, the greater burden of bearing the cost of government spending, at least that portion not borrowed, lies on the shoulders of the middle class. The concern arises that its ability to sustain that burden is now in serious jeopardy. In 2016, the number of people earning less than the annual $60,000 required to pay for necessities rose to over 50 percent of the country's population (Pew Research/ US Census Bureau/Economic Policy Institute).

This simply means that, given the real rate of inflation, less middle class members are able to cover their basic survival costs. It also points to a desperate need to re-define poverty and the parameters of the middle class, particularly its lower strata. Yet this has not happened. To accommodate this need would be tantamount to admitting that the system of taxation and spending is failing. Instead, Congress and the executive have paid lip service to middle class erosion by passing, for example, tax legislation that is touted to be aimed at resolving the issue, but simply does nothing to ameliorate the problem. The middle class, however, is ever and increasingly aware that its financial stability is eroding at an increasing pace. This recognition, as pointed out previously, has led to support for outre political candidates, ranging from Trump and Clinton to Sanders and, most recently, to Ocasio-Cortez, and their ideas, which run the gamut from tax reform to more jobs in the private sector, to free universities and federal jobs for all, then culminating in the abolition of "capitalism." Not a single one of these people is offering actual solutions aimed at resolving the economic crisis we are facing. They are baiting their respective hooks for votes. This is meeting with some success because people are beginning to get desperate, most certainly those who have begun to rapidly lose financial traction. Unfortunately, each of these pols, along with their compatriots, are also attempting to carve supporters out of the most afflicted groups of people by separating them on the basis of race, nationality, ethnicity and the like, while denigrating others of other groups.

The bait, blame and hate game has become the new norm of American politics. It is a device borne of a desire for political power and to divert attention from two harsh realities: the first, that none of the promises being made will be substantively realized and the second, that things will get worse. It is a game that heralds the decline of our Placebocracy because the ability of the federal government to manage the frustrations of its constituents has abated. It is irrelevant who wins the next political rounds. Arguably, Trump and his Congress have somewhat addressed the issues by raising employment rates through corporate tax relief; however, nationwide, incomes relative to inflation remain inadequate, savings rates are abysmal and we are seeing a heady increase in people running into financial trouble. Bankruptcy filings amongst the elderly, for instance, have increased at alarming rates.

Amazingly, the political establishment is mute as to the national debt, which has grown to about $23 trillion dollars. This translates into well over $62,000 for every man, woman and child counted by the US Census Bureau. To the contrary each, in their own way, continue to promise ever increasing deep government pockets for their respective supporters. The result is an unintentional war on what remains of the middle class. This, because in order to sustain the promises made, the individual economic liberty interests of the class will, of necessity be further curtailed. Until Peter becomes financially incapable of shouldering the burden and joins Mary and Paul. Then, the pols will make efforts to replace Peter with large corporations and the so called one percenters. This will fail, because the latter may simply vanish and the former, driven by profit seeking, will shrink in their activities or relocate which, in turn, will have adverse consequences for employment and inflation. We will see an increase in civil unrest and managed tensions between various groups will become unmanageable. The outcome can only be a detriment to individual political liberty interests because, when all is said and done, and placebos become ineffective, the State will act to ensure its own continued existence.

There are most assuredly other samples, mostly diversionary, of public frustration management that satisfy the earmarks of Placebocracy. Perhaps the most noteworthy is the legalization of marijuana in a growing number of states, Oregon, Colorado and California among them. Marijuana is still illegal under federal law. The feds have opted not to overtly enforce the law, but have quietly continued to selectively exercise federal forfeiture laws, whereby without any requisite for a criminal conviction, the government is able to seize and sell assets purportedly paid for with illegal activities. The proceeds are retained by the government. Where the federal government has abstained from otherwise engaging in the marijuana issue, the states legalizing it have not established any regulatory standards over the industry, presumably wary of trespassing into the bailiwick of the Federal Drug Administration (FDA), which, if it were federally legal, would have jurisdiction over the regulation of marijuana production and distribution. As a result, pot plants have been genetically engineered by growers to boost levels of tetrahydrocannabinol, or THC, which is the major psychoactive attribute of marijuana, found in plants to inordinate levels, in some cases surpassing 60 percent. In the interim, THC has proven to be highly addictive and presents users with psychological risks never imagined by those who indulged in smoking weed during the 1960s. Nor are there any restraints on growers regarding the use of pesticides or any other agents to raise productivity. For states, legalization has provided a mechanism to both distract their constituents without any capital expenditures and simultaneously has introduced a new taxable revenue stream. Federally, we can expect the legalization of marijuana to come to the fore in the context of a national debate at a politically opportune time; when our pols advance the question to escape public scrutiny of other issues portending greater negative consequences.

At heart, Placebocracy is an intermediate stage of a failing system. It is also a natural consequence of the relationship dynamic between states and their constituents that evolves in a democracy. This process morphs individual self sufficiency into an unhealthy codependency between government and its populace. And, economic considerations then fall sway to appeasement politics. The irony in this is that the very economic principles that are necessary to sustain a democracy are thus voluntarily discarded. ✑

CHAPTER 4

CAPITALISM IS THE ONLY
ECONOMIC SYSTEM . . .

C apitalism is the only economic system that can be said to exist. In today's parlance, much the result of the Cold War, capitalism is deemed the antithesis of socialism. The two systems are popularly distinguished by the notion that capitalism embodies private sector control over economic activity, while socialism entails public, or governmental, dominion over the economy. Advocates of these diametrically opposed ideas proclaim the other to be systemically contrary to the well being of humanity as a whole. The collapse of the Soviet Union has been heralded as the triumph of capitalism. As we march through the second decade of the 21st century, as an economic model, capitalism is both touted as the cat's meow and reviled as the root of all evils—largely dependent upon the financial perspective of the commentators, or of politicians, whose votes they are courting. Throughout the related public debate, of late, the terms capitalism and "free markets" or "market capitalism" have all become interchangeable. The problem is that all of this is abject nonsense and serves to negate the very real need to understand the nuanced distinctions between economic systems, particularly economies of scale.

First, a universal definition of capitalism: "Capitalism" is the process by which one or more of the factors of production are employed to generate capital. The factors of production are, in modern terms, land, natural resources or ideas, labor, information and available capital. And, while all money is capital, not all capital is money. It can also take the form of goods, used as barter or for consumption. This is, without exception, the sole mechanical structure of all economies.

Now to the crux of the matter. And, as Trump might say, though you can be sure he will not, it is a "beautiful" thing in its simplicity. The means of distinguishing between economic structures, is to divine the degree of centralized control by any person or entity, public or private, over one or more of the factors of production. Obviously, the plural forms of person and entity are applicable here.

There are, in essence, two extremes of capitalism and a panapoly of variants that lie between the two. The extremes serve as idealistic models. Neither has been, nor ever will be, realized. The two propositions bear some striking similarities, but diverge in methodology. Both suggest an ideal circumstance depicted by an absolute lack of centralized control over any of the factors of production. The first, espoused by Karl Marx in "Das Kapital," a work of some gazillion words, later condensed for dummies in the "Communist Manifesto," boils down to this: The ideal state is one which embodies a classless society, without government, where production and distribution of goods is based upon the principle of "From each according to his ability, to each according to his needs." The penultimate requirement for attaining the communist Utopian ideal entailed manifestation of a socialist, totalitarian regime, with absolute centralized control over all of the factors of production, through which humankind would remodel the world according to its nature. The Marxist model, where implemented, most notably the Soviet Union, has never survived the totalitarian phase. Instead, the achievement of absolute centralized control over the factors of production, save for black market activity, which tends to burgeon in order to meet supply for the demand of items otherwise unattainable, leads to collapse.

The contrarian ideal, pure "Free Market Capitalism," was most succinctly described by Adam Smith in *Wealth of Nations,* another somewhat unwieldy tome. That wily Scot proposed greed as the primary motivation for all economic endeavors. Flowing from this, the notion that left to their own devices and absent state interference, people will pursue individualized control over their labor and as much of the remaining factors of production as possible, thereby diffusing control over the factors of production. An imbalance in centralized control is certainly likely under this model. However, it would remain relatively fleeting; the idea being that when an entity becomes too large, it becomes inefficient and succumbs to its leaner, more recent competitors.

Unlike its Marxist rival, pure market theory does not anticipate nor want the elimination of government. It simply seeks a circumstance whereby the state maintains a level economic playing field for its constituents through its restraint in interfering in the market place or asserting control over the factors of production, save to the limited extent necessary for national security and the like. Hong Kong, during its governance by England, might be deemed a near example of a free market system. However, this is misleading in that the British taxpayers heartily subsidized this jewel of the crown, and its government wielded considerable power over the economy and its participants. It is safe to assume that a pure free market economy of scale has never been realized.

The inherent flaws in both Marxist and pure market ideology are matters of human nature and the nature of governments. The communist ideology is dependent upon the evolvement, under a socialist regime, of a collective esprit de corps that would require the utter abatement of the present human condition, including propensities for greed, laziness and dishonesty. Equally naive is the notion that a centralized state economy would ever be ceded to the masses at the expense of the state's perpetuation. As we now know, for instance, the Soviet state never even made the pretense of adhering to its purported

Marxist ideology; rather, upon seizing power, the Bolsheviks entrenched the Soviet Union in political and economic totalitarianism until its ultimate implosion, followed by a brief stint of quasi anarchy, after which it emerged as a collection of states largely ruled by authoritarian oligarchs. Economic communalism has, of course, occurred in the context of ancient tribal groups and small scale communal enterprises, peopled by like-minded folks with a common purpose and the collective power to weed out any unsavory characters or uncooperative participants and exile these into a different reality.

The foibles of pure market theory are threefold. First, of lesser concern though significant, is that all people are not driven by greed. Were this the case, we would have no musicians, poets, artists or others who opt for a calling unlikely to generate wealth. The second is the unspoken assumption that successful enterprises prefer continued competition. They do not. They seek profits at any cost in order to placate their investors. Hence, once they become inefficient, due to size, they will seek to develop political power in order to influence decision makers in undertaking to eliminate any emerging, more efficient, competitors. And finally, lies the altruistic concept that states can be compelled or convinced to curtail their involvement in the economic activities of their constituents, even if this can be shown to be in the state's best interests. This is an impossibility; it belies the very nature of states.

States are subject to a number of fluid conditions that reshape their characteristics and lead to their inexorable growth. Conjunctively, it must be held that no State will voluntarily cede power, once amassed. There are four truisms that most profoundly influence the evolution, or devolution, if you will, of States.

First is the tension that arises within the State between its moral and amoral attributes. The values of government are imposed by its political leadership which, in turn, are forged by personal ambition and political pressures from constituents. The morality or immorality of these values is a matter of perspectives based upon whose political choices gain power. The effect of value based policies on governance, however, are always dampened by the degree to which prior, conflicting policies are entrenched within the bureaucracies charged with their implementation. It is in the hands of bureaucrats, tasked with devising the mechanics of their execution, that the moral imperatives of political creatures become the amoral attributes of States.

The second defining aspect of States lie in their bureaucracies. They are tumorous by nature, sprouting from the corpus of State in exponential proportion to the demands made upon them to implement an ever increasing array of policies. Simply put, in addition to serving the needs of their hosts, bureaucracies are organic; expanding for no other reason than self-perpetuation, in response to increasing inefficiency. They deplete State resources, while producing less than the cost of maintaining themselves. Though necessary to the functions of government, bureaucracies negate any opportunity for States to establish and maintain a status quo once an optimal level of government, necessary to meet its obligations, has been realized.

Next, States are defined to a considerable extent by external political and economic factors. For the US in particular, this translates into issues related to national defense; sating domestic demand for foreign resources; and establishing an international realm of influence for both the private and public sectors. These endeavors demand the expenditure of vast amounts of capital to implement and maintain.

And, finally, States are characterized by demands to address public needs and fulfill promises made to constituents. This, in turn, defines the relationship between government and its public. All States must, by definition, impose their wills, by force if necessary, over their populations. They are compelled in this to enforce the mores of their political leaders and to sate the expectations and manage the frustrations of their constituents. The more resources are expended to do so, the more the State must, and does, intrude into the liberty interests of those constituents. This includes direct and indirect engagement in the State's economy. Given these dictates of realpolitik, it is inevitable that government exercise some degree of centralized control over one or more of the factors of production. The extent and method of that control identifies the type of capitalism embodied by the economy of every State. And, globally, none of these are represented by the ideals of free markets or communism. They lie well within the two.

The outcome of all of this is predictable. States can not maintain the status quo when the demands made of them exceed their available resources. Every instance of increased demand leads to a corresponding increase in centralized control over the factors of production by the State and/or its proxies—governmentally protected private interests. Whether arrived at incrementally or in rapid steps, failure to stem the tide of expenditures in excess of resources culminates in economic totalitarianism. And, absent some form of externally provided intermediate relief, this condition can only lead to collapse of the State. The only difference between modern democracies and politically totalitarian regimes, in this regard, is that the former may defer the problem because they have greater access to global factors of production. In this, the modern State may emulate the former Roman Republic; however, as with this precedent in history, the inevitable cannot be forestalled if diminishing returns are not stalled.

Ancillary to all of this is another truism; that there is an inverse relationship between increasing centralized control over the factors of production, whether privately, publicly or both, and individual economic liberty interests. This in turn must result in a corollary diminution of individual political liberty interest.

Applying all of this to the present condition of the US economy raises the specter that an entirely different boogeyman than the oft blamed free market is responsible for our economic woes. ༄

CHAPTER 5

THE US DOES NOT HAVE
A FREE MARKET ECONOMY. . .

The US does not have a free market economy because there is too high a degree of centralized control over the factors of production. One must bear in mind that, while ownership may denote control, control does not necessarily mean ownership. The federal government owns 28 percent of all land in the United States. According to the US Bureau of Land Management, this ownership is not proportionate across the country. Federal ownership extends to 61.3 percent of Alaska and 46.4 percent of the contiguous western states in the lower forty-eight. State and local governments account for an additional 8.7 percent of land ownership across the US. According to the Federal Reserve, in 2007, 1 percent of the population owned about 33 percent of all investment holdings, including real property, directly or indirectly, in the US. Taken in sum, then, the interests of governments and 1 percent of the population account for the ownership of roughly 60 percent of all land in the US. The remaining 40 percent is held by the balance of the population, though not in equal proportions. If one extrapolates from the Federal Reserve's data, coupled with various economic studies cited by *Bloomberg* and other publications in 2017, that 80 percent of the population accounted for ownership of 7 percent of the country's wealth, one can likely assume a similar distribution in ownership of real property. The remaining 33 percent of US real property interests would then be held by some 19 percent of the population. Generally speaking, there is a relatively high degree of centralized control over land in this country. In a global context, there are countries with higher degrees of centralized control; in Canada, federal and provincial governments account for 90 percent of all land ownership, and in

China, absolute control over all real property is vested in the State. Conversely, there are countries in which private ownership is not only prevalent, but is also weighted towards ownership by a greater percentile of the overall population. Sweden presents one such example.

The notion of private ownership of real property is, however, somewhat illusory if one accounts for the stark certainty that non-payment of real property taxes will vitiate any such interest. Nor is this a new phenomenon. Largely levied by state and local bodies, property taxes have been a revenue raising mechanism in the US since Colonial times. The nexus between tax rates and values was widely implemented during the five years leading to the American Civil War and has led, most assuredly during the last several decades, to the imposition of increasingly regressive taxes. Regressive in the sense that home values, and the assessments on these, have outpaced net incomes in inflationary terms, based upon decreases in purchasing power of a dollar, coupled with increasing income taxes. This has become harshest for lower and fixed income tax payers, who find themselves becoming wealthier in terms of assets, while losing ground in relative incomes. In essence, taking all of this into account, the more likely descriptor for land ownership by individuals in the US would be as a tenancy or, more precisely, a fee interest in property ultimately owned by the State.

Control over the natural resource factor of production in the US is not dissimilar to that found with respect to lands. Farms, with the exception of most large scale grazing areas, owned by federal and state entities are privately held in this country. Farm land comprises some 40 percent of all land in the US, constituting about 2.1 million farms, which correlates with the US Department of Agriculture's (USDA) assessment that there are about that number of farm owners. According to the USDA, 73 percent of all farmlands, or 28 percent all US real property, is owned by 130,000 corporations, institutional investors, real estate investment trusts and individuals, each owning more than 1,000 acres. Small operators hold 27 percent of all farm lands, farming anywhere from 5 to 999 acres. This means that 6.2 percent of farm owners control almost ¾ of all agricultural property. Further, the present trend, according to the department, suggests a material decline in the number of farm owners, while the average size of farms is increasing. So too, is there a trend away from owner operations, marking a significant and ongoing increase in operators leasing farm land from owners. As a result, while families may still be dominant in operating farms, ownership control over agricultural property is shifting away from the traditional family owned and operated small farm. Interestingly, according to United Nations Food and Agriculture Organization census data, globally, 75 percent of all farms are small family run operations, with 12 percent of all farms scaled at less than 4.4 acres, The sum of these family farms is estimated to produce some 80 percent of all agricultural products. Clearly, while the US model at first blush suggests relatively decentralized control over farm lands, based on the numbers of farm owners, actual control over acreage of agricultural holdings suggests to the contrary and, further, indicates an ongoing trend towards increased centralized control there over.

Timber lands comprise some 33 percent of the US land area, of which about one-half is owned by federal and state governments. The US Forest Service reports there are some 11 million private landowners who own forested property in this country. Of these, private ownership by about 7.5 million people of one to nine acres encompasses five percent of all privately held forest lands. An additional 4 million individuals and families hold an average acreage of sixty-six, comprising some 61 percent of all privately owned forest lands. Six percent of all timbered property is held by non-profits, mostly conservation.

Most interestingly, some 160,000 corporate owners control, though direct ownership, 28 percent of all privately held forests. Of these, 1,600 entities, or one percent, own 73 percent of all parcels of 5,000 acres or more. Federally owned timber lands present a somewhat different story, given that a good portion of these are not given to the harvesting of merchantable timber. That said, the bulk of timber sales on federal lands fall to large commercial enterprise, with a relatively small portion being sold to small businesses. Keeping in mind that most forest lands described in this paragraph do not constitute holdings sufficient to support commercial harvesting of trees, the indicia of centralized control over this natural resource seem readily apparent. For comparisons sake, it is worth noting that in the US, centralized control over timber is not as draconian as in Russia and China, where all forested lands are state controlled, though it is less, if marginally, than in countries such as Sweden, which seems fairly typical in Europe, where 50 percent of timber lands are owned by families; 15 percent by larger industrial concerns; and 25 percent by the government. There does, in those countries however, appear to be a stronger tendency towards a greater number of smaller enterprises engaged in commercial lumber activity.

Energy production and distribution in the United States are most assuredly subject to a high degree of centralized control. The US Department of Energy reports that coal and natural gas are the primary sources of energy in the US, accounting for some 61.8 percent of domestic consumption. 41 percent of all coal is extracted from federal lands. Four companies produce about 50 percent of the coal mined in the US, while some 500 companies of various sizes, produce the balance. Nuclear power plants, owned by sixty-five companies through various subsidiaries, generate 20.1 percent of America's energy needs. The balance of our energy needs are derived from renewable resources, such as power dams, windmills, and solar energy. These industries are also represented by a relatively small, concentrated group of corporate entities. Moreover, distribution of energy to consumers is undertaken by national and regional monopolies that are regulated by state and federal governments.

Oil and gas production, a large portion of which is produced on federal lands and offshore dominions, is another factor of production that must be characterized as suffering a high degree of centralized control. Ten companies account for 40 percent of global oil production, while another ten produce 30 percent of the world's natural gas. Three of these, BP, Conoco-Phillips and XTO are among the top ten in each category. In 2015, these ratios also held true for domestic US Production.

Labor is the most widely diffused factor of production in the United States. Each of us is free to determine how and where to apply our efforts. Once this decision is made, there may be constraints put upon these by employers, although we can not be forced to work for a particular employer or in a specific field of endeavor. We are free to work for ourselves, if we choose and enter any arena we elect to, hampered only by our talents, education and the scope of our connections. The connotation of this freedom suggests that our labors are for our own benefits. However, if one takes into account the requisite to pay taxes, of every type, a somewhat more realistic picture emerges. In 2018, the entirety of US federal taxes is expected to be $3.4 trillion and state taxes are estimated at $1.8 trillion. The total, $5.2 trillion, represents 30 percent of the nation's gross income and exceeds the gross amount Americans will spend on housing, food and clothing. This, according to the non-profit Tax Foundation, which further calculates that our collective efforts will pay these tax burdens by April 19, coined by the Foundation as "Tax Freedom Day." Statistically, from a historical perspective, Tax Freedom Day landed on January 22 in 1900 and extended through latter March by 1950. As of 2000, this date has generally fallen in April, from the 7th through the 27th.Comparatively speaking, the US Tax Freedom Day arrives earlier than in most other developed countries. This date does not, however, incorporate national debt. In this context, it is worth noting that the US has the second highest per capita national debt in the world, roughly $62,000 for each of us, and is only one of a handful of countries whose annual debt exceeds its GDP, the gross value of everything produced within a year. Given all of this information, one can only surmise that control over labor is centralized for at least one third of every year. In essence, it is a sophisticated form of feudalism. We work to pay our liege in order to gain the fruit of our efforts. And, though we are free not to work, exercising this option plants us squarely within the aegis of the poverty industry.

The control of information is concentrated in a handful of private entities, such as Google, Amazon, Apple, Microsoft and Facebook, as well as government agencies, most certainly including the National Security Agency. This is not only true as to the acquisition of data, but also applies to its dissemination. In the modern world, this centralized control over information, particularly where, as is the present case, private and public control are interwoven, a lack of competitiveness becomes a manifest reality.

Regulatory control over capital in the United States is high centralized. The US Department of Treasury is responsible for the printing of money. Decisions as to the supply of money, interest rates and other monetary policy are dictated by the US Federal Reserve. The Fed is a quasi-public body that is generally autonomous. Its directors are nominated by the President of the United States for confirmation by the US Senate. Economic decision making is vested in the Fed's so-called

"Federal Open Market Committee," and is not subject to governmental oversight. There are twelve Regional Federal Reserve Banks throughout the country, which are owned, proportionately to their investment therein, by private financial institutional shareholders. Although these regional banks are not members of the Open Market Committee, they are able to render advice to that body. Investors in the regional Federal Reserve Banks are paid dividends on their shares, based on a floating rate tied to the Federal Reserve's fund rate, on their shares. Dividends used to be fixed at six percent. We are asked to trust in the integrity of those charged with managing our monetary policy and the economy it stakes, yet it is difficult to believe in the altruism of those endowed with absolute power over anything, much less the finances of this country. As Mayer Amschel Bauer Rothschild, an international banker of yore, whose financial legacy yet endures, famously avowed, "Give me control of a nation's money and I care not who makes its laws." This adage comes to mind when one considers the infamous bailout of banks, to the tune of $16.8 trillion, commencing in 2008. Many of these were, and remain, shareholders in Regional Federal Banks. So too might one dwell on the risk of temptation for whispered asides to insiders related to looming Fed decisions. This no less than one might wonder whether fortuitous shorting of the Turkish Lira might have preceded Trump's tweets regarding his decision to impose tariffs on imports of steel and aluminum originating in Turkey. Perhaps I am too great a cynic, but the humans involved are not altruistic beings—they are absolute monarchs in terms of the decisions they are empowered to make.

Physical control over capital wealth is also highly concentrated in this country. The Federal Reserve reports that in 2016, 62 percent of Americans had savings account deposits of less than $1,000. A good portion have no savings accounts. Statistically, average savings deposits, which are heavily skewed due to the larger deposits held by high income earners, range from averages of $6,000 for lower income groups to $37,650 for those earning up to $159,999 per annum. Deposit averages for those earning in excess of this amount rise to $117,771. Average checking account deposits tell a similar story. Further more, based upon interest rates established by the Federal Reserve, funds held in savings accounts deteriorate in value due to the fact that interest rates on these accounts are less than the rate of inflation.

Also deeply weighted by the statistical biases due to higher balances held by those earning above $160,000 annually, average checking account balances range from $2,018 at the lower income brackets to almost $13,000 for those earning up to $159,999. Average balances increase to $42,253, for those earning in excess of $160,000. Of note, 27 percent have no checking accounts, partly attributable to the use of electronic payment methods and otherwise to simply living on cash on hand.

Retirement benefits are even more dismally distributed. The US General Accounting Office reported in 2013 that one-half of households, of people aged fifty-five and older, had no retirement savings. Twenty-nine percent of the same group had neither retirement accounts or defined benefits plans. Conversely, analysis undertaken by the Economic Policy Institute of Fed and government data for 2013 indicates that the 90th percentile of income earners have combined retirement savings averaging $274,000, while the top 1 percent are secured with an average of $1,080,000. Ultimately, the bulk of Americans will depend upon Social Security benefits to survive upon retirement, which inadequately meets the real cost of living.

These disparities are likewise reflected in the distribution of wealth in this country. In a speech delivered on October 17, 2017, Federal Reserve Chair, Janet Yellen, relying upon data collected for

2013, reported that 5 percent of American families held 63 percent of all US Wealth. The lowest 50 percent of families accounted for 1 percent of all wealth during that year. Translated, 62 million households owned wealth averaged at $11,000 per household and 25 percent of those 62 million households had 0 or negative wealth. The top 5 percent of wealth owners in the US controlled two-thirds of all financial assets, such as stocks, bonds, mutual funds and private pensions, while the bottom 50 percent owned none.

The underlying problem with all of this is that mounting public frustrations, among the middle class and those enduring economic poverty, is aimed at the perception of glaring deficiencies in so-called market or laissez faire capitalism. In truth, our economy is not principled on the tenets of market principles. It is more akin to a socialistic-techno-feudal capitalistic regime. And, the current populist trend towards the embracement of "socialism" will only exacerbate the problem because it will lead to further centralization of control over the factors of production, creating even greater disparities. The present inequitable distribution of factors of production is not a result of market forces. Rather, it is a symptom of direct government intervention in the market through subsidies, protectionism, cronyism, preferable tax treatment, bid rigging and the like. ⌖

CHAPTER 6

CORPORATE WELFARE
AND PROTECTIONISM ARE . . .

C orporate welfare and protectionism are not market economic mechanisms. Nor are government mandates creating captive markets; purchases of products to reward overproduction and artificially "stabilize" prices; inequitable tax relief; or bidding processes designed to assure the success of specific corporate entities. In fact, the employment of these is antithetical to the notion of free markets or any other economic model even leaning towards that form of capitalism. Yet, these forms of governmental intrusions into the economy are the rule, rather than the exception, in this country. Furthermore, aside from enjoying a more competitive, robust economy, even if all other conditions remained static, our national debt would not be exceeding $22 trillion dollars which translates into over $62,000 for every man, woman and child in the US or, put another way, about $170,000 plus per tax payer.

Corporate welfare is nefariously difficult to pin down because it takes a multitude of forms and has become the device of all manner of imaginative schemes. Among these are direct subsidies; targeted tax breaks; low interest loans; tailored bids; regulatory limitation of competition (creating rules that only large companies can afford to comply with); creation of captive markets (Obamacare); and acquisition of products to maintain high prices (agricultural products). Assigning a dollar value to the extent of these programs is difficult because many are simply not a matter of overt public domain and the origin of these is spread throughout every aspect and department of government. One example: in December of 2007, the *Baltimore Sun* reported that the National Institute of Health was leasing a lab it could not use for over $15 million dollars a year. Another in 2005, as reported by the *Anchorage Daily News,* entailed a $500,000 Congressional grant to Alaska Airlines to paint a fish on one of its planes. A third, widely reported in 2001 and 2002, was then Secretary of Defense, Donald Rumsfeld's announcement that $2.3 trillion dollars in Department of Defense transactions could not be accounted for. The money had been paid out, over time, but it could not be ascertained to whom. Presumably, a good portion of those funds, if not the entirety, were paid to third-parties. A fourth, according to Subsidy Tracker, Boeing, a substantial beneficiary of tailored government contracts, received about $13.1 billion dollars in federal, state and local subsidies between 1997 and 2014. Fifth and finally, *Vanity Fair* reported in August of 2018, that the Pentagon's request for a $10 billion dollar cloud services contract was tailored to an extent that only Amazon, Jeff Bezos' behemoth, will be able to sate its specifications. These are but some of literally tens of thousands of examples of corporate welfare, most of which are hidden within the labyrinth of the federal budget. In some instances these entail relatively small amounts of money, while others are of considerably greater significance. All said, it would be worth bearing in mind that chicken shit makes manure. In other words, it all adds up. Others aspects of the corporate welfare scheme are more overt, but require some thinking to ascertain their financial impact.

There are two critical elements to understanding the deeper consequence of welfare in the form of low interest loans and subsidies. The first is that a subsidy requires the federal government to pay interest on the amount thereof because it is borrowed money. Also part of the federal mix is the spread between low interest loans made to corporate entities by the government and the cost of that money in interest payments on the federal debt. In the simplest of terms, if I were to give you a hundred dollars that I borrowed at an interest rate of

3 percent, not only would I lose the hundred I gave you, that loss would be compounded by the $3 dollars a year in interest I have to pay on the loan. Or, if I borrow a hundred dollars at 3 percent interest a year and lend it to you at an annual interest rate of 1 percent, I would lose two percent a year on the spread. Even better, in the latter case, how about I lend you the money that I borrowed at 1 percent, and you re-lend it to me at 3 percent. If these scenarios sound stupid, it is because they are. Yet the federal government has done all of these to the tune of hundreds of billions of dollars at a time which, when stacked up, adds up to trillions.

Painting with a broad brush, solely utilizing readily accessible and large examples of government largesse in underwriting the private sector, it is possible to divine some hard numbers and measure their cumulative effect on the current national debt. In 2012, the Cato Institute, relying upon data included in the Budget of the United States Government, Fiscal Year 2013, determined that the annual federal outlay for corporate welfare amounted to approximately $100 billion dollars per year. Of note, about 25 percent of this amount is directed at agricultural subsidies. Of these, the top 10 percent of farmers, generally corporate, received 77 percent of all direct cash subsidies. One consequence of this is that cheese, some 1.5 billion tons, and about 2.3 billion tons of meat products, are stockpiled by producers receiving subsidies, allowing elimination of market forces in setting the values of these products. Absent subsidies, these stored items of food would be released to the market place and consumer prices therefore would be markedly lower. Energy companies have likewise benefited. Department of Energy subsidies to oil, gas and solar companies total about $17 billion dollars a year while similar subsidies from the Department of Interior amount to roughly $2.6 billion annually. These figures <u>do not</u> include discounts to oil, gas and coal producers on federal leases and royalties. In 2013, the Department of Interior's Inspector General reported that the Agency was undercharging for coal leases on federal lands. The actual loss, over the preceding thirty years, was calculated to be $29 billion dollars by the Institute for Energy Economic and Financial Analysis. This sum is nearly matched by the losses to the taxpayers of some $730 million dollars a year, if factored by the same time period, in royalties on oil and gas produced by private companies on federal property, due to undercharging by the government (Center for Western Priorities—Reported by *Newsweek* in 2015). Leaving these aside to focus only on the 100 billion per annum suggested above, and adjusting for inflation over time, this translates into corporate subsidies of $2 trillion dollars from 1998 through the present.

Low paying corporations are also indirectly subsidized by the federal government which pays public benefits to underpaid workers otherwise unable to subsist on incomes alone. The Labor Center of University of California, Berkeley, reported in 2015 that real incomes, adjusted for inflation, remained flat or entered negative territory for the bottom 70 percent of hourly wage distribution throughout the country between 2003 and 2013. The result, the Center reported, was that 73 percent of the people enrolled in major public assistance programs were from working families. In essence, this is because the spread between hourly wages and the cost of living leads to unsustainable circumstances for hourly laborers working at low paying jobs. Absent federal social programs, supplementing the needs of this labor force, exemplified by fast food industry and box store workers, the wages paid by employers of such, as well as the ability to expand and/or compete would be driven by realistic, rather than subsidized labor costs. Although at present, wages have risen somewhat, the result of lowered unemployment, the fact remains that the social safety net in places is directed at underwriting low wage paying corporations more so than individuals. The cost to the American taxpayers, according to the Labor Center, some $153 billion dollars per year. Again, allowing for inflation, this amounts to over $1.5 trillion dollars over the course of ten years. Added to the amount of direct corporate subsidies, we arrive at a subtotal of $3.5 trillion dollars.

Now we come to the great bank bail out of 2008. Ostensibly the failure of the financial sector in 2008, the result of activities which, if emulated by any of us individually would lead to long term incarceration, was averted through the very publicly created "Troubled Asset Relief Program," funded with $700 billion dollars. Privately, the reality was somewhat different. A federal audit of the Federal Reserve Banks in 2011, as well as numerous Freedom Of Information Act (FOIA) requests, resisted vigorously by the Fed on ground that it is a private corporation, ultimately revealed that the funds made available to financial institutions amounted to $7.7 trillion dollars. These were not solely supplied to domestic institutions, but to an almost equal extent benefited foreign banks, including the Bank of Libya. It has been reported that funding to the extent of $16 or even $29 trillion dollars was made available. However, this is misleading because the initial seven some odd trillion was rolled over from time to time as some banks repaid their loans and others borrowed. These were all low interest loans, bearing interest of well below one percent and were made at a time when government securities were yielding between two and four percent. According to the US Office of Management and Budget (OMB), the net direct losses to the federal government in the wake of this fiasco amounted to about $68 billion dollars. This is simply an inadequate representation of the net effect of the bailout, financially and otherwise. There were no conditions attached to the secret Federal Reserve loans made to banks. They were free to use this money as they saw fit. And so they did. Funding of the banks directly led to a number of mergers. Bank of America merged with Merrill Lynch, Wells Fargo with Wachovia and so on. The net result was that twelve banks ended up in control of 70 percent of all the nation's bank assets. Of further import, is that in order to meet the immediate demand for loans, the money supply had to be expanded. Logically, an unplanned increase in the supply of money reduces its unit value. Hence, the dilution of the US Dollar reduced its value to those holding it—think American wages and savings. This is an inflationary event which led to rising prices, including those for necessities. Accordingly, the ability of Americans to meet the cost of living was diminished.

More dire consequences flowed from the financial institutional melt down. The US economy lost about $648 billion dollars in economic growth between the fall of 2008 and the end of 2009 as a result of the crisis. During roughly the same time period, real estate values dropped $3.4 trillion dollars; stocks lost $7.4 trillion; and $5.5 million jobs evaporated. These figures are based on data collected by Pew Research in 2010. The effect on Americans was devastating. Bear in mind that these losses catastrophically impacted the average person's retirement accounts, home values and savings values. This triggered 500,000 home mortgage foreclosures. Between 2008 and 2013, enrollment in the federal food stamp program escalated 70 percent, ultimately adding 47.8 million people, or one out of seven US residents, to the program. The Congressional Budget Office predicts, or hopes, that this number will fall to 43.5 million by the end of this year, 2018.

The losses to the federal government attributable to the financial crisis are somewhat quantifiable. In *Staff Papers*, published by the Dallas Fed in July 2013, the authors, examining the costs and consequences of the financial crisis, point out that the post 2008 economic downturn reduced economic activity which, in turn, led to a decrease in federal tax revenues. Though not quantified in that research, the paper assigned credibility to the International Monetary Fund's 2009 calculation that direct governmental commitments in excess of normally expected expenditures, directed at ailing households and businesses, totaled $12.6 trillion dollars. Further, 2008 Congressional Budget Office projections for public debt in 2012, that portion of the national debt held by third parties, undershot the realized public debt by $4.6 trillion dollars. This was caused by the government's unexpected efforts to meet public needs and stimulate the economy. The authors of the Dallas Fed paper, referenced above, posit unequivocally that the US government debt would would have been "trillions" lower, but for the financial crisis.

The irony of the great bank bailout is that the Federal Reserve, the US central bank, loaned money to the financial institutions that caused the crisis at near 0 percent interest rates, while acquiring our public debt and earning an average 2.5 percent from the American taxpayer. Adding insult to injury, some of the institutions requiring the bailout, many of whom were foreign owned and located, utilized US Treasury issued securities to collateralize their loans and in some cases, utilized Fed loan proceeds to acquire US debt instruments, earning money on the spread between interest they were paying on the loans from the US central bank and income earned from loans to the federal government. To illustrate, if the borrowing banks had invested all of their loan proceeds, some $7.7 trillion dollars, in our national debt, their earnings on the spread would have amounted to some $192 billion dollars a year.

To characterize federal expenditures in response to the financial crisis of 2008 as anything other than a form of corporate welfare would be sheer nonsense. The federally created central bank, as well as some federal regulators, such as the FDIC, establish the rules of operation for banks. As cited above, the twelve Federal Reserve Banks are owned by the banks regulated and the larger the financial institution, the greater its shares in a Reserve Bank. This creates a murky situation on multiple levels. Federal regulators are subject to the whims of Congress which, in turn, is deeply influenced by the wishes of banks proffered through lobbyists. Financial institutions expended $2.7 billion dollars lobbying Congress between 1999 and 2008 alone. Moreover, there is no bar on federal employees moving to well paid positions in the financial sector and political appointees have moved at will between finance and positions of power related to bank regulation. Jamie Dimon, CEO of J.P. Morgan Chase, once commented that his bank receives "a good return on the company's seventh line of business—government relations." While CEO of J.P. Morgan, Mr. Dimon also sat on the board of the New York Federal Reserve Bank, the largest of twelve such banks, a not uncommon condition, and was thus in a position to influence Fed decisions related to regulation of banks, including J.P. Morgan. Only a naif would believe that the latent conflicts of interest represented by such circumstances are not realized, given the amounts of money involved. The trilateral relationship between politicians, the Federal Bank and financial institutions can only be described, if modestly, as incestuous. Significantly, it protected the growth of larger banks and allowed them to take financial risks simply because they could. This set the stage for the defects in their conduct that resulted in the crisis. The mere fact that federal legislation and policy allowed our financial institutions to reach the level of requiring public assistance is sufficient to paint the bailout as welfare.

Of longer term concern, the bailout vitiated all moral and fiduciary responsibilities on financial institutions regarding future endeavors. They have become a protected class to the extent that even their failure has become an impossible horizon. The characterization by critics of the bailout as a flaw in market economics baffles me. In a market oriented system, the federal government would not have intervened, nor would it have needed to. Inefficient practices would have weeded out non-performing financial entities long before they became "too big to fail."

All said, there is nothing to question the position that the national debt increased by $4.6 trillion dollars as a result of the banking crisis. Adding this amount to the $3.5 trillion dollars attributable to direct corporate subsidies and federal subsidization of low wage jobs, we reach a staggering $8.1 trillion dollars of corporate welfare. This excludes the costs of non-bid contracting; benefits of captive markets to health insurers and providers; government waste and fraud; discounted federal land leases and royalty income; and a myriad of other programs too hidden to readily ascertain. Nor does it include tax write offs taken by banks due to the financial fiasco. These instances of corporate welfare, totaling $8.1 trillion dollars, represent 38.57 percent of our national debt, or almost $24,000 for every person in the US Service on this debt, assuming a conservative 2.5 percent interest rate, amounts to $202.5 billion dollars per year or $2.025 trillion dollars over ten years.

There are other forms of corporate welfare. So called free trade agreements tend more to protectionism than competitiveness in the marketplace. ∾

CHAPTER 7

I'LL BELIEVE IN
FREE TRADE AGREEMENTS WHEN . . .

I 'll believe in free trade agreements when I can cross the border from Mexico with a few hundred dollars worth of gifts or furnishings and not be required to pay import duties to bring them home.

Free trade is the unfettered trans-border movement of raw materials, goods, services and labor. Operationally, these items are only subjected to import duties or tariffs to the extent they are subsidized, directly, indirectly or through artificial currency value manipulation, in their country of origin. The purpose of such taxes is to eliminate an unfair competitive advantage which creates a corollary disadvantage for domestic sources of the same items.

The benefits of true free trade are threefold, each flowing from from the other. First, countries of origin will develop a comparative, rather than competitive, advantage because they are naturally able to produce the items exported for less money than the importing country can. The immediate effect is that prices for such items are lower in the importing country than would be the case if it were to produce those things domestically, its resources then freed to produce items based on its own comparative advantages. Ultimately, this fosters domestic economic efficiency in both the exporting and importing country.

As applied, for instance, prior to external disruption of its culture, in Melanesia, coastal villages engaged in fishing would trade their fish for produce farmed by inland villagers. Although the distances between the two were often not great, it was more efficient for those living on the shore to fish, while those in proximity to superior soil conditions farmed. Framed in the context of present conditions, although the principles of the Melanesian case may yet be applied, there are additional complexities. Technology and other forms of intellectual property may create a comparative advantage where otherwise there might not be one. National security issues will discourage reliance on imports for items deemed strategic necessities, such as food, energy resources and rare minerals. And, artificial labor costs, whether derived through employment of slave labor or some other totalitarian control over individual productivity, as in the People's Republic of China (PRC), aside from a moral consequence, establishes an often overlooked, ignored or covert unfair competitive advantage. These issues are surmountable. Intellectual property has a shelf life as long as it takes to develop the next innovation, provided there is no restriction on the flow of information; national security issues are abated through widespread economic well-being; and untoward labor practices are thwartable through import duties on discrepancies these cause on labor costs or through the illegalization of imports that are the fruits of such practices. At heart, the principles of free trade are sound because they foster economic development based upon efficiency and tend to create a mutually beneficial interdependency among participants that erode the perceived benefits of conflict. Detractors of free trade are prone to point to wage disparities between trading partners as a fundamental detriment to free trade benefits. However, the real issue is not one of disparities in income, rather the issue turns on incomes relative to the cost of living, which varies wildly in a global context. That said, however, and most deliberately overlooked, in order for free trade to be effective, there must be an ability for labor to move freely. The free, trans-border movement of working people will effectively lower labor costs in a target country, due to an increased abundance of workers, while leading to increased wages in the countries of departure, if these are to retain their labor forces. This is a function of free markets that has been completely suppressed.

In addition to eliminating market functions for labor, the euphe-mistically labeled free trade agreements now employed are designed to foster competitive advantages, rather than enhance comparative advantages. They are crafted to protect the interests of more power-ful signatories, trade unions and a relatively small number of large corporations. Indeed, in many instances, these agreements have undermined the relatively free trade that preceded their formalization. Most importantly, while a tenet of free trade is one of mutual benefit between trading partners, trade agreements are increasingly aimed at tipping the scales. As pointed out by the World Trade Organization (WTO) in 2016, these "tend to go far beyond tariff cutting exercises. They provide for increasingly complex regulations governing intra-trade (e.g. with respect to standards, safeguard provisions, customs administration, etc.) and they often also provide for a preferential regulatory framework for mutual services trade. The most sophis-ticated RTAs [Regional Trade Agreements] go beyond trade policy mechanisms, to include regional rules on investment, competition, environment and labor."

Foremost among the issues that have dominated trade agreement negotiations are Trade Related Intellectual Property Rights (TRIP); the flow of cross border capital; regulatory standards; and litigation. Though seemingly benign, these issues have been, and continue to be, the subjects of intense lobbying by corporations and have nothing to do with lowering tariff barriers to trade. TRIP entails the imposition of increasingly longer, stringent monopoly restrictions on intellec-tual property. This includes pharmaceuticals and research intensive products. The inclusion of TRIP conditions in trade agreements allows drug manufacturers to hold drug prices at inflated values. These firms argue, amongst other things, that the cost of developing and introducing new drugs justifies these protections. Absent from these laments is that the costs of introducing new drugs in the US is, in large part, due to the lobbying efforts of pharmaceuticals seeking to institute regulations restricting the financial ability of upstart companies to enter markets with new drugs. The TRIP manifesto of provisions also eliminates the ability to reverse engineer technology a practice oft employed in the past to not only duplicate, but improve upon existent technology.

Restricting the rights of host states to govern cross border cash flow has also become the norm in conditional free trade agreements. Under the aegis of such terms, banks and other financial services entities are given free rein to move capital resources without the imposition of any domestic managerial oversight of capital movement, even if this is to the detriment of the economic well-being of the affected country.

The enactment of common regulatory standards among free trade agreement partners has increasingly evolved to the forefront of conditions sought by corporations in seeking to influence the terms of trade agreements. Ostensibly directed at the promotion of greater ease of trade through the establishment of common standards amongst signatories, the underlying end game is markedly different. In essence, normative standards provisions in free trade agreements are designed to forestall the imposition of any regulatory standards by the governments of export targeted countries. Agreement to these terms bars countries from promulgating or enforcing regulations even under circumstances where the importation of a particular product would present a detriment to public policy, consumer protection or cultural mores. This has included the acceptance of genetically modified organisms (GMOs) or derivatives of these, such as processed commodities, dairy products, for example, where GMOs are found in the food chain leading to the final product. So too, have these agreements entailed prohibitions on labeling that might lead fully informed consumers to avoid certain products.

Empowering foreign operators to seek legal redress against host countries for actions, whether regulatory or otherwise, characterized as reducing profits of the complaining entity is a final leg that has found traction in free trade agreements. In addition, these disputes, together with other trade related conflicts to be resolved by arbitrators empowered with final authority, are often at the expense of applying the legal and regulatory schemes of the country involved.

As pointed out by Harvard Economist, Dani Rodrik, in the Spring, 2018 issue of the *Journal Of Economic Perspectives,* the inclusion of the four foregoing conditions, now evermore routinely incorporated into free trade agreements, is the result of intense political pressure brought to bear by those entities most likely to benefit therefrom. Not surprisingly, these count among their numbers Monsanto; pharmaceuticals, such as Pfizer and Bayer; information and technology firms; automobile manufacturers; dairy and other agricultural producers; labor unions, most notably the United Steelworkers and the AFL-CIO; textile firms; banks and other financial services providers; and the entertainment industry.

The principles evoked by these attributes of so called free trade agreements are antithetical to the philosophical tenets of true free trade. Rather than promoting the development of comparative advantage economic dynamics as a means of arriving at mutually beneficial trading arrangements, these agreements have bastardized the concept into a form of corporate and cultural imperialism. They are protectionist and promote inefficiency within their protectorates. These agreements denude the right among consumers to make informed choices; unfairly co-opt producers and manufacturers who, but for the agreements, would enjoy a comparative advantage in their endeavors, vis a vis domestic and foreign markets; and, completely exploit labor, rather than allowing its value to be the subject of market forces.

Ultimately, in their present manifestation, free trade agreements are short sighted because they cannot achieve the long term goal of economic, and consequent political, stability envisioned by free trade concepts. They are corrupting in that they serve to undermine all but lip service to any market capitalist orientation and instead, are the result of an unholy alliance between politicians and large private sector entities, to the exclusion of the vast majority who cannot afford the purchase price of political influence.

The by-product of the fuzzy lines now existent between politics and protected corporate interests has been the evolution of a two tiered hierarchy. The first, an entitled minority imbued of elitism and entrenched corruption. The lower tier comprised of mere commodities —the rest of us. ∽

CHAPTER 8

THE PROBLEMS OF CORRUPTION, FRAUD AND ELITISM . . .

The problems of corruption, fraud and elitism in this country are not so much that these exist, an unavoidable societal attribute of the creatures we are, but that they have permeated our culture and noticeably affected our economic well-being. In fact, all three maladies have become so rampant that they are no longer undertaken sub rosa, but are conducted in a blatant manner.

Public trust in America's institutions has plummeted, lending credence to the notion that things have gotten out of control. This is as true for medical systems, media, corporations, the judiciary and scientists, as is, not surprisingly, for Congress and the executive. Nor is this trend a manifestation of the Trump presidency, although mistrust has grown in that office; rather, it is a downward spiral that has been apparent for more than a decade. Moreover, the data supporting this conclusion is confirmed by a myriad of pollsters, nonpartisan and otherwise. A Rasmussen poll published in 2016, tracking voters between 2012 and 2015, found that 81 percent of American voters think government is corrupt. Of these, 60 percent believed members of Congress would sell their votes for cash or campaign contributions and 56 percent were of mind that their representatives had done so. In 2017, NPR, in conjunction with PBS, reported poll results indicating that only 29 percent of Americans trust Congress, while two thirds did not. Thirty percent of those polled trusted the media and 37 percent trusted President Trump. More recent polls show a decline in trust for the president. According to Gallup, in 2016, trust in media was at a record low at 32 percent, a number that has subsequently declined to a nadir of 30 percent. Pew Research polls indicated that only four of ten Americans trusted scientists—the negative connotations of this result were attributed to a disproportionately high degree of mistrust of scientists associated with climatology and genetically modified foods. Public trusts in institutions was measured by Pew in 2014 with the results that public institutional trust was at 32 percent. Broken down, 27 percent trusted banks; twenty trusted media; 19 percent trusted the federal government; 39 percent trusted the medical system, down from 80 percent a few years earlier; and 50 percent trusted the judiciary. Trust was highest for small business and the military. Military, in the context of such polls, should not be confused with the Department of Defense, rather it is an indication of public trust for the men and women in uniform. Also telling were Gallup's poll of 2015, indicating a belief that individual freedom in the US is declining and Pew's research, undertaken in 2017, reporting that 66 percent of Americans are dissatisfied with the country's direction.

A comprehensive examination of corruption in this country would provide sufficient meat for an entire book, or even a compendium of volumes. For purposes of this chapter, then, the inclusion of a sampling of forms, types and extents of public—private corruption will have to do. Other instances will be touched upon in subsequent chapters, directly and inferentially. It should also be made clear at the outset, that public corruption, and the protection of corruption by private interests, be they of sufficient size, is entirely nonpartisan. Taking the latter first, one need only look to the proceeds of drug trafficking. In 2010, the United Nations Office on Drugs and Crime estimated the value of the global drug trade to be $1.6 trillion dollars, or 2.7 percent of global GDP. One suspects this amount has risen during the intervening eight years. That aside, the laundering of proceeds realized by drug cartels is simply not possible by acquiring a few cash oriented businesses and slipping money into the stream of reported income.

Money laundering on the scale required can only be done through the cooperation of banks and other financial institutions, with involvement at the highest levels. Indeed, some years ago, Congressional investigators, former bank officials and finance experts estimated in the late 1990s, as put by Senator Carl Levin, that "half of this money finds its way into the US" through its banks. This does not include other forms of corrupt money laundered by US banks, such as funds siphoned out of developing countries, the former Soviet States economies and other aspects of global underground economic activity. Laundered money finds its way into US treasuries and corporate investments; the overall impact is sufficiently pervasive so as to created a dependency on money laundering in the overall US Economy. The amounts involved run to the trillions of dollars, over a few years, and absent this flow of capital, there is every reason to believe that our trade deficit would have considerably more than the present marginal effect upon the domestic economy. Contrary to the popular lament that the drug market in the US fuels the drug trade, it is this addiction to illegal capital that denudes the will of the government to effectively combat illicit activities.

When banks get caught laundering money, a relatively rare occurrence, they are fined a small proportion of the amounts involved and no one at the upper levels of management goes to prison. HSBC's American division, for example, was fined $1.9 billion dollars of an estimated $881 billion dollars it had laundered for the Mexican cartels, as per the US Justice Department, and no prison sentences were issued. Other institutions alleged to have been involved in money laundering are US Bank, J.P. Morgan, Wachovia, Western Union and, more recently, Rabo Bank. Remember too, that under civil forfeiture laws, the federal government is empowered to seize all assets suspected of being employed in, or derived from, illegal activities, regardless of whether there is a related criminal conviction. No bank has suffered such consequences. Yet, our prisons are filled with small time dealers and users and civil forfeitures have been used and abused on a vast scale. As one young gang-banger told an acquaintance working with inner city youth in Portland, Oregon, some years ago, "The government is just a big gang trying to keep the rest of us out of the game."

In order to reconcile well documented and suspected activity by banks and federal agencies, such as the Central Intelligence Agency (CIA), in the drug and laundering rackets, with well publicized take downs of drug trafficking kingpins, such as Carlos Lederer, Pablo Escobar, Manuel Noreiga and El Chapo, one need only consider that each of these individuals were causing embarrassment to their fellow Cartel leaders or had a falling out with the US Government.

In essence, the decision to arrest or prosecute such people can only be characterized as an extension of US Foreign policy, albeit conducted covertly. Let's face it, in order to succeed at their endeavors, traffickers and launderers require the complicity of government, both bureaucratic and political. Government has the ability to detect cash deposits by small businesses, a frequent happenstance, and seize these on accusations that they are depositing too much cash into their business accounts, skating too close to the ten thousand dollar reporting limits. One would think, then, with the technology available to government agencies, that it could readily identify trillions in illegal funds moving through the banks. They do not. Nor is there any ebb and flow to this corruption related to which party controls the White House or Congress. Corruption is rampant and it is non partisan.

No bid contracts awarded by government also provide incalculable opportunities for corruption through fraud. As pointed out by the Office of Budget and Management, no-bid or cost plus contracts pose a risk of overspending because "they provide no direct incentive to the contractor for cost control." In spite of this, the Department of Defense

(DOD) alone, in fiscal 2016, awarded more than half of its contacts, totaling in excess of $100 billion dollars, non-competitively. It has been increasingly embarked on this course for more than a a decade. Even where bids are said to be competitive, specifications are often tailored specifically, so as to preclude all but a single company from winning such bids; this appears to be the case with the recent call for proposals to develop a $10 billion dollar data cloud for the DOD, which apparently greatly favors Jeff Bezos' Amazon. A similar contract was accorded to Amazon by the CIA, to the tune of some $600 million dollars. This tactic is decades old, having gained eminence during the cold war. No bid and tailored contracts are issued by every government agency in the hundreds of billions of dollars. Contracts thusly awarded are generally the result of cronyism, campaign contributions and lobbying efforts, not just directed at politicians, but to sway military leaders and other agency decision-makers. In addition to costing taxpayers money well beyond the value of the work done, these practices promote inefficiency and bar smaller companies and start-ups from participating by virtue of their inability to pay large sums to politicians and lobbyists and thus gain access to the process in a meaningful way. Moreover, every administration has been guilty of issuing no bid contracts. It is, again, a nonpartisan practice.

Although the effect on US spending and the national debt is likely immeasurable, one need only look at Rumsfeld's announcement, referenced earlier, that the Pentagon had essentially lost $2.3 trillion dollars, a problem there is no reason to believe has been ameliorated. Or, the Institute of Medicine's assessment in 2012 that the post Obamacare US Health system, enacted in 2010, loses $750 billion dollars annually to fraud, inefficiency, inflated prices and other abuses. These two issues, taken at face value, amount to about $8 trillion dollars, not adjusted for inflation, through the present, or well over a third of the US national debt.

From before Bush, to Obama and beyond, the beat goes on. Volumes, quite literally, have been written about the corrupt practices of the Bush family and the Clintons. Some highlights regarding the former include: the first Bush's dismantling of regional, independent organized crime task forces and the CIA's involvement in the drug trade during his tenure as director; family business alliances with the Saudi government and bin Laden Construction; obstruction of the 9-11 Commission's investigation into the terrorist attacks of that date by the latter day Bush's administration and its creation of false information to justify the invasion of Iraq; the institution of warrantless domestic information gathering by the intelligence community; and, of course, the wholesale theft of money throughout the Iraq war.

The Clintons fare no better, though as pikers when compared to the Bush family. There is a great deal of evidence to support the claim that while Secretary of State, Ms. Clinton formulated a pay to play scheme, requiring beneficiaries of her official largesse to make charitable contributions to the Clinton Foundation; itself the subject of considerable debate in light of disproportionate overhead as compared to actual expenditures for good causes. According to *Fortune's* 2016 article, lawyers hired by the Foundation had reason to suspect its dealings were not entirely above-board. The investigation in to misdeeds was effectively killed by the Obama administration, as was scrutiny of Ms. Clinton's illegal use of personal email for public business. Historically, aside from allegations related to Bill Clinton's frequent peccadillos, the couple was engaged in questionable real estate transactions and at least one figure, Barry Seals, a notorious drug smuggler, claimed Clinton involvement in that business while Mr. Clinton was the governor of Arkansas. Along the same vein, it was reported by WND in 2000, that a career undercover officer investigating narcotics and public corruption in Tennessee was informed by a senior FBI official that protection for these illicit activities originated from then Vice President Al Gore's office.

In a glaring headline, dated April 21, 2013, the *Huffington Post,* generally sympathetic to President Obama, raised the question of whether his presidency was the most corrupt ever. Aside from shielding Ms. Clinton from potential judicial scrutiny, the *Post* pointed to legislation quietly signed in to law by Obama in 2013, that rendered unenforceable the STOCK law, forbidding insider trading by Congress and congressional aides, that he had signed to much fanfare only a year earlier. Under Obama, the US plummeted in scoring by the World Bank on public corruption to a nadir not even reached by Bush or Clinton. The *Huff* further cites evidence of Obama's collusion with financial institutions during the "bail out," in any number of ways inconsistent with public interests. In discussing whether to support Obama or Elizabeth Warren, the author of that piece suggested that the question did not concern a white woman versus a black man; it concerns a nation of equality under law, versus a champion of 'Too Big To Fail.' In fact, Obama has been disastrous for Blacks, and not just for the rest of the 99 percent."

As for our current President, Mr. Trump, he is relatively unique. Not because of some unassailable moral virtue; rather, because he brings to Washington a fresh cadre of nefarious deed doers. I do not believe for a moment that the disdainful remarks made about Trump by former intelligence officials or past presidents giving eulogies at celebrity funerals are borne of deep philosophical differences. Instead, these are tantrums about being cut-off from getting a piece of the pie by people who are no longer invited to sit at the table. There are indications that the Trump charities are somewhat akin to personal piggy banks; he has clearly succumbed to the Israeli lobby, though there appear to be opportunities in the shambles this has created in the middle east; government spending, and the fraud that comes with it is increasing at an alarming rate under this president; and conflicts of interest between Mr. Trump's personal endeavors and his office seem to have moved beyond latency. While I do not think there was serious collusion between Trump and Russia leading to the election, the culture of garnering information about opponents and cash contributions by politicians is bipartisan and in all cases has played into Russian hands, which are busily sowing discontent and discord in order to confound their enemies—which includes us.

Congress. Need one really say more? Every aspect and instance of fraud and corruption referenced in the preceding, and subsequent, pages is done with the acquiescence and support of this millionaires club. Moreover, this august body, time and again, exempts itself from the laws, rules and regulations that govern our conduct. Whether it be insider trading, or having tax payers pay their share in the Affordable Health Plan, for which they could otherwise receive no subsidies due to high incomes, this group of elitists is beyond despicable. As a group, no pause is given to consider the impact of its spending on future generations or the consequence on our national security in the wake of selling votes and adopting short term, misguided policies in the face of lobbying by the 1 percent and foreign public and private interests. But fear not, Elizabeth Warren has a plan. She would ban lobbying by foreign governments, but not foreign corporations; lobbyists would be required to register and disclose all of their contacts with government officials; make it difficult to cash in on government service; and require release of candidate tax returns, as well as subject the president and vice president to conflict of interest laws. None of this will be effective. It is an attention getting, vote inducing notion designed to further manage the frustrations of the American public. It is Placebocracy in action. As long as Congress does not legislatively overcome the

Supreme Court's determination that corporations are people too, for 1st Amendment electoral purposes; ban lobbying with money or future job prospects; cap spending in proportion to revenues; illegalize protectionism; bar corporate subsidies; and, other forms of discrimination aimed to underpin the 1 percent, Warren's proposal is no more than rhetorical nonsense, much as STOCK legislation was. She would not propose these things if there were any prospect that Congress would enact them.

Congress. To borrow a phrase from the inimitable Hunter S. Thompson, a "Generation of Swine," indeed.

At least in those countries where corruption is deemed an overt societal norm, it can be said to be somewhat egalitarian—a process available to all. In our country, corruption is the bailiwick of the elite; the rest of us obliged to pay and pay and abide by the rule of law.

And what of our wars? Are these aimed at bolstering national security, or are they further examples of officialdom's descension into moral turpitude? ⌒

CHAPTER 9

WARS
AGAINST EVERYTHING . . .

Wars against everything seem to permeate our national psyche to an extent that has become numbing. They are decreed in either the name of patriotism or ideology—or both. Yet one might do well to question the validity of such rationales as applied to our post World War II declarations of war, with an eye towards Machiavellian principles of governance. Thus, one might, as a cynic or realist—take your pick—characterize ideology as the mechanism commonly invoked to garner popular support for the realpolitik objectives of the political and economic elite. Thereby are the virtues of true idealism marginalized and the masses manipulated, all in one fell swoop. The promotion of fear and divisiveness are other such tools.

In dissecting the efficacy of our wars, it seems most logical to examine their geneses, costs and final resolutions, or outcomes. The longest of these, now almost faded from the national memory, was the war on communism, pronounced as a global totalitarian threat to individual liberty interests. Our greatest adversary in this war was the Soviet Union, its territory and access to natural resources assured by Franklin Roosevelt's unnecessary concessions at Yalta, in 1945, over the objections of allies and some American military leaders alike. Stalin, in spite of having slaughtered even more people than had Hitler (23 to 40 million v. 17 million) was, nonetheless, our ally and deserved rewarding. During the ensuant forty-one years, until the Soviet Union's collapse in 1991, the United States expended trillions, in current dollars, combating the Soviet Union in various locales around the world and, most notably, in an ever escalating arms race. According to a Cato Institute paper, about $7 trillion dollars, adjusted to 1996 dollars, was spent during the Cold War, a great portion of this on Pentagon purchases from defense contractors. As reported to shareholders by Retired Army Gen. Richard Cody, a vice president at L-3 Communications—the seventh largest defense contractor at the time—in 1996, the end of the Cold War marked the moment when "all defense budgets went south." The Cold War was fraught with technology transfers into the USSR, whether through espionage or deliberate leaks, necessitating a constant need to advance war technologies. We built a mousetrap, they built the same mousetrap, and then we built a better mousetrap—and so it went. And, it appears we have not yet won. After some years of turmoil, the new Russia, a totalitarian oligarchy embarked on visions of re-expansion under Vladmir Putin, has emerged; it is, for all practical purposes, the same entity, marked only by the greater sophistication of its leadership. Hence, the boom went bust, and now some twenty-two years later, we have defense contractors lobbying to have the Pentagon increase weapons spending to meet this new (old) threat.

Before the end of the Cold War, no actual direct battles were fought between the US and the USSR; though the Vietnam war was a form of proxy war, on the part of the USSR, which we lost at a cost of over 58,000 American lives and about 350,000 wounded, and, corrected for inflation, a trillion dollars, excluding ancillary costs. In toto, the war cost an estimated 1.5 to 3.5 million lives in Vietnam, Laos, Cambodia and to Americans. Vietnam is still a communist state.

The only upside to the war, other than its benefits to defense contractors, were to those who reaped the rewards of the lucrative heroin trade that blossomed during the war years. As a footnote to that war, one wonders at the first Bush's embracement of the Khmer Rouge, a regime that wiped out well over 1.7 million of its own people in Cambodia some simply because they wore glasses, stacking their skulls into well documented stacks for all to see. It was ideology; the war against communist totalitarianism, that must have motivated him. In the end, it was Vietnam that put an end to the Khmer.

We are still technically at war with North Korea, another abjectly totalitarian regime, although the shooting war between North Korea, supported by the Soviets and the Peoples Republic of China, and South Korea—with US allied backing—ended in 1953. Approximately 2.5 million people, military and civilian are thought to have lost their lives, including 38,568 US Military personnel. Another 103,284 Americans were wounded. And now, over half a century later, we are confronted with the same North Korea, only now under new (old) leadership and armed with nuclear weapons technology. We are barred from exporting bazooka gum to North Korea, yet ABB, a European company in which Donald Rumsfeld was a director at the time, remember he went on to become little George Bush's Secretary of Defense, sold key components for nuclear reactors to North Korea for $200 million dollars in 2000. According to the Guardian and other sources, this sale was just fine because it was part of then President Clinton's policy to have North Korea engage positively with the west. A couple of years after Rumsfeld left ABB, as Secretary of Defense he declared North Korea to be a member of the so-called Axis of Evil, together with Iraq and Iran, while the Bush administration was waving the flag and extolling the idealist imperative to go after Saddam Hussein.

The last of the great Communist regimes, with whom we have never had a direct war, is, of course, the Peoples Republic of China (PRC). However, our anti-totalitarian ideology has conveniently been by-passed by the opportunity to make money, through trade, with that Communist regime. In 2017, trade with China was worth some $636 billion dollars for the year, and the US trade deficit with China for that period ran to $375 billion. There is no real advantage here. Perhaps, the real impetus for our ideological and patriotic stance as regards this country lies in the fact that it currently holds $1.18 trillion dollars of our national debt. The war on communism and totalitarianism: ideology or realpolitik—you choose.

Now for a look at the War on Poverty. Declared by President Lyndon Johnson in 1964, at a time when 20 percent of the population was said to be living in poverty, this war has been going on through the present—although President Trump, in mid 2018, did declare the war to be over, that it had been won. While it is true that unemployment is down, indeed, to the extent of historic lows amongst Blacks and Latinos, it is also true the spread between incomes and the real cost of living is growing rapidly. The questions then remain, how many people are still living in poverty and what has the cost of that war been. According to the US Census Bureau, 12.5 percent of the population is living in poverty. On the surface, this would suggest an improvement.

Unfortunately, the standard utilized to define poverty by the Census Bureau, is misleading. The US government calculates that for a family of four the poverty threshold lies below an annual income of $24,565. As pointed out in previous chapters, this benchmark is artificial and bears no semblance to reality. The Pew Foundation and others calculate that the average household requires, at minimum, $60,000 per year to meet needs. The US Census Bureau reports that 32 percent of American household earn less than $35,000 per year. In other words, about 32 percent of households earn enough to meet one-half of their expected needs. Given this, as a possible indicator of poverty levels, one must conclude that the war on poverty is far from over; it is lost—this is more evident if one uses the benchmark of all families unable to meet the expected cost of their needs. If the war is lost, how much has it cost. Depending on who is doing the calculating, whether the Heritage Foundation or the Cato Institute or the federal government, in inflation adjusted dollars, we have spent anywhere from $15 to $23 trillion dollars in the War on Poverty. And, had we succeeded in this war, could we have won the accompanying war—the War on Drugs.

The drug war, famously declared by Richard Nixon when he formed the Drug Enforcement Agency (DEA) in 1973, has fared no better than the War on Poverty. It is a war that has been fought against users and small fry dealers, by and large because, as pointed out in the preceding chapter, the economic costs of taking out large scale purveyors of drugs, cartels and pharmaceuticals are simply too high. Accordingly, there is no political will to win this war. To the contrary, there is an impetus to lose. For instance, reported by *Politico* in July, 2018, DEA agents on the ground in Afghanistan developed plans to eliminate the heroin trade utilized to finance the Taliban and allied insurgent leaders. These were rejected out of hand by the Bush League, the Obama administration and, more recently, by the Trump White House—supposedly because such disruption did not take into account the "bigger picture."

In truth, the drug war, which has cost the US well over $1.5 trillion dollars since its inception, has been directed at small time dealers and users. In 2014, the *Washington Post,* relying on FBI data, reported that 620,000 people, one per minute, had been arrested for possession of marijuana. In 2013, about 1.5 million people were incarcerated for non-violent drug crimes. In 1973, when the war was declared, some 38,000 people were imprisoned for similar crimes. At this juncture, there are more people per capita in imprisoned in the US than anywhere else in the world, save perhaps China. The costs of such incarcerations are not included in the government's tally on costs of the war on drugs. In the meantime, over 205,000 people have lost their lives killed in Mexico, since 2006, as a result of cartel violence. And, opioid addiction, addiction to prescription drugs manufactured by pharmaceuticals, has sky-rocketed. According to Reuters, in 2017, two-thirds of patients were over-prescribed opioids, such as Oxycontin, by physicians. One thousand people a day were being treated for overdoses, of which ninety-one died. While a handful of doctors have been prosecuted, the war has not been taken to the doorsteps of companies manufacturing these drugs and then shipping them, in unmonitored quantities, to healthcare providers. Of further note, of course, is that while banks and other large scale participants in the drug trade have been immune therefrom, the government has seized assets of individuals, valued in the hundreds of billions of dollars, under civil forfeiture laws that do not require accompanying criminal convictions, or even charges

It has been repeatedly asserted by the political world that the problem with drugs lies with the market, rather than the supply, yet no substantive commitment has been made to abate demand. Instead, the actions taken have driven prices up, forcing consumers to shift to other forms of drug abuse. It is incontrovertible that there is a nexus between poverty and substance abuse. This has been affirmed by a number of studies, including ones undertaken by the National Bureau of Economic Research and Duke University. However, these get bogged down in chicken and egg debates, about which causes the other. Ultimately, it is clearly evident that persistent poverty leads to a loss of hope, which then begs for some form of escape. The unfortunate reality is that the wars on poverty and drugs are marked by symbolism rather than substance. Small time dealers and users, disproportionately minorities, are incarcerated while money launderers an wholesale distributors remain unpunished. This state of affairs will prevail until poverty is not treated as a political tool and we are willing to face the economic consequence of curtailing wholesale drug manufacturers, distributors and their money launderers.

In the wake of the the attacks on September 11, 2001, then President

Bush declared the War on Terrorism. Since then, the war on terror has encompassed operations against Al Qaeda in the Middle East and Afghanistan and the Taliban in Afghanistan. It involved prosecution of the war in Iraq and subsequently against the Islamic State (ISIS). And, it has enveloped military actions and military expenditures in Libya, Syria and Yemen. The War on Terror was also the basis for creating the Homeland Security department and mounting an unparalleled assault on American privacy interests by the National Security Agency and the other alphabet agencies of the federal government. The costs of this was are only partially calculable. Between 2001 and the present, according to research done by National Priorities, the US has spent about $3 trillion dollars in military costs; $300 billion for the care of war on terror vets; $850 billion on Homeland Security; and, $620 billion in interest on the war debt. Bush also managed, in the context of his declaration of war, to alienate Muslims, collectively, while taking great care to protect his family's and cohort's business relationships with Saudi Arabia.

Not much thought is given to the underlying roots of our middle eastern conflicts; however, it is readily apparent that these stem from decades of unilateral support for Israel and unfettered exploitation of natural resources, mostly oil, through despotic leaderships that do little to allow public discourse or the flow of oil revenues into the general populace. This is, of course, a gross oversimplification of a highly complex compendium of problems.

The outcome of the War on Terror is somewhat nebulous, yet discernible in some important instances. First, as to the war in Afghanistan, it has been lost on the ground, militarily, politically and culturally. Coalition force casualties have numbered 3,556, while 31,000 civilians have been killed. Moreover, as reported by the Pentagon in 2009, some 360,000 troops had suffered some form of traumatic brain injury in both the Afghanistan and Iraqi wars. Our success in Afghanistan has been no less dismal than that of Alexander the Great, Britain or the Soviet Union—the latter whom we helped defeat by aiding the very people we are now fighting. During our tenure, a natural gas pipeline across the country has been constructed and opium production has reached a zenith. The country remains factionalized in terms of competing tribes and clans. Tens of millions of dollars, in cash, have been distributed among these by military and intelligence agencies, in the hopes of purchasing loyalties, with the end result that in spite of these and conventional military efforts, ground has been lost, rather than gained.

The war on terror's expansion onto Iraq, by the Bush League, was predicated upon the realpolitik objective of destabilizing the region, while drumbeats of ideology and national security were sounded. Saddam Hussein, installed by our government as the Iraqi leader, was accused of harboring weapons of mass destruction—a myth that has been exposed countless times by as many sources in the aftermath of the war. Indeed, these lies were exposed by the Knight Ridder news organization well ahead of the invasion—while mainstream media elected to blindly ignore the facts, a disturbing harbinger of media's present condition.

The Iraq portion of the War on Terror accomplished many things. It made a vast fortune for Vice President Dick Cheney's affiliated Halliburton and its subsidiaries, as well as other Bush Leaguers. It disproved the notion that Iraq possessed weapons of mass destruction. As reported by *National Geographic* in 2013, the war caused the deaths of about 500,000 civilians and, as further reported by the United Nations, resulted in the displacement of 4.4 million people and the exodus of a further 265,000. American military deaths numbered 4,424 American, with another 32,000 wounded by 2009. The war accomplished the

looting of Iraq's museums, galleries and banks. The Iraq war desta-
bilized the region in accord with Israel's realpolitik interests and, ultimately, it eliminated one of few secular leaders in the region, creating
a power vacuum that was subsequently filled by ISIS.

ISIS. Daesh, as ISIS is otherwise known in the region, initiated a
reign of terror in Iraq and Syria that can only be described as publicly
murderous. ISIS initiated a campaign of genocide against the Yazidis,
an ethno-Christian minority and embarked on the wholesale slaughter and subjugation of any group that falls even marginally outside
of its narrow interpretation of Islamic Sunnism. ISIS is distinguishable from Al Qaeda in that its ambitions are aimed at the creation
of a pan-Islamic state in the Middle East, based upon its worldview,
while the latter is directed at a misnamed "jihad" against Israel, the
United States and its allies. Both organizations have, according to various well publicized reports, received financing from Saudi Arabia and
other Sunni Gulf states, with an eye to the notion that they serve as
useful proxies in combating Islamic Shiites, most notably Iran, which
employs similar tactics. In March of 2016, after conducting a 4 month
investigation, the *International Business Times* reported that ISIS was selling oil, at a peak rate of about $300 million dollars per year, to partially
finance itself. ISIS oil, often mixed with oil produced in northern Iraq
by the Kurds, was steadily sold to European and Israeli markets, as
well as the U.S, through two of the world's largest oil trading companies. Indeed, the product was used to pave tarmac at the new airport in
Portland, Maine. The US Department of State acknowledged knowledge of these sales, as of 2014, to the Times investigators, deeming these
generally irrelevant. Throughout the ISIS conflict, the US has done
very little to assault the sources and transportation of ISIS oil, nor has
it curtailed the flow of cash back into ISIS coffers. Not content with the
power vacuum it created in Iraq and the rise of ISIS, the US further

expanded its war on terror to seek the overthrow of Bashar al Assad, the president of Syria, another relatively secular leader, by backing rebel groups with the same objective. This resulted in US support for rebels associated with Al Qaeda and ISIS. Iran and Russia threw their support behind the al Assad regime with the net result that the conflict in Syria has evolved into wars between various proxies. The outcome, as reported on NPR, to date, is that over 400,000 people have been killed, 4.1 million have fled the region and, another 7.1 million are internally displaced. Added to the mix, both the US and Israel have bombed sites in Syria, to deter the use of chemical weapons by the Syrians and forestall Iranian entrenchment near Israeli held territory. At the time of this writing, Syria, with Russian and Iranian aid, is on the brink of success, though this is a relative term. Conflict will continue in the region.

From an ideological standpoint, the removal of despots is an admirable goal. Unfortunately, this has been neither the goal or the outcome. The war on terrorism is a cynical war, borne not of idealism, but out of greed and the satiation of Israeli interests in the region. While Israel cannot be blamed for asserting self-interest in inveigling the US in furtherance of its perceived national security interest, which to me appear to be short sighted, these do not coincide with our national interests—which should be directed at long term national security, both militarily and economically. Neither has been accomplished as a result of the war on terror.

The war on terror was a preventable war. Aside from misguided foreign policy stances in the middle east, there was clear failure by the intelligence community to thwart the initial 9/11 attacks and, in the aftermath, there was an equal failure to provide an honest assessment of actors underwriting the attacks. Indeed, as noted by the 9/11 commission, the Bush administration, particularly the CIA, proved obstructionist in providing that committee with information necessary to its deliberations. Above all, the war on terror has been a profitable war. And, finally, lest we forget, every aspect of the so called War on Terror, has been fully supported by both parties of the United States congress, with only a small handful of exceptions.

The above said, terrorism is certainly a threat; however, the larger picture points to enemies of far greater import and consequence. ❦

CHAPTER 10

AMERICA HAS
REAL ENEMIES...

A merica has real enemies, readily identifiable and who present an existential threat to democracy, national security and our continued relevance. The first and most dangerous of these is the People's Republic of China (PRC). In 1983, an acquaintance attached to a civilian intelligence analysis group in Honolulu, opined that political decisions vi a vis trade and other relations with the PRC, as of the Nixon era, did not recognize the fact that we are at war with that country. And, in spite of incompatible ideologies, that this war was predicated upon pragmatic, rather than ideological, considerations. In short, our conflict with the PRC turns on what he and his co-workers considered to be the PRC's insatiable demand for resources. Although our ideological dichotomy with the PRC has lessened, by virtue of our government's assault on individual liberty interests and its growing inclination towards total surveillance, the practicalities of the conflict have widened the gap.

Interestingly, at a time when pundits and pols alike are criticizing President Trump for being enamored of dictators, no such criticism has been leveled at preceding presidents, from Nixon to Obama, the latter having famously kowtowed his way through meetings with foreign heads of state, many of them despotic, for fully embracing the PRC and its leadership. The PRC is governed by the Communist Party of China, and has been since the success of Mao Zedong's revolution in 1949. It is an abjectly totalitarian regime that is estimated to have killed between 49 and 78 million people during its tenure. It has, and continues to be, embarked on missions of cultural genocide directed at every ethnicity not encompassed by the Han majority. This includes the Tibetans, whose organizations report some 1.2 million killed, and the Uighars, of whom some 1 million are imprisoned in so-called re-education camps, according to the United Nations, and an untold number have been slaughtered.

According to the Central Tibetan Administration and other groups the following methods are employed against people, as a matter of course, by the government of the PRC: shooting, beating, crucifixion, burning alive, mutilation, stoning, strangulation, live burial, drawing and quartering, beheading and boiling alive. The PRC has instituted a citizen social credit score system, whereby persons scoring unfavorably, for such transgressions as opining their views on social media or buying foreign made goods, are deemed untrustworthy and are stripped of the ability to gain employment, travel, buy property and enroll their children in schools.

In 2006, supplemented by a follow-up study published in 2016, David Matas, a Canadian human rights attorney; David Kilgour, a former Canadian politician and diplomat, and, Ethan Gutmann, a researcher, reported that since 2000, a likely upward of 1 million organ transplants have taken place in the PRC. They report that most of these were the result of forced or live organ harvesting and that the majority of victims of this practice are Uighars, Tibetans, Christians, Falun Gong practitioners and other political prisoners. Contrary to PRC government assertion that the practice of ripping organs from the unwilling was abating, the authors posit, based upon their research, that it is actually increasing and that there is a burgeoning market for foreign recipients of organs harvested in the PRC.

This is lovely stuff. Added to all of that, is the fact that the PRC has now engaged in the practice of kidnapping Chinese people who are residents, or even citizens, of foreign countries, and its total surveillance of its citizenry, dispatching technology to monitor activities, including facial recognition, social media and some 176 million CCTV cameras (expected to expand to 676 million by 2020), and a picture of the so-called Middle Kingdom emerges.

Yet, we are not deterred. In 2017, according to the US Department of Commerce, trade between the US and the PRC was valued at $636 billion dollars, with US exports accounting for $130 billion, leaving the US with a $375 billion dollar trade deficit with the PRC. So much for the idealism of American government or, for that matter, its constituents. One questions whether we would be trading with Germany if Hitler had won and the Nazis were still in power. Given that the Nazis were novices at slaughter and totalitarianism, when compared to the PRC, one supposes that the answer would be, yes. Hence, if the nature of the beast is insufficient to cause alarm, perhaps an examination of the pragmatic risks posed by the PRC bear mentioning. Aside from the current trade deficit we enjoy with the PRC, the PRC presently owns about $1.18 trillion dollars of the US national debt. Its military budget for 2018 is $175 billion dollars. Some researchers believe this to be an understatement, with the Stockholm International Peace Research Institute estimating the PRC actually spends some $60 to $80 billion more than its official figures. Nonetheless, while these sums may seem a paltry sum compared to our $700 billion dollar budget, if one takes into account the PRC's relative efficiency and its exponentially lower costs of production and military pay, a different reality becomes apparent. *Bloomberg* reported in late 2017, the minimum wage in the PRC is about $333, monthly, and the national average is $1,111 per month. The average US military service pay is $57,000 per month. Average pay, according to the US Department of Labor, is about $3,900 per month. Translated into relative terms, then, the PRC military budget, realistically, almost parallels our own.

The PRC has transformed its economy from agricultural towards industrial at an incredible pace—to the extent that it now consumes one-third of global mineral, fossil fuels and other primary resources. This is the driving force behind the exercise of its claims in waters around the South Pacific, which are rich in oil deposits, and has led to tensions with Brunei, Vietnam, the Philippines Japan and others. This has led to the PRC's military expansion, through the creation of island military bases, throughout the region. In addition, the PRC has invested heavily in Africa, a continent replete with resources, and while US investments in Latin America have doubled since 2000, the PRC's have increased twenty-two fold. Indeed, our abandonment of the Monroe Doctrine, designed to protect our regional interests, in favor of playing in middle eastern sandboxes and immolating ourselves politically and socially, has allowed the PRC free and easy access into our backyard. Research undertaken by the Center for Strategic and International Studies concluded that the PRC is likely to soon replace the US in terms of regional economic and political influence.

The PRC finds itself in the same position as did Japan, prior to WWII, thwarted in its growing demand for resources by US interests, albeit on a much larger scale. From a security standpoint, it is surrounded by US allies and our military presence. Geopolitically, the only country standing between the PRC and a dominant position is the US. The PRC is not solely driven by its ambitions; it is also in dire need of resolving the economic dichotomies within its own borders.

Hence, while our pols dither about reelection strategies, formulated on the backs of reaping social discord and sating lobbyists demands, the PRC has mounted a multi-faceted assault on the US. It has given money, intelligence and technology to countries and organizations with whom we are in conflict, including Iran, which is dependent on the PRC for trade, and North Korea. In doing so, the

PRC has not only harangued us through proxies and depleted out resources, but it has studied our responses in order to learn our tactics and strategies, assessed our willingness to engage in conflicts on multiple fronts and, tested our overall political will. It has invested heavily in Hollywood productions, which promote a picture of benevolence on the part of the PRC and its people, and has established organizations in universities throughout the US with similar objectives. The PRC has invaded our technology with data traps and the like, while harvesting advances to out technological abilities, covertly and on the open market. It has engaged in spying and the intimidation of its Chinese, Tibetan and other critics in the US and elsewhere. In addition, the PRC has diligently worked to undermine US influence and exercise its dominion—militarily, economically and politically in every corner of the world we have turned a blind eye towards, and in those where we are ineptly engaged.

It is also worth noting that the PRC has refused to share information regarding infectious diseases with the west and is embarked on the wholesale export Fentanyl; an opioid responsible for some 50,000 deaths in the US during 2017.

We are at war with the PRC, and have been for decades. And, it is financed by us as consumers. It is not a war of ideologies, although it ought to be; instead, it is a war of appetites. Russia represents a further, serious threat.

Not only has Russia expanded its military and concomitant ambitions, as it has always been wont to do when troubled economically, but Russia has scored the greatest intelligence coup against the US since it had James Jesus Angleton, the CIA's then chief of counterintelligence, chasing his tail in the great mole hunt of 1963 through 1974, which severely damaged the agency's efficiency. Now it has managed to paralyze the US political, law enforcement and intelligence establishments in a bitterly divisive witch hunt to pin the tail of collusion with the Russians on the president.

The Russians accomplished this by stealing and leaking stolen emails and other data, combined with a well-directed social media campaign that has manged to pit all sides against each other. In truth, it is a non-issue, unless one believes that Trump is working with the Russians to undermine the US. Ultimately, getting dirt on political opponents, by any means, has become the norm of American politics.

As for financial gains, I doubt that Trump is any more of a money whore than Clinton or Congress—most of whom have histories of taking money in return for pandering to foreign interests. One need only look to Hillary Clinton's role in the sale of US uranium mines to Russian interests and the subsequent contributions to the Clinton Foundation by interested parties. Regardless of this, as with Angleton's long sought out mole, the existence of such a specter is far less damaging than the process to ferret it out. In this context, Russia's wildest dreams would be realized if Congress, abetted by insiders in the Justice Department and the Alphabet intelligence agencies, were to invoke a Constitutional crisis by seeking to eject Trump on grounds that he is an "outsider," and not entitled to the same corrupt practices as establishment figures in public office.

Russia's game is one of smoke and mirrors. While the US is contemplating its collective navel, Russia has expanded its rule into Crimea, taken a role in Bashar al Assad's civil war in Syria and, is threatening the security of the Baltic states under guise of its security interests in Kaliningrad, its non-contiguous seaport on the Baltic. Russia's strategic interests have aligned with those of the PRC in seeking to corral America's military and political-economic influence and supplant the US dollar with an alternative, controllable, global medium of exchange. Russia is particularly dangerous in that, unlike the PRC, this oligarchy's expenditure of resources has outstripped its means. It cannot hold the course unless relatively quick and decisive action is taken. This, in the context of Russia's history, both Czarist and Communist, is the harbinger of increased conflict. In this, it is worth considering that Russia is emboldened by its alignment with the PRC and its abilities to wage campaigns of disinformation and capitalizing on roiling unease in areas of traditionally American influence.

There are other enemies. Some, such as Venezuela and Cuba, are relatively inconsequential. Others, more specifically, Pakistan, North Korea and Iran are of concern. Pakistan and North Korea have nuclear weapons, while Iran is clearly intent on obtaining these. All three serve to varying degrees as proxies for the PRC and, to a lesser extent, have aligned interests with Russia. Pakistan is subject to the caprices of governance and the risks of radicalization. It has been unreliable insofar as US interests are concerned, having harbored bin Laden and other terrorists, while serving the PRC's interests in arresting India's ability to focus on a single front of threats. Pakistan poses a greater direct threat to India than it does to the US and this further turns on who is governing both countries at a particular moment. If Pakistan succumbs to a radical Islamic leadership at an instance where India allows the rise of radical Hinduism, the stage may be set for a serious conflict—beyond the present tensions in Kashmir. North Korea depends on the PRC for survival, but is more intent on gaining global legitimacy and standing than it is on launching a nuclear war. Iran, of the three, is the most dangerous.

Iran, for all intents and purposes, is a theological state; an Islamic Shi'ite state governed by its clergy through oversight of its elected bodies. It is a major sponsor of terrorist organizations and is presently said to have implanted sleeper terrorist cells within a number of western countries, including the US. Iran has openly declared hostilities with the US, our allies and Israel—having promised to obliterate the latter. Iran is further dedicated to acquisition of technology that would allow it to produce nuclear weapons.

The notion that its agreement to hold this ambition in abeyance is misguided because it presumes in Iran's leadership a western rationality that it simply does not have. An integral aspect of the Shi'ite doctrine is the coming of the Mahdi, said to be the last Prophet or divine ruler, whose manifestation will signal a golden age of Islam, for a period of seven to nine years, and culminate in the end of the world, or the end of days. In the fundamentalist Shi'ite view, this is an objective to strive for, rather one to be feared. This is akin to fundamentalist Christians, having pulled the notion of "The Rapture" out of their rear ends, yearning for the Apocalypse; scary stuff because it points to an irrational sense of consequences for earthly actions. Coupled to this is the fact that Iran is ripe for an internal regime change due to worsening economic conditions and the imposition of severe religiously invoked sociocultural restrictions. If it fails to quash the unrest of its constituents, the Iranian government is likely to escalate tensions outside of its borders in order to unify the country against the common existential threats it will declare to be ever looming. Moreover, any revolutionary groups within Iran could count, perhaps, on support in the form of lip service from the US but, if history in the region is any indicator, should be leery of counting on material support from an ally that has proven prone to abandoning such ventures in the eleventh hour, as was the case for the Shi'ite and Kurds in Iraq.

Iran is not simply a threat to western interests, it too poses risks for the PRC and Russia. Iran's alliance with these two countries is not an embracement of friendship, rather, it is a case of "the enemy of my enemy is my friend," in only the most pragmatic of terms. Once its objectives are met, through these alliances, or they are no longer deemed profitable, Iran is quite likely to turn its sights on either or both, particularly in light of their internal treatment of Islamic minorities.

Ultimately, our ability to deal with our enemies and protect our national security interests turns on whether we can overcome our present bent of being our own worst enemies. ∾

CHAPTER 11

PERHAPS WE SHOULD
DISBAND CONGRESS . . .

Perhaps we should disband Congress, given that it has all but abdicated its constitutional duties.

Or, preferably, we could ask its members to get off their asses and do their jobs. The indicia of Congresses' infirmities lie in the unprecedented accumulation of power by the executive branch of government and the growing public expectation that laws should be enacted, rather than interpreted, by the US Supreme Court.

This is not a particularly new phenomenon; there have been past instances of Congressional acquiescence to executive authority, during both the Lincoln and FDR presidencies, for example. However, there has been a growing wholesale refusal to act on its full authority and constitutional mandate over the last several decades, which has accelerated since the advent of the attacks of September 11, 2001, and the Bush administration's accumulation of raw, unchecked power in the executive branch. Congress, as it sits today, is comprised of a majority of members, both in the Senate and House, that are ill-inclined to promulgate laws that pose risks to reelection prospects. In so doing, as a body, Congress has manged to politicize the judiciary and create an over-abundance of weight to the importance of presidential elections because both the judiciary and the executive are now publicly perceived as having dominant roles in instituting public policy.

Some examples of the problem are called for. First, most legislators do not draft proposed laws. These are, often as not, written on behalf of the executive branch in order to promote its agenda; by lobbyists, with the same purpose; and by Congressional aides. More problematic is that most proposed laws are not read by members of Congress before they vote on them. As Senator Rand Paul pointed out on the floor in 2012, while holding a bill awaiting a Senate vote, "600 pages, no one will read it. No wonder our [Congressional] approval rating is 10%. Nobody knows what we're voting on."

The failure to read legislation prior to its enactment is exemplified by passage of the massive US Patriot Act. Proposed by the Bush League, the Patriot Act was introduced to the House on October 23, 2001 and passed by it the same day. It was passed by the Senate on October 25 and signed into law following day by President Bush. In spite of its drastic, long term consequences on the liberty interests of their constituents and portent effect on the budget, most members of Congress failed to read the act.

Similarly, passage of the Affordable Healthcare Act introduced by the Obama administration, comprising some 2,700 pages, together with an additional 22,000 pages of regulations, was undertaken with a vast majority of legislators remaining clueless as to what it contained. Indeed, when Senator Max Baucus of Montana was asked if he had read it, the *Flathead Beacon,* a local Montana publication, quoted Baucus as offering "I don't think you want me to waste my time to read every page of the healthcare bill. You know why? It's statutory language . . . We hire experts." This statement is not only notable for its arrogance, typical of Washington's elite, but it is also suggestive of an imperative to simply do away with Congress and have us hire "experts" in its stead.

The passage of the Trans Pacific Partnership trade bill, or TPP, as it became known, presented a debacle of Congressional abdication of responsibility. Classified as secret by the Obama administration, legislators were given limited access and time to read the bill, which was housed in a secured chamber, before voting on it. This, in spite of the fact that the legislation addressed commerce, rather than issues of national security. Moreover, Congress had the right to "declassify" the bill. Nonetheless, Congressional leaders acquiesced to Obama's demand that it not be discussed publicly or that even an inkling of its contents be revealed in any manner to the American public. The TPP is no more, but Congressional malaise continues.

The list of bills that are of such length that they would be impossible to read between the time of dissemination throughout Congress and when they are voted on is endless—being the rule, rather than the exception. Worth a final note on the subject is the federal budget. The Office of Management and Budget, in reviewing the 2017-2018 federal budget, concluded it would result in an $813 billion dollar operating deficit, based on expenditures of $4.173 trillion dollars in the face of revenues expected to total $3.34 trillion. In conjunction to this, on April 7, 2018, after a mere 24 hour review, Congress passed the 2,232 page Stop Gap spending bill in the amount of $1.3 trillion dollars. Not only was this spending bill generally unread, as reported by the *Times Ledger* of Queens, New York, it was largely drafted by lobbyists and key Congressional aides, violated the 2011 Budget Control Act passed by Congress and signed into law by the president. If one takes the time to read comments and opinions rendered over the years by members of Congress on the subject of federal spending, it becomes self-evident that their individual votes, particularly as to discretionary spending, comprising over a third of the overall annual budget, are not predicated upon a holistic understanding of its parameters, but are focused on whether the spending demands of specific lobbyists, constituents and pet pork barrel projects have been funded. Absolutely no thought is given by these people to the national debt and its effect on future generations. Moreover, Americans have become so indoctrinated to the notion that the executive submits a proposed budget to congress for approval, rather than the reality which is that Congress is charged with preparing a budget, but has avoided this responsibility by tasking the president with this chore.

Nor is there any inclination to remedy this problem. Congress has outright rejected the proposition that its members be required to read legislation prior to voting on passage of bills.

Most recently, in 2015, Senator Paul introduced S1571, which would have imposed a requirement that all proposed legislation be circulated at least seven days prior to introduction on the floor, that every such bill be fully read aloud in each chamber of Congress and, that every member be required to execute an affidavit attesting that he or she had heard the oral presentation or, in lieu thereof, had read the legislation in its entirety. Bluntly put, a bill to impose on Congress a duty to fulfill its obligations failed.

The accumulation of power in the executive branch is now unsurpassed and has taken three distinct forms. First, in passing laws, Congress grants to the executive branch the power to promulgate rules and regulations ostensibly designed to implement Congressional intentions. In reality, and as a general rule, the regulatory schemes devised by the various agencies of the federal government, which fall under the aegis of presidential authority, have expanded upon bills passed by Congress to the extent that they have become legislative in and of their own—their scope exceeding anything envisioned by Congress. As posited by Senator Ben Sasse of Wisconsin, on the first day of the early September 2018 Senate hearings to confirm President Trump's Supreme Court appointee, Brett Kavanaugh, ". . . more and more legislative authority is delegated to the executive branch every year . . . that a 'self neutering congress' has ceded its constitutionally mandated legislative duty to 'a bunch of alphabet soup bureaucracies.' These are, of course, unaccountable to the public. Hence, by passing the buck, Congress can, and does, deny responsibility for the outcomes to its constituents with the accompanying mantra to "blame the president." Yet, in its fervor to avoid responsibility, and likely unknown to most Americans, Congress has also created independent agencies that are self-governing and wholly unaccountable to the president. Three such agencies are the Consumer Financial Protection Bureau, the Securities and Exchange Commission and the Public Company Accounting Oversight Board—which was not even created by Congress, but was established sua sponte by the Securities and Exchange Commission.

Congressional "dysfunctional[ity]" was cited expressly by President Obama, as reported by *ABC News* on October 24, 2011 as his rationale for superseding Congressional authority on multiple occasions by employing rule making authority, executive orders and simple refusals to enforce laws that had been enacted. Obviously, examples are called for. On July 2, 2013, the Obama Administration unilaterally extended the December 31, 2013 statutory Obamacare deadline requiring business with more than fifty full time employees to provide health care coverage. On November 14 of the same year, the Administration stated it would decline, in spite of legislation to do so, enforcement of requirements against insurance companies not in compliance with the requisites of the Affordable Health Care Act. In spite of the Senate not being in recess, in January of 2012, Obama sought to bypass the constitutional confirmation process by making four appointments to the National Labor Relations Board, by declaring that the Senate was in recess—a folly subsequently struck down on constitutional grounds by the Courts; the ruling was initially ignored by the Board, which continued to meet with the illegal appointees in place and implement regulations that were found to be illicit as well. On September 23, 2011, the President offered states a waiver of the No Child Left Behind Act proficiency testing requirements, if they agreed to implement his Administration's educational curricula and standards. No allowance therefore was provided for in the Act and federal law forbade the institution of a federally mandated, nationwide curriculum. A final example, though these are not not representative of the exhaustive list of his constitutional transgressions, lies in Obama's creation of the Dream act by executive order. Long debated, yet unresolved, by Congress, was the question of whether amnesty should be granted to a specific class of illegal immigrants, known as Dreamers, comprised of persons under the age of thirty who arrived in the US prior to the age of sixteen. Impatient with Congress' lack of resolve in addressing the issue, the Obama Administration simply opted to not enforce immigration laws as to these people. The issue was not whether this class of immigrants should be allowed to remain the US; rather, the question is one of whether the president has the right to usurp the law by refusing to enforce it. Congress to this day, despite repeated requests by the Trump Administration, has refused to legislatively resolve the Dreamer dilemma. As a body, it members fear the political outfall of acting.

Obama was not alone in this conduct, although his abuses of office were perhaps more blatant and frequent than those of other presidents—though Trump may yet outstrip him, and little Bush did no less damage to the constitutional separation of powers scheme. Bush's nebulous war on terror led the charge on an all out assault against the constitutional protections offered by the 4th and 14th Amendments to the US Constitution, assuring due process and protection from government intrusions in to privacy and the rights of free speech enumerated under the 1st Amendment. Moreover, with increasing frequency, the executive branch has assumed from Congress the right to declare war, under the guise of exigent circumstances, which has resulted in years of multiple conflicts—and the specter of more in the offing.

If it is not enough that Congress has created a latent monarchy in the presidency, it has sought to create a legislative body in the judiciary. It has done so by politicizing the confirmation process to the extent that appointees to the Supreme Court are deemed worthy only if they will act as suitable finger puppets for the prevailing congressional party. Potential Supreme Court Justices are seen as partisan surrogates, rather than independent arbiters of the law, most pointedly in regards to the application of Constitutional law.

This partisan approach to vetting judicial nominees took on it most extreme visage during the hearings on Robert Bork's failed nomination by President Reagan and has become the norm since then. As Judge Bork subsequently pointed out, the clear evidence of malaise in the separation of powers scheme, envisioned by the founders, lay in the fact that people are more prone to protest outside the Supreme Court than they are on the steps of the Congressional edifice. Nor are nominations for judges by the executive offered on the basis of legal intellect and judicial impartiality. Both Hillary Clinton and Donald Trump, as have other presidential candidates before them, expressly campaigned, in part, on promises that their respective nominees to the highest court would have to pass a "litmus test" on how they would vote with respect to specific issues that could come before the Supreme Court. In sum, whether these nominees to the bench would imbue the Court with a politically conservative or liberal viewpoint and craft their decisions accordingly.

Likewise, in questioning prospective jurors, senate members are ill inclined to pose their inquiries in terms of a nominee's judicial qualifications; ability to present objectively reasoned opinions based on existent law; willingness to defer to congressional legislative authority to amend infirm statutes, rather than step into the legislative process by curing such deficiencies from the bench; and, perhaps most importantly, whether the candidate's impartiality will rise above the political processes that led to nomination and, if being the case, to confirmation.

Instead, hysterical objections to nominees are posted on social media by Senators within hours of announcement of their selection without any sense of who the prospective juror is or what might be their qualifications. The questions posed of them are directed at specific issues and how a nominee will be expected to vote on these—as if these interviews are directed at the appointment of an additional member to the Senate, rather than an independent jurist. This was blatantly clear during the confirmation hearings of Judge Brett Kavanaugh, a Trump nominee to the Supreme to Court. While I am convinced that Judge Kavanaugh was a terrible choice, given his tenure in the Bush League and generally statist views, the process leading to his nomination and the ensuant confirmation hearings were appalling and embarrassing. Trump nominated Kavanaugh as a stopgap to potential consequences of the investigations into his campaign, and Senate Democrats skewered him with emotional, unsubstantiated accusations and rhetoric.

These proceedings, as has become the norm, and with a handful of exceptions, portrayed the Senate Judiciary Committee as being comprised of members verging on doddering senility, coupled with younger members that appear functionally illiterate and inescapably ignorant, in the most drastic terms imaginable, of the separation of powers and functions of government envisioned by our country's founders. They are egged on by an equally inept activist constituency, whether leftist or right, that would cheer the subversion of the Constitution when judicial decisions support their world view and lament its demise when they do not. No thought is spared for the concept of universally preserving the Constitution and Bill of Rights.

Congressional empowerment of the executive and subversion of judicial independence, while failing in its obligations, have created a partisan divide that encompasses all three branches of government and ultimately has merged them into a single entity composed of two factions; a president, his congressional supporters and fellow travelers on the judiciary, on the one hand and on the other, the party opposed to the executive, with its league of congressional members and federal judges, with each side vying for absolute control. All of this has set the stage for a constitutional crisis that if unabated will culminate in the devolution of democratic principles to the absolute detriment of individual liberty interests and the increasing entrenchment of special interest power brokers. This portent future pales, however, in comparison to the constitutional crisis posed by the US Intelligence community and federal law enforcement agencies. This, because the former may yet be cured, while the latter presents a fait accompli. ⤾

CHAPTER 12

WE FACE A CLEAR
AND PRESENT DANGER. . .

We face a clear and present danger in the form of our federal intelligence and law enforcement communities because these have moved beyond the tasks legally assigned them into the realm of seeking to determine the course of this country and who its leaders shall be. If this sounds akin to conspiracy theory nut conjecture about the existence of a "dark state," let me unequivocally state that it is not. It is not speculative conjecture about some nebulous cabalistic endeavor, though a degree of conspiracy must be involved; rather, it is an effort that is, in large part, very much in the public eye. Nor is the concept of untoward conduct by federal agencies unprecedented. What has changed are the objectives.

It is a matter of well-publicized history that J. Edgar Hoover infamously leveraged information obtained about politicians, among them the Kennedy brothers, and bureaucrats to secure his continued tenure as director of the Federal Bureau of Investigation (FBI) and ensure the Bureau's funding objectives were met in the federal budget. Hoover also demanded, and was granted, complete autonomy in his management of the Bureau. Though reprehensible, Hoover's blackmail did not significantly deign to govern beyond the shell of his fiefdom. This is no longer the case.

The FBI, with other agencies, has actively sought to direct the political processes of this country. As described by former FBI director, James Comey, while promoting his book at Barnes and Noble, in Union Square, New York City, on April 18, 2018, "There is a deep state in this sense. There is a collection of people, CIA, NSA, FBI, in the United States military services who care passionately about getting it right, who care passionately about the values we try to talk about. . . . No president in a single term could screw it up. It would take generations to change the culture of the United States military in its essence, federal law enforcement, of [the] intelligence community. It would take generations, and that should comfort us." The heart of these statements is the clear inference of agreement among these powerful bureaucracies to ensure the direction of this country, based upon the collective values of their senior officials. The arrogance of this position is both frightening and chilling. Each of these agencies serves at the direction of the executive—the president, in accord with all laws passed by Congress and subject to judicial scrutiny in cases of excess. The mere suggestion that each may act of its own accord to fashion policy, rather than as directed by the electorate, through the president and congress, is replete with totalitarian overtones and signifies an aura of unaccountability. This is not a question of who is president or sits in Congress; rather it is one of who does not and the power they presume to have.

Though likely simmering for some time, the FBI's culture of interference in the democratic process erupted during the 2016 election cycle, particularly as to the candidacies of Hillary Clinton and Donald Trump. It continues to this day. During that campaign, Wiki-leaks, an organization helmed by the notorious Julian Assange, released packets of hacked emails obtained from the Democratic National Committee (DNC), Hillary Clinton and some of her aides. Among these, were gems of underhanded dealing by the DNC, classified information and nuggets of incriminatory evidence that Ms. Clinton, while Secretary of State, had run a "pay to play" scam, in which her office would give favorable treatment to foreign states and nationals, in return for donations to the Clinton Foundation and the Clinton Global Initiative (CGI). Additional corroborating evidence was obtained by *Judicial Watch,* the *International Business Times,* and *The New York Times.* For instance, in

November 2014, email correspondence indicated that Ms. Clinton, in her official capacity as Secretary of State, would host a CGI meeting in Morocco, from May 5-7, 2015, at its King's request, after the latter had committed some $12 million dollars in funding. Ms. Clinton's attendance was canceled when her campaign team pointed to the untoward effect this might have on her campaign for president.

Data obtained from the State Department and the Clinton Foundation, analyzed by the *International Business Times,* showed that while Clinton was Secretary of State, the Department had approved weapons sales worth $165 billion dollars, double that of the prior administration throughout its second term, to twenty nations that had donated to the Clinton Foundation. Similarly, a *New York Times* investigation, published in 2015, showed that Clinton's State Department approved the transfer of 20 percent of the US's uranium production to Vladmir Putin's Russian government, while the Clinton Foundation received $145 million dollars in donations from investors in the deal, who were linked to the Kremlin. Uranium, amongst other things, is used to make nuclear bombs.

The response by the FBI was startling, at best. It completely ignored Ms. Clinton's questionable dealings, most interestingly the likelihood of collusion with Russia in the uranium deal (of note, in spite of touting its significance in 2015, on November 14, 2017, *The New York Times* walked back the story, claiming it inconsequential). The FBI then conducted an investigation into the transmission of classified material by Ms. Clinton and her aides on unsecured servers and found that these had been intercepted by foreign actors, but, in the wake of a meeting between then Attorney General Lynch and former President Clinton, on the tarmac of an airport, exonerated her conduct. On July 5, 2016, then FBI Director, James Comey, announced that Clinton had been "extremely careless" in her actions, but that "no reasonable prosecutor," would opt to prosecute her, in spite of the fact that it was not his decision to make, rather, it was a matter for the Attorney General to decide. Clinton was never charged, although the Obama administration prosecuted multiple other people for mishandling classified information. Contemporaneous rumblings from rank and file FBI agents suggested some dissatisfaction with that outcome. Turning to Wiki-leaks, the FBI's leaders immediately branded the organization as a Russian agent and, on these grounds, together with other scanty connections, has since embroiled Trump in allegations of collusion with Russia through purported cooperation with Wiki-leaks. It seems likely that Wiki-leaks is serving Russian masters—it's dissemination of information having historically assailed US interests; however, the information leaked was not false and the Trump campaign's capitalization thereon the unfortunate norm of American politics.

Indeed, were the acquisition and dissemination of information about candidates from foreign actors a crime, one would expect prosecution of James Comey and other senior FBI, intelligence community officials and members of the Clinton campaign for purchasing, accepting and leaking the so-called "Steele Dossier." Said to enumerate a variety of Donald Trump's sins, the dossier was created by former British intelligence officer, Christopher Steele, released during the presidential campaign and was ultimately paid for by the DNC and the Clinton campaign. Its contents were subsequently discredited by a variety of sources, including by Steele during the course of sworn testimony. Nonetheless, despite having been advised of its lack of veracity by other members of the intelligence community, and knowing of its origins, including who had paid for it, FBI Director Comey sought to enter it into the official intelligence record. The dossier was leaked, in part, if not fully, by James Clapper, an Obama appointee to the nation's highest ranking intelligence office, Director of National

Intelligence. Mr. Clapper subsequently lied to Congress about his role in the leak.

Comey, on being fired as director of the FBI by President Trump, admittedly contrived to leak a dossier of his creation on Trump. In his words, during testimony to a Senate panel, "I asked a friend of mine to share the contents of the memo with a reporter. Didn't do it myself for a variety of reasons. I asked him to because I thought that might prompt the appointment of a special counsel." Comey's intent; clearly to seek ouster of the president at any cost. Rank and file agents of the Bureau were not impressed with Comey's actions. As opined by former agent Bobby Chacon, in an interview published by the *National Review* on April 9, 2018, Comey had been ill-advised in his actions by "senior leadership, which seems to have been infected with people who did not spend enough time in their careers working cases at the street level and rose up the ranks to fast." And, that FBI leaders have forgotten "about a lot of FBI traditions that were in place for a reason, such as not getting involved in politics." Deputy Director Andrew McCabe was also dismissed from his job for making unauthorized leaks related to the related to Trump and for lying under oath on multiple occasions. McCabe led the investigation into Clinton's email debacle and her "pay to play" scheme.

Disdain, not only for Trump, but also for the election process and those who voted for him, was expressed in numerous emails between Senior Agent Peter Strzok, Lisa Page and other senior FBI agents. Strzok, a counter-intelligence chief, was working for Robert Mueller, the special counsel investigating purported collusion between Trump and the Russians. Page was a bureau attorney as well as Strzok's mistress. Among these text messages were the following excerpts, all released by the FBI's Inspector General Horowitz, an Obama appointee:

Page: "Trump's not going to become president, right? Right?"

Strzok: "No. No he won't. We'll stop it."

Strzok would subsequently tell page that he would devise an "insurance policy" to stop Trump if he were to win the election. Another senior agent wrote: "Trump supporters are all poor to middle class, uneducated, lazy POS [pieces of shit] that think he will magically grant them jobs for doing nothing. They probably didn't watch the debates, aren't fully educated on his policies, and are stupidly wrapped up in his unmerited enthusiasm." Yet others on a senior level disparaged lower ranking agents within the bureau who might vote for Trump: "I find anyone who enjoys [this job] an absolute fucking idiot. If you don't think so, ask them one more question. Who are you voting for? I guarantee you it will be Donald Drumpf." Similar emails described Trump supporters as retarded.

As if these arrogant, privileged elitists, living quite well off tax-payer salaries do not sufficiently bring one's blood to boil, the suggestion allegedly made by Deputy Attorney General, Rod Rosenstein, that he wear a wire in meetings with President Trump to gain information leading to invocation of the 25th Amendment to the Constitution, allowing for removal of a president deemed unfit or unable to serve, takes the cake. Rosenstein now denies making this suggestion; however, if true, the most chilling aspect of this is the notion of an effort to engineer a putsch by bureaucrats not even contemplated by the Amendment as being empowered to invoke it. Rosenstein is no longer in office, but the beat goes on. The Central Intelligence Agency (CIA), though more surreptitious than its sister agency, is no less culpable in undermining our democratic principles.

The CIA is prohibited, by law, from conducting its operations domestically. Domestic intelligence and counterintelligence activities are within the exclusive bailiwick of the FBI. The CIA has had important, though little known, successes since its replacement of the Office

WE FACE A CLEAR AND PRESENT DANGER ⌒ 109

of Strategic Services (OSS) after WWII, and it has had well-publicized failures. In spite of its propensity to avoid oversight by engaging in illegal activities, such as the smuggling of heroin from Southeast Asia during the Vietnam war and the import of cocaine from Columbia, to finance its off-book clandestine operations, the Agency serves a necessary function in the realm of global realpolitik. That said, its mandate and methods are ill-advised for domestic employment precisely for the reasons that it is is effective overseas—the institution of regime changes, blackmailing foreign leaders and business people into aligning with US interests and the like are the aims of its trade. However, it has become clear that the CIA has overstepped its bounds by foraying in to the domestic arena.

In March of 2014, Senator Diane Feinstein leveled accusations that the CIA had spied on the US Senate Intelligence Committee by breaching a firewall in the RINet network, that had been provided by the Agency, to monitor the Committee's activities. CIA director, John Brennan, ultimately fessed up, admitting that the Agency had done so, after having originally denied the allegations.

Feinstein characterized CIA's actions as unconstitutional and she was quite right. And, in spite of other Committee members calling for Brennan's resignation, nothing came of it. At the time of the illegal intrusion by the CIA, the Intelligence Committee was investigating the post 9/11 rendition and torture practices of the CIA. In an ironic twist, in August 2018, it was widely reported that in about 2013 or 2014, Feinstein was notified that an aide of the Senator's had been a spy for the Peoples Republic of China (PRC) for some twenty years, including during Feinstein's chairing of the Senate Intelligence Committee. Coincidentally, during two years of her tenure in that position, 2010-2012, some eighteen to twenty CIA sources in the PRC were either killed or imprisoned. Feinstein, an ardent supporter of the PRC, did not lose her security clearances and her aide, though dismissed, was never charged.

Whether there is a nexus between Feinstein's failure to act against the CIA for its violations of law and the mole in her ranks is a matter for Freedom Of Information Act (FOIA) requests in the distant future; however, the events are tainted by an aura of impropriety. So too is the conduct of senior intelligence officials in the overt political arena.

Senior officials in the intelligence community, including Brennan and Clapper, for inexplicable reasons, are permitted to keep their secrets clearances after leaving office. Though no longer working on behalf of the country, these clearances allow such past political appointees and bureaucrats access to the nation's secrets in order to forward their personal fortune and agendas. They are afforded back-door entry into the official intelligence community in the form of private contracts and utilize their access to information in public forums as pundits and critics of subsequent administrations and, in some cases, to sell their services to foreign interests. Given these circumstances it is untoward for these actors to strive to undermine the foreign policy of any president's administration, regardless of what these are or who holds executive office. Brennan and Clapper have done so relentlessly, as to the Trump presidency, without thought for the effect it might have on US interests or its diminution of the right of American voters to institute policy through the electoral process that seats a president. These are not elected officials and it is beyond hubris for such individuals to believe they are privileged beyond all account-ability. The revocation of Brennan's security clearances by President Trump were long overdue—not just in the present sense, but as a policy that should be adopted by every executive with respect to for-mer intelligence community employees. Out should mean out; when they leave their positions, there is no justification for their continued access to information related to national security interests that is not available to any citizen of this country. If they disagree with a particular president or policy, they may avail themselves of the same political processes open to all Americans. Admittedly, I experienced a bout of schadenfreude to hear Brennan whine when he lost his clearances. Welcome to the real world, pal.

If the specter of constitutional breaches is apparent in the activities of other agencies, it is the National Security Agency (NSA), The US' electronic spy ship, that bodes the greatest ill to individual privacy interests and the integrity of our republic. Having largely operated out of the public eye, moving deep within the shadows of the intelligence community, Edward Snowden's dramatic revelations thrust the NSA into the limelight. Snowden's disclosures are well documented and have been acknowledged as true. Among these, which affect ordinary Americans, the NSA obtained a secret court order requiring Verizon to daily provide the NSA with millions of American's phone records. AT&T provides these voluntarily. It can manipulate social media and has developed and employs XKeyscore, which allows collection of anything on the internet. As described by Snowden in an interview with *The Guardian,* "I, sitting at my desk [could] wiretap anyone, from you or your accountant, to a federal judge or even the president, if I had a personal email." Snowden also revealed that the NSA has unfettered access to "private emails" and that it harvests millions of email and messaging contacts and messages, as well as data stored by Google, Yahoo and others. It tracks the online sexual activities of people in order to garner information to discredit them if the need arises. Snowden collaborator and journalist, Glenn Greenwald, in his book, *No Place To Hide,* reported the express objectives of the NSA's data collection were to "Collect it All," Process It All," Exploit it All," "Partner it All," "Sniff it All" and "Know it All."

While Snowden's revelations, particularly as to legitimate foreign operations, may have had adverse effects on US national security interests, and Snowden's purposes perhaps debatable, or somewhat naive in some instances, the fact remains that all of them are incontrovertible. Equally troubling, as detailed in an unsealed Foreign Intelligence Surveillance Court (FISA) document, dated April 26, 2017, the Court held that the searches by NSA were illegal, widespread and raised a "very serious Fourth Amendment issue." Although likely that the NSA has crossed the Rubicon of illegality throughout its existence, it gained momentum in this under the executive leadership of little Bush in the post 9/11 years, which was further augmented by the Obama administration, even to the extent of having the agency spy on Trump transition team members, and has not abated under Trump.

The NSA's response to critics has largely posited that "if you have nothing to hide, you have nothing to fear." This Orwellian stance belies the Fourth Amendment principle that if reasonable suspicion arises that you have something illegal to hide, the state gains the right to obtain a court order to find it—and that may be something to fear. Instead, we have an unfettered bureaucracy that develops profiles on every American. Hence, if you want to watch a little porn, read political treatises, research the Fourth and Fourteenth Amendments, make reservations at an Indian restaurant, buy a new truck, write a letter to the editor and the like, your profile is evolved within the NSA's data chambers. The purpose may be to use this data against you, should you be deemed subversive, or to develop a social credit score to determinate the scope of any future rights you might seek to enjoy—akin to that employed in the PRC.

From a presidential viewpoint, the capabilities of a totalitarian surveillance state, to be commanded at will, have proven to be irresistible. As pointed out by Snowden, employees at every tier in the NSA used its technology to spy on acquaintances, friends, partners and even strangers of interest. But, we are asked to believe, that such excesses would not tempt senior level bureaucrats within the agency, or other agencies with access to the NSA's wherewithall. And, here we come to the real crux of the problem, which is certainly germane in the present political atmosphere.

If the decimation of our privacy interests are not sufficient to cause alarm, the ability of bureaucrats to direct the course of this country should be. To put it more succinctly, there is absolutely nothing to bar a director of the NSA from gathering information about the FISA judges, appointed to curtail NSA abuses; presidents; members of the house; and senators, and flat out using that information to force acquiescence to whatever policy demands might be in the offing, whether by that director, individually, or as a participant in James Comey's coalition of bureaucrats, as referenced above. Nor are there any limits to how the technology at stake could be used for personal gains. If information is power, as the adage goes, and power corrupts, what of absolute information?

The ultimate chill factor is that we now have bureaucrats with the means and the mentality to govern this country through proxies. This has the prospect of rendering the electoral process completely moot and, if realized, marks the end of our democracy. The real problem is that we, the American public, have no inkling of whether this has already happened. Nor do we seem to have a sense of other consequences wrought in the name of homeland security. ∽

CHAPTER 13

A FEW WORDS
ABOUT HOMELAND SECURITY. . .

A few words about homeland security are merited in the context of whether our domestic national security faces a greater threat from within than without. The Department of Homeland Security (DHS) was conjured out of thin air by President George W. Bush, following the terrorist attacks of September 11, 2001. In fact, the attacks were the rationale offered by Bush for its necessity. The DHS was created by Congress, at the behest of Bush, on November 25, 2002. It amalgamated twenty-two federal agencies, comprised of some 180,000 employees, under a single banner, ostensibly to further domestic security. By 2017, the DHS had grown to some 240,000 people and consumes an annual budget well in excess of $40 billion dollars. It is the third largest cabinet department, overshadowed solely by the Departments of Defense and Veteran Affairs. Although governed by a Secretary, DHS policy is set by the White House, through the Homeland Security council, which reports directly to the president. To understand the ramifications arising in the wake of DHS's establishment, it is worth noting the preceding events.

Whether one subscribes to the theory that the attacks of September 11, 2001 arose through some conspiracy involving the Bush administration; that the attacks were simply a manifestation of the inevitable; that these were a matter of sheer luck on the part of the perpetrators, coupled with the complete ineptitude of the intelligence community and the FBI's counter-intelligence subdivision; the result of inter-agency rivalries and a lack of cohesion in the sharing of known information between intelligence agencies; or, as many believe, a truncated combination of all of these. To be clear, this is not meant to underwrite the notion that some vast conspiracy on the part of the executive branch led to the assaults of 9/11, or that there was participation therein by federal agents. However, the evidence unearthed by Congress's 9/11 Commission and other credible investigations do suggest the following: During Bill Clinton's tenure at the White House and that of his successor, Bush, intelligence regarding the identities, support networks and differing aspects of the activities of many of the 9/11 attackers were known to both the CIA and the FBI. Bin Laden was a creature of the CIA's creation—it supported him in resisting the Soviet invasion of Afghanistan. Bin Laden's posture regarding the US was well known throughout the intelligence community in the years after the Soviet withdrawal from Afghanistan because he was quite overt in making these views known, even going so far as to announce them during interviews with American media outlets. Each agency had snapshots of what the perpetrators of the attacks on the US were up to, but by not sharing the data, an actionable picture did not timely emerge. Reaction by the Clinton administration to the 1998 attacks on the American embassies in Kenya and Tanzania in effect elevated the stature of Bin Laden and his cohorts in Al Qaeda to that of enemy combatants, rather than as the international criminals they were, thereby legitimizing them among the Islamic radicals. Further support for the terrorists was generated by the employment of bombs against suspected Al Qaeda positions due to the consequent loss of life among innocent bystanders incinerated and injured, all characterized as "collateral damage." Where Clinton's engagement and impetus in addressing the problem was distracted by his domestic travails, Bush was oft influenced by his advisers and unwillingness to confront the Saudi Arabian role in terrorism—likely because of his family's business dealings with members and citizens of the Kingdom. Leadership in both the CIA and FBI refused to take seriously information about the terrorists that had been accumulated by agents in the field. There was, throughout the years preceding 9/11, a dearth of understanding related to the culture, mores and nuances of middle easterners. And, finally, I suspect, there were those, likely within the intelligence communities, who believed that successive administrations were not taking the risks posed by terrorist groups with sufficient seriousness, perhaps due to public apathy, and thus were of mind that a successful attack might serve to ignite those fires. This said, I choose not to believe those elements anticipated the scope and severity of the attacks mounted on September 11, 2001. Regardless of one's belief, it is inescapably true that the 9/11 attacks have served as the rationale for the unprecedented accumulation of power in the presidency and the simultaneous, unequaled dilution of civil rights constitutionally guaranteed to Americans.

In this context, and supplementing the abuses of civil liberties by the intelligence community, the DHS is another of the elephants in the room. Its mandate encompasses control over our borders, through US Customs and Border Enforcement and Immigration and Customs Enforcement, US Immigration and Customs Enforcement and US Citizenship and Immigration Services, as well as the US Coast Guard. It controls access to travel, both domestically and internationally, under the aegis of the Transportation Security Administration (TSA), and is the parent agency of the Secret Service and the Federal Protective Service. DHS is responsible for managing national disasters via the Federal Emergency Management Agency (FEMA), countering weapons of mass destruction (whatever that means), training federal law enforcement officers, overseeing the office of science and technology, gathering intelligence and working as a clearing house for intelligence gathered by other agencies. Other subsets, equally varied, of the DHS permeate the federal landscape. Ultimately, the DHS has proven to be an unwieldy, inefficient bureaucracy of the worst order, at least in terms of its mandate—to secure the country against terrorist attacks. Its machinations have been markedly more effective in undermining the rights of those it was designed to protect.

Since its inception, the DHS has received few laudatory comments, while criticism of the agency has been consistent and mounting. Most notably, the department is deemed to have failed miserably in consolidating intelligence related to terrorist threats, its effort resulting in internecine hoarding of information and inter-agency conflicts, exponentially worsening the shortcomings in intelligence sharing that were the DHS's basic raison d'etre. This was demonstrated when Border Agents, having apprehended a number of middle easterners illegally crossing the border with Mexico in 2017, queried the DHS terrorist data base and finding no information related to whether they posed a risk, took the initiative to likewise inquire of the FBI. The FBI had flagged these individuals as having likely affiliations with terrorist organizations. Some two years earlier, it was reported by House Representative, Stephen Lynch, a Democrat from Massachusetts, that a congressional investigation had revealed some seventy-two employees of the DHS to be on the terrorist watch list authored by the Department. As a result of this and other failings on the part of the DHS in screening foreign entrants into the US, Lynch, well before Trump's echoing of the sentiment, supported legislation aimed at tightening the vetting of Syrians seeking asylum in the US. Her rationale was based upon the DHS's failure to do so of its own accord.

The Department was charged, in 2015, through a Senate oversight report, issued by then Senator Tom Coburn, with failing to enforce the nation's immigration laws. The report offered that only three out of 100 persons illegally entering the US faced deportation. While this was a case of policy under the Obama administration, little has changed in the intervening years. The Senate report characterized the DHS as a "dysfunctional" body, citing abysmal failings in its tasks to ensure American cyber-security, its inability to demonstrate the effectiveness of its counter-terrorism programs, its ineffectiveness in dealing with natural disasters, coupled with a propensity for declaring minor events as national disasters in order to justify its ever burgeoning budgetary demands and the threat it poses to civil liberties. Indeed, the Senate report found that in addition to being fraught with instances of fraud and corruption, the DHS had, as it continues to do, an utter lack of respect for the Constitutional rights of Americans.

The DHS established so-called "fusion centers," around the country which were designated as clearing houses for local, state and federal intelligence related to latent terrorist activities. The upshot of these is that the exercise of First Amendment rights by average, law abiding citizens has resulted their being labeled as threats to national security. Among them, the ACLU's admonition to a school regarding Christmas celebrations, all military veterans, Muslim lobbyists, anti-war activists, anti-death penalty activists, pro and anti-abortion activists, Second Amendment (the right to bear arms) activists, environmental activists, Tea Party members, third-party voters and Ron Paul supporters. The DHS labeled one half of American voters as "right wing extremists." All of this is well documented throughout the Department's archives. The Cato Institute, on February 2, 2011, published a paper by David Rittgers, entitled "We're All Terrorists Now," with links to DHS sites listing its transgressions through that date. Subsequent searches of the Department's site offer the revelation that its mentality regarding the civil rights of Americans to express themselves has only become more deeply entrenched. One need only examine the well publicized practices of the Transportation Security Administration (TSA), a subdivision of the DHS, to confirm this.

The TSA, charged in bulk with providing passenger screening and security at the nation's airports and on board security through federal air marshals, employs about 50,000 people. Inspections of TSA's efficiency in thwarting weapon toting passengers from clearing through security have resulted in failure rates, over the years, from 70 to over 90 percent. TSA has not, by its own accord, prevented any terrorist attacks. Although this may present a chicken and egg debate, if one takes into account post 9/11 hardened cockpit entries, passenger awareness and the employment of air marshals, the likelihood of aping the methodology employed by the hijackers in that attacks somewhat scant. The TSA has encountered serious problems regarding the conduct of its purported mission. It has improperly vetted employees with dubious histories, employees have been engaged in growing incidents of thefts from passenger bags and other passenger abuses and it has compiled lists that have proven to adversely affect the travel rights of Americans included thereon. There are three such lists.

The first of these is the "No Fly" list, a compendium of persons deemed to be latent or actual terrorists derived from multi-agency databases and maintained by the federal Terrorist Screening Center. Well founded in principle, unfortunately this list, to the extent information has been made public, from time to time, over the years, is fraught with nonsense. It includes the names of terrorists, such as Bin Laden, who are long deceased and fails to include others who are still active. In 2006, as was reported by CBS's *60 Minutes* on October 5, 2006, eleven British subjects who had been investigated for over a year for plotting to blow up airliners were not on the list. Nor was one David Belfield, thought to be working for Iran's Ayatollah Khomeini as an assassin on the list. Intelligence agencies justified omissions like this on grounds that terrorist organizations would be alerted as to names on the list, if the list were leaked by operatives on foreign governments that are privy to the names on it. Yikes! So who is on the list. The exact number of persons on the list is classified, as are their identities. Nonetheless, one gleans a sense of the skewed criteria used to compile the list from those few instances the names have been publicized as a result of abuse of the lists, or simple mistakes. Senator Ted Kennedy and the singer Cat Stevens, whose crime apparently was that he converted to Islam, appeared on the list, as have numerous children and people with names similar to those of legitimate entries. More chilling are the scintilla of indicia that inclusion on the No Fly list may be a matter of simply exercising one's rights to free speech or assembly. As reported by *The Guardian,* April 27, 2007, Walter Murphy, a professor of jurisprudence at Princeton, on being denied boarding because he was on the Terrorist Watch List, recounted the following exchange with the airline employee that had denied his his pass:

Airline Employee: "Have you been on any peace marches? We ban a lot of people from flying because of that."

Murphy offered that he had not marched, but had given a lecture at Princeton that was "highly critical of George Bush for his many violations of the Constitution."

Airline Employee: "That'll do it."

Others have found themselves on the list for no apparent reason, other than peaceful political activity and some, it appears, are found there because of data entered at the above-mentioned, "fusion centers" operated by the DHS. For American citizens, the list has, for all intents and purposes, negated the concept of due process and it is reportedly beyond onerous to have one's name removed.

The second list, "Quite Skies," it was revealed by the *Washington Post* and other media in early 2018, is not quite a list; rather, it is a program, arbitrarily instituted in about 2011, whereby travelers are targeted based upon their travel histories, bathroom visits, body odor, alertness and a litany of other subjective and inane criteria. Perhaps mismatched socks, books held in hand, music played and similarly suspicious indicia are also employed. Or, a la Pol Pot, it may be merely sufficient to be wearing glasses—a clear indication of unsavory intellectualism. In any event, once identified, air marshals are charged with following these folks around airports and watching them on flights to monitor the subjects' behaviors. Whether this or some other secret lists include such criteria is unknown. Nonetheless, the sheer gall and arrogance by which this federal agency rationalizes its program is indicative that this could well be the case—yet another assault on our rights.

And, were this not enough, we are informed there is another list. This one compiled by TSA, as reported by *The New York Times* in May of 2018, which had obtained a copy of the relevant TSA directive, is directed at monitoring "unruly" passengers. These latent troublemakers include people who linger outside of security checkpoints, perhaps parents watching their children go through security, as I often do; those who voice displeasure over pat downs, or perhaps rude behavior on the part of TSA personnel; and, of course, others who are deemed a physical threat to TSA officers. This list, again, is entirely subjective and "permits TSA officials to blacklist people for conduct that can be wholly innocuous," according to Hugh Black, of the ACLU. Ultimately, the list is a power ploy that is designed solely to arm the TSA in cowing passengers into accepting anything that is done to them, regardless of whether such acts contravene any constitutional rights. It is the manifestation of the "Us verses Them" mentality that has come to permeate public service attitudes.

A multitude of commentators, the ACLU and, even to some extent, federal watchdogs, such as the GAO, have suggested disbandment of the TSA on a variety of grounds, ranging from inefficiency and cost to the ongoing disruption to civil liberties represented by the TSA's operations. And, while these are all valid concerns, they miss the most glaring argument for change. That being the fact that 77 percent of all flights in the USA are not subject to TSA's or any other security measures.

According to the Federal Aviation Administration (FAA), there are some 14,485 private airports in this country, of which 4,211 are equipped to handle jet traffic. By way of contrast, there are 5,116 public airports. Private jet traffic in the US, during 2017, constituted some 25 million flying hours. In its "Security Guidelines for General Aviation Airport Operators and Users," of July 2017, TSA openly acknowledges the lack of any requirement for TSA's presence, or any mandated security, at private aircraft facilities (FBOs), save for those which are in close proximity to Washington, DC. Some of these share runways with commercial airliners and others do not. Some lie in remote areas, while others adjoin major urban areas, such as New York, Los Angeles and the like. Those that can accommodate jets are generally equipped to handle aircraft of sufficient size to make overseas flights.

Private jets employing the services of FBOs range in size from light, short haul aircraft to mid size jets, capable of crossing the country or the Atlantic, and jumbo jets, such as those owned by many of the well over 4,000 members of the Saudi royal family, including those the Bush league allowed to soar out of the country in the wake of 9/11, when all other flights were grounded. Remember the Saudis? Some of them flew planes into buildings on 9/11, while others, in the upper echelons, still stand accused of financing them and, most recently, the royals of that country appear to have ordered a journalist hacked to pieces within the confines of Saudi Arabia's consulate in Turkey on October 2, 2018, after which they very publicly executed dozens, among them women and children, for such heinous crimes as protesting and being gay. Lest we lay to much criticism for Saudi indulgence on little

Bush, it must be said that Obama and Trump are equally culpable for coddling the Saudi regime.

The security exposure presented by these FBOs literally renders the TSA as an archaic, utterly useless federal entity. It serves no useful purpose other than to inure Americans to the concept of enjoying any rights what so ever, and to indoctrinate us into acceptance of being treated like cattle, while our upper echelon bureaucrats; select pols; media elites; entertainers; and, oligarchs flit about impervious to the realities we face in airports. If the TSA has any other function, it is to sustain a stable of butterballs unlikely to gain useful employment elsewhere.

Were I not included on some federal list to date, it is a circumstance that will likely be remedied should this book, or at least this chapter, come to light. I must hope, then, for torrential sales so that I might afford soaring away in the comforts of a private bird. Or, I suppose, I can always drive.

There is, of course, another world of lists; that of the information technology cartels and their deliberate furtherance of the existential crisis facing democracy. ⌒

CHAPTER 14

WE ARE LITTLE MORE
THAN COMMODITIES . . .

We are little more than commodities to the behemoths that govern the increasingly inescapable digital world. Our role as commodities has become the lifeblood of commerce and sociopolitical manipulation. In essence, we are the sum of our data, which is comprised of our telephone calls; text messages; internet searches; on-line and in store purchases; travels, whether by car, plane or train; restaurant choices; medical records; dating patterns; work habits; political choices; bank and credit card accounts and financial activities; television and musical preferences; and every other thing that we do that entails the direct or indirect employment of digital electronics. Our homes, cars and telephones have become listening and data collection outposts. Once gathered, our personal information is stored, sold or traded to third parties and, invariably, to the federal government. In the case of Facebook, users are scored for "trustworthiness," pretty much a privatized version of what the PRC is utilizing to monitor, categorize and ultimately punish its citizens. All of this is done without our consent or through our agreements, mostly unread, in the dozens of pages of incomprehensible conditions we must consent to when we sign on to open accounts with Facebook, Amazon, Google, Twitter, Instagram, AT&T, Microsoft and their ilk.

Worse, it has become all but impossible to function in our jobs, schools and daily lives without mandatory utilization of one or more of the "services" provided by these data sucking entities. Nor are we afforded any legal rights to protect our individual data and privacy interests. To the contrary, should protest arise, we are admonished with the Orwellian mantra that we have "nothing to fear, if we have done nothing wrong." Protected by their fiscal relationships with politicians and contractual entanglements with federal agencies, such as the NSA, the Pentagon and the CIA, operating under the guise of creating a transparent society, these mega corporation have stripped us of every right to lawfully live our lives without scrutiny. This dystopian world view will ring the death knell of every principle of democracy and the precious freedoms it embodies.

Moreover, by manipulating our data, the information available on line and the dissemination of both, these omnipotent information caliphates are hell bent on having us accept a virtual interpretation of events and society that has no basis in reality. Except, of course, to the extent we can be convinced to react and live our lives according to these contrivances, thereby giving them life—much as the Catholic Church engraved its views of the universe into the minds of its adherents, branding as heretics all those who disagreed, in spite of the scientific evidence that vindicated them. More draconian in effect, people may become exalted or vilified simply by elimination of public access to contravening information. Debates regarding issues are increasingly decided through the expungement from the ether of all material referencing one position or the other.

Though often couched in rationalizations of encouraging acceptable social mores, these manipulations are blatantly aimed at the social engineering of a global society that conforms to the paradigms imagined by its designers; to sew a crop of of manageable, compliant and docile commodities and consumers that are entirely bereft of access to the competing avenues of information that are necessary to the employment of critical thinking. Thus, we are witness to the institutional implementation of the mechanics that will culminate, quite rapidly, in the utter demise of critical thinking and its replacement with blind acceptance of the pablum we are fed. In turn, as noted previously, democracy will perish.

While perhaps the notion of governance under a sophocracy, Plato's ideal of rule by the wise, might be more appealing than our present system, I would be hard pressed to accept the personae of Mark Zuckerberg, Jeff Bezos, Bill Gates and their fellow titans of digitally imposed totalitarianism in such roles. Each, in their own way, as reflected by both deeds and words, have exhibited traits of narcissistic sociopathy. All hold elitist views borne of their knowledge and exploitation of digital technology and the wealth derived therefrom and have, to varying degrees, encouraged cultism within their respective enterprises. These folks are more aptly defined as tyrannical oligarchs than the philosopher kings necessary to a sophocratic state and I, as many others have begun to, would advocate a severe curtailment of their powers, and that of their corporate entities, rather than any further expansion of these.

On an ongoing and increasing basis, countless, readily verif able revelations by tech companies, usually on being outed by news organizations or challenged by governments other than our own, unambiguously support the foregoing concerns. AT&T, for instance, voluntarily entered into an agreement to turn all customer data over to the federal government. This company, I believe, also sells the content of conversations to third parties. My \experience is that conversations on my telephone, without corresponding texts or emails, have led to email solicitations relevant to the subject matter of the calls. Verizon is under a court order to turn over customer data to the US government. Samsung and its competitors in the Smart television sector include cameras and microphones in those devices allow monitoring of people in the vicinity of television sets. Samsung's privacy statements, as far back as 2013, allowed that private conversations would be captured and could be passed on to third parties.

In 2017, Wikileaks revealed that the CIA, through its "Weeping Angel" program, likewise can and does monitor Americans through their television sets. Microsoft, through its Xbox gaming device, listens to, saves and stores all conversations that occur within its range. Amazon TV does likewise and all digital providers of entertainment and in home smart devices record and video everything within the confines of the home. All digital television content providers track viewing habits. Google's Alexa famously has recorded conversations within the home and transmitted these to third parties. Google and Yahoo admit to scanning, storing and selling information gleaned from its email account holders. Computer webcams and microphones have been found to record the data of their users, a fact acknowledged by then FBI director, James Comey, who admitted to covering the cameras on his computers to mitigate this issue. Cookies, regardless of user preferences, are routinely installed on computers and monitor all internet activities of the users—that data then turned over to third-parties for marketing purposes and to the government to aid in constructing profiles on ordinary, law-abiding people. Data is collected in much the same way with respect to the occupants of cars that are digitally connected.

Alphabet, Inc.'s Google was caught and admitted to capturing people's wireless data while mapping neighborhoods. It was also proven, in 2018 by researchers at Princeton University, to have illegally tracked the movements of millions of iPhone and Android telephone users, even when preventive settings had been employed. Apple iPhone users were exposed by merely downloading Google apps. Likewise, Twitter is under investigation in Ireland for tracking users' internet browsing histories and marketing that data to third parties. Facebook is also the subject of multiple privacy violations in Europe, where, contrary to the US, there are some statutory protections against privacy intrusions. On a similar note, Uber stands accused of tracking customers whose privacy settings have been activated and even those who have deleted its app.

In 2018 it was also disclosed that Google had entered into an arrangement with MasterCard, the credit card company, to acquire data on MasterCard's some 2 billion card holders' spending habits and patterns. Google, in turn, makes this information available to its advertisers. Both corporations claim that personal information is not shared; however, given the lack of any accountability to anyone by both entities, the veracity of this claim is questionable. Google further claims to have access to the data of some "70 percent" of US Credit and debit card holders through partnership arrangements, though it refused to name those partners. Amazon likewise collects and disseminates all of the "customer" data it can lay its hands on and, given its relationship with the CIA and the Pentagon, it would be naive to believe that it does not have a data "sharing" arrangement with the federal government. Its cloud based systems, given voice by Alexa and Echo, reside in some 40 million American homes, tracking, recording, transmitting and storing our tastes, moods, problems and every other imaginable form of personal data. This is buttressed by Amazon's drive to monopolize the retail sector, a problem in and of itself, which gives it further access to consumer data and its ownership of media outlets, such as the *Washington Post,* which ensures a positive media spin on its endeavors. It is utterly amazing to me that people are paying to be spied on for the sake of convenience. More incredible, is the fact that most public school systems require students to work on projects through Google's platforms without any consideration for the privacy implications this has for these future adults.

Facebook is no less intrusive and is perhaps even more so. With over 2 billion users, all spilling their guts detailing the most intimate aspects of their lives, as well as having their movements, communications and on-line habits tracked, Facebook has become a veritable vacuum cleaner of data. It employs facial recognition which, as time passes, will allow identification and tracking of anyone almost anywhere. It gleans from its users every kernel of information, which is not limited to that of its users. Data is mined about friends, relatives and acquaintances, whether or not subscribers to Facebook, and once harvested, is simply, though very profitably, traded on the data commodities market. Most recently, Facebook has suggested it may recommend "friends" to users based upon who is in proximity to those users.

Not surprisingly, where personal data is collected it, is also lost to hackers or marketed without permission to entities other than those engaged in basic retail sales. The news has been replete, over the last several years, with acknowledged instances of wholesale data hacking. Recent incidents have involved Google and Facebook accounts, as to the former, a breach of some 500,000 accounts resulted in its shutting down Google+, the consumer version of its social network, while the latter, Facebook, was hacked by Russians now offering to sell the data of some 81,000 account holders on a claim, not verified, that some 120 million accounts have been compromised. Aside from the obvious risks, hacking of data is most assuredly designed to achieve the end results of identity theft and blackmailing of people who, in spite of their online indiscretions, actually do have something to hide. More chillingly, in 2014, the data of 50 to 60 million Facebook users was sold by a professor, who had harvested the data with Facebook's apparent acquiescence, to Cambridge Analytics. Cambridge ultimately employed that data to have affected account holders vote Republican in the 2016 elections.

The actions of Cambridge Analytics are suggestive of the greater threats posed by the data collection of digital giants such as Facebook, Google and the like. Those risks lie in the establishment of data monopolies and the manipulation of information sought by anyone utilizing a particular company's technology. One would be foolish and naive to assume that whoever controls information is not going to control its dissemination. Ninety percent of all internet searches undertaken globally are, for example, done through Google. It also owns You Tube and about 200 other companies in the tech sector. Algorithms developed by Google determine the search results. These operate as data sifters, ostensibly producing objective results, organized in order of relevance, but, in truth, results are presented on the basis of a number of criteria—including preferential treatment for Google customers and partners. Moreover, search results are imprinted with sociocultural and political values and objectives as are determined by Google, or its parent, Alphabet. In Google's case, these happen to be progressive, to the extent its finances are not adversely impacted. In short, Google has the power and will to withhold information from people using its technology. This flat out signifies its abilities to shape public opinion, purchasing habits and promote the Google vision of a perfect society. Although it faces no repercussions in the US, save political rhetoric, it was fined $2.7 billion dollars by the European Union for manipulating search results for economic gain, and is yet again under investigation in Europe for similar practices.

Facebook and Twitter are equally culpable of data manipulation and censorship. In November of 2018, the British Commissioner on Information referred Facebook to the European Union's supervisor for social networks in Europe, citing concerns about Facebook's practices regarding the dissemination of false information, particularly related to politics, and its disregard for the privacy of its users. More recently,

Mark Zuckerberg, Facebook's co-founder and CEO, was asked to testify at an international committee, representing at least five governments, investigating disinformation and interference in elections. Zuckerberg refused.

Unfortunately, the political focus on so-called fake news is somewhat of a red herring. Certainly, the issue of foreign interference in domestic affairs through the employment of propaganda and planted news is problematic. It is an age old problem that has been exacerbated by advanced information technology. However, the real problem is that under the guise of resolving this issue, Facebook, Twitter and other social media entities outlets have embarked on a course of quashing legitimate ideas and news by denying these access to their advertising rosters, news feeds and public dialogue, based strictly upon whether or not these agree with the host company's world view. Compounding the problem is the fact that governments and political parties, under guise of the same artifices, are demanding censorship of competing ideas. American political proponents of this position are using these arguments as a workaround to circumvent the Constitutionally guaranteed right to free speech—by inveigling privately owned social media to implement one-sided standards within the context of their monopolies on the flow of digital information.

At present, at least from varying statistical viewpoints, reported by *The Free Beacon, The Gateway Pundit, Western Journal* and others, the algorithms employed by Facebook, Twitter, Google, YouTube and company, have directly affected conservative media and other information outlets, as well as individual conservative viewpoints on topics such as immigration, abortion and the debate of numerous other valid issues as well as, in the case of Facebook, the views of moderate Muslims. The term, "illegal alien," for instance, has been labeled as verboten "hateful" speech by Twitter, in spite of the fact that this is a legal term. In this context one might wonder what comes next? Will we be required to call a rapist "choice challenged," lest the legal term be deemed "hateful." Meanwhile, pro-terrorist sites and accounts are left to trundle along untroubled by worries over censorship.

While the biases under development and that have been utilized in stifling free speech are oriented in favor of the political left at the moment, given the tenor of polarization in this country and Europe, the right is no less inclined to suppress opposing views and would be singing a very different tune were the tables turned. Indeed, while supporting so-called "progressives," in the west, these very same social media entities have utterly acquiesced to the demands of totalitarian regimes, in other parts of the world, to impose blanket censorship on views and information deemed by them to be hostile or disadvantageous. Among these are the PRC, Saudi Arabia and Russia. For instance, Google's "Dragonfly," a search engine developed for the PRC, will eliminate results for terms such as "human rights," "student protest," and "Nobel Prize," while enabling the PRC government to add censured terms and extract users' search data. There has been internal dissent at Google over its work for the PRC, however, according to its CEO, Sundar Pichai, who refused to release details of the search engine to US Senators, its benefits will be substantial both within and outside of the PRC. To me, and I leave it to the reader to deem this as cynical or realistic, Google's position is the harbinger of things to come in our digital world and the thought frightens me.

Advocates of censorship would be well advised to bear in mind that history clearly indicates that sociopolitical trends are prone to reversal. Of further import is that the suppression of ideas, even those that are clearly bad, forces these into an underground where they are prone to fester and re-emerge in often violent and unpredictable ways. It is far better to leave these in the public realm, to be debated and addressed openly, than to add disenfranchisement to the mix of grievances that generally accompany some good, and all lousy, ideas.

In the final analysis, the ultimate question that requires consideration is who should be the final arbiter of which ideas are acceptable or not. Of what information should or should not be allowed into the public forum. Given that the express objective of the digital information industry is to increase profits, it follows that collectively its implicit purposes must entail the subjective suppression of information, beliefs and ideas that may interfere with the objective realization of its goals. Meanwhile, the scions of technology hide behind walled compounds with armed security, their private lives bereft of any discernible data.

Among the rest of us there are ample human commodities and consumers who adamantly and emotionally support the implementation of censorship on varying grounds—most commonly to thwart totalitarian or fascist ambitions, popularly denoted as Nazism, which, incidentally, is socialism (National Socialist). In net sum, however, and regardless of the labels relied upon, the success of these endeavors will engender the institution of totalitarianism to an extent that can never be remedied because of the technological wherewithall in the public and private sectors to forestall any resistance.

All of this, naturally enough, recalls the common thread, found throughout this book, of the effect of education's demise in this country and, increasingly, throughout the western world. In the present case, it has paved the way to institutionally replace critical thinking with indoctrination, justified by the increasingly accurate presupposition that we, as constituents, are too stupid and ill-informed to make individual choices as to the good and bad of ideas and beliefs on the basis of our knowledge and experiences.

Exacerbating this dilemma are those of our other institutions which, though endowed with the means and historical impetus of injecting objective information into the framework of encouraging critical thinking, have opted instead to become part of the problem. This is particularly true of the fourth estate, traditional media, which has corrupted its role of objectivity by replacing it with advocacy. ❧

CHAPTER 15

TRADITIONAL NEWS MEDIA ARE GROWING INCREASINGLY IRRELEVANT . . .

T raditional news media are growing increasingly irrelevant because they have abdicated from the role of objectively providing information to instead assume the mantel of advocacy. This may be, part, attributable to abandonment of the Fairness Doctrine by the Federal Communications Commission in 1987. Under the doctrine, enforced from the 1940s through 1987, media outlets were mandated to present relatively balanced points of view. As a result, public faith in the media, collectively, has declined dramatically. Americans no longer trust the media. This is reflected in a number of polls on the subject. For instance, results of a poll conducted by NPR, *PBS NewsHour,* and Marist, released on July 2, 2018, found that 37 percent of adults had no trust in the media, while another 31 percent indicated having very little trust therein. The poll did find that Democrats were more inclined to trust the media than were Republicans or independents. As an aside, and certainly worth noting, only 35 percent of Americans purported to trust political polls. By way of contrast, Pew polls conducted in 1985 and 2009 found that during the intervening period, pubic trust in media's ability to "get it right" had waned from 55 percent to 29 percent.

Another poll, released in May, 2017 by Media Insights Projects, as reported by the *Huffington Post,* indicated that only 24 percent of Americans judged the media to be generally "moral," although far higher marks were given by respondents regarding the media they used most frequently. More telling, the same poll resulted in only 17 percent of Americans giving the media high grades for being "very accurate." Only 34 percent of those polled would say the same about their favored media outlets. The statistic related to the nexus between perceived "morality" of media outlets and their more frequent consumers is most troubling. From a logical standpoint, if media were inclined to report events objectively, they should be perceived as amoral, rather than adjudged as moral or immoral on the basis of news content. This points to the crux of the cancer that has consumed media—particularly in the mainstream.

Contrary to President Trump's allegations, oft parroted by the far right and, as it serves them, others on the political spectrum, media's greatest transgressions do not lie as much in the dissemination of "fake" news, as they do in in selective reporting and the editorialization of news. In net effect, these practices have culminated in the absence of news, if defined as the unbiased and impersonal reporting of all information relevant to a particular issue. Endless examples of both selective reporting of news and entwining personal, emotional rhetoric in its dissemination abound.

The case for selective reporting is underpinned by a number of examples, most recently as related to the reporting of news related to President Trump. On October 9, 2018, the Media Research Center (MRC), an admittedly conservative non-profit entity oriented towards tracking anti conservative media activity, released a verifiably credible report based upon its analysis of all evening news stories reported by ABC, CBS and NBC between June 1 and September 20, 2018. Aside from reporting biases and negative coverage of the Trump White House, MRC's study showed that in spite of the administration's significant gains in fostering an economic recovery, which included tax cuts, significant increases to US GDP and decreases in unemployment, notably among minorities, and repatriation of a large number of jobs, of a combined 1,960 minutes of airtime during that period, a mere 14 minutes were expended on reporting on those accomplishments. The study further found that during the Senate hearings related to the nomination of Justice Kavanaugh to the US Supreme Court, some 32 minute were devoted to coverage by the three networks; however, once allegations of sexual misconduct on the nominee's part surfaced, an additional 249 minutes were dedicated to this topic. It must be noted that when some of the alleged victims' stories were firmly debunked or recanted, coverage was scant, at best. Among the same networks, between January 1, 2017 and January 26 of the following year, only 20 of 82 record high closings of the Dow on the New York Stock Exchange, while declines received more coverage than all gains combined.

In 2016, the Southern Poverty Law Center, together with the American Federation of Teachers circulated a questionnaire to some 1.6 million educators, asking them to report instances of derogatory or racist conduct towards students. The ensuing report stated that 40 percent of the respondents had "heard derogatory language directed at students of color, Muslims, immigrants, and people based on gender or sexual orientations." No differentiation was recorded to the ethnic or racial sources of that conduct, which could be of significance and of use to combat biases. Equally telling, the Southern Poverty Law Center self censured the results. An additional, initially unreported question in the survey, asked whether respondents had encountered any "derogatory language directed at white students." Twenty percent of the respondents reported that they had. While the former statistic was widely reported by the *Washington Post, The New York Times* and others, none of these reported the latter statistic, once reluctantly released under pressure from the *New York Post*.

Similarly, while news covering of global warming is well reported, contrary scientific findings are not. For instance, in 2017, Polar Portal, publisher of climate research undertaken by the Danish Meteorological Institute, the Geological Survey of Denmark and Greenland and the National Space Institute published the annual Arctic ice surface mass budget summary, which reports on how much ice glaciers gain, compared to how much is lost due to warmer temperatures. The findings were that the amount of ice on the Greenland ice sheet in 2017 was the "fifth highest out of the 37 year record." This information was never reported by any mainstream media. Emerging reports over concerns of a global cooling trend due to decreases in solar activity also receive minimal coverage.

Perhaps the most egregious example of media's refusal to cover news arose during the Bush League's foray into Iraq on grounds that the regime of Saddam Hussein had supported the 9/11 terrorists and amassed weapons of mass destruction. In spite of the heroic efforts of then Knight Ridder's reporters and editors, that irrefutably proved the premises for invading to be sheer fabrications, not a single other mainstream media outlet, print or televised, refuted the Bush administration's assertions. Instead, bedazzled with the prospect of embedding reporters with the military, so that news from Iraq could be filtered and photos of body bags and civilian casualties underplayed, the Fourth Estate flat out, sold out.

Editorialization of the news is more readily discernible because there is no need to prove a negative. Insofar as news coverage of the Trump presidency is concerned, studies by a range of entities, academic, political and apolitical nonprofits, are in clear agreement of its negativity and biased presentation. Harvard's study, conducted by its Harvard Kennedy School and Shorenstein Center on Media, Politics and Public Policy reviewed coverage by *The New York Times, Washington Post, Wall Street Journal,* CNN, CBS, Fox News, NBC and European media outlets, The *Financial Times*, BBC and ARD. During the first 100 days of Trump's presidency, the study found that negative coverage never dropped below 70 percent and had often reached the threshold of 90 percent, setting a "new standard for negativity" in presidential press coverage. According to the results, Trump was the topic of 41 percent of all news stories, three times that of prior office holders. On average, coverage of Trump during his first 100 days in office ranged from 98 percent negative for issues related to immigration and 53 percent negative for reporting related to the economy. While the study's author, Thomas Patterson, allowed that Trump's conduct contributed to the negative coverage more so than in the cases of any of is predecessors, Patterson did opine that, "Nevertheless, the sheer level of negative coverage gives weight to Trump's contention, one shared by his core constituency, that the media are hell bent on destroying his presidency." Subsequent studies conducted by MRC and Pew Research clearly indicate that the trends revealed in Harvard have not abated to any extent.

Of interest is the fact that, while negative media coverage of the Trump administration has remained constant within the 80 to 90 percent range, Trump's approval rating in various polls, including those conducted by Gallup, have averaged between 43 and 52 percent. During the first 100 days of his presidency, Trump's approval ratings averaged 45 percent. By way of contrast, during President Obama's first 100 days in office, negative coverage was at about 41 percent, while his approval ratings were at 45 percent; In Little Bush's case, approvals were at 66 percent, with negative media coverage at 57 percent, although this was reduced drastically in the wake of 9/11; and during Bill Clinton's first 100 days of office, public approval ratings were at 45 percent and negative coverage at 60 percent. These comparisons suggest, particularly in the case of Trump, that the media is utterly out of sync with public sentiments and, more so, is possessed of considerable arrogance in deeming itself entitled to sway public opinion by couching its opinions as news.

Quite frankly, the blatant editorialization of news has reached the point of ridiculousness that can only be appealing to those who prefer emotion rhetoric to news or who prefer the news to take on the character of the old *Jerry Springer Show.* Breathless, outraged "reporters," panting with indignation, voices asqueal, lamenting a worldview contrary to their own, have become the norm. It all reminds me of the *Saturday Night Live* skits, back when SNL was still comedically relevant, where the response to any and all "bad" news, was to "blame it on Canada." Worse, most certainly as to CNN, MSNBC and Fox, is the newly evolving tendency to become part of the story, whether by campaigning for pols in the midterms or acting insufferably uncivil or rendering opinions, rather than asking questions, at press conferences.

Accompanying this ignorance, and there really is no other way to characterize it, we have the institutionalization in media of intellectual mediocrity, intolerance and racism, as in the case of *The New York Times'* hiring of Sarah Jeong, a Korean born "journalist," who tweeted, amongst other racist commentaries, her joy in being "cruel to old white men," utterly insensitive to the likelihood that her right to blather was ensured by "old white men," and others who fought in the Korean war. Another example of media hate baiting includes CNN's Don Lemon's pronouncement that the "biggest terror threat in this country is white men." Then we have the *Financial Times'* admonition to its writers, in which they were asked to avoid quoting too many males, ostensibly to garner increases in female readership.

All of this seems to make clear that media has developed an innate inability to understand context or hold empathy for the issues and people about which alleged journalists report. Furthermore, and perhaps of greater societal import, is that through media driven partisanship, we are losing track of real issues. It is time for some reality checks here. Much is re-hashed about the historic role of ethnic

Europeans in the miserable trade in slaves, yet very little is reported on the present slave trade: within the last year African refugees were openly sold as slaves in Libya; Saudi Arabia still keeps slaves; children in Cambodia are sold to, or kidnapped by, slavers to work as domestics, to be abused as sex toys for pedophiles or, if it could possibly be worse, their organs are forcibly harvested to be used in transplants performed in Thai medical clinics for the benefit of wealthy recipients from the PRC. Looking at media's stance on these circumstances, or the lack thereof, the conclusion easily reached is that slavery, more so its prevention, is not as worthy an issue as flagellating white men for the sins of the past

The same is true of reporting and dissemination of information regarding the abhorrent, though common, practice of genocide. The atrocities committed by Hitler's Nazis against Jews are oft revisited, yet the plight of the Roma, oft referred to as Gypsies, at Hitler's hands remains unmentioned. Nor are modern examples of genocide of import in the mainstream of news. And, the list of these is formidable. The Turks sought elimination of the Armenians; people are slaughtered on a daily basis in various African countries, singled out on the basis of their religion or tribe; The PRC's ambitions towards Tibetans and Muslim minorities are clearly genocidal; and Myanmar's government is hell bent on eradicating the Rohingya. While the latter has received some news treatment, the rest, by and large, have not. So the question arises, can we truly combat future genocides if we generally acknowledge only one historical example of this?

Racism in the United States is widely reported by media as the perpetuation of hateful conduct by whites against minorities, most often blacks. In reality this paints an incomplete and lopsided picture. There are ample instances of racist conduct against whites by minorities and among minority groups, as well as displays of bias predicated

upon gender and sexual orientation. Yet these are, as they say, inconvenient truths. The impossibility of solving the problems of racism
and other forms of prejudice turn increasingly on media's failure, and
outright refusal, to portray these as a fully completed landscape.

In refusing to provide a repleteness of information, absent any
emotionally charged spin doctoring, media is not only contributing
to sociocultural divisions and political partisanship—it has become
a driving force behind these phenomena. Ultimately, together with
the burgeoning tendency to publish news without verification of
purported facts, these will become the most dangerous hurdles to
maintaining a free press in this country and abroad. The so called
issue of "fake" news arises from all of the foregoing, woven together
with an increased propensity for reporting, the seamier the better and
most often on political topics, unverified information. This is coupled
with recalcitrance at retraction when contradictory facts emerge, as
was exemplified by the pillaging of Supreme Court nominee Kavanaugh
regarding allegations of sexual misconduct and more historically, the
unconscionable, unsubstantiated vilification of the Ramsey family
regarding the murder of their daughter, JonBenet, in 1996.

While partisan salaciousness and malice, whether left or right, is
a factor, much of this is caused by a desire to increase audiences, and
thereby advertising revenues, through sensationalism, and just plain
old, piss poor reporting. It is definitely not journalism. The traditional
journalists' questions requiring answers prior to publication of a story
were: "Who, Why, What, Where, When and How." Once sated, the
subsequent criteria were to: "Verify, Verify, Verify." Hence, the gravitas attached to Woodward and Bernstein's breaking of the Watergate
story and Knight-Ridder's revelations regarding the Bush League's
embroiling the US in the second Iraq war under false premises. These
have become largely irrelevant, not strictly the result of journalistic

incompetence, but further because media outlets themselves have lost their independence in the wake of corporatism—the traditional stalwarts of print, for example, *The Washington Post, The New York Times,* and *The Los Angeles Times,* are now owned or controlled by oligarchs, while CNN, perhaps the greatest television news outlet while under Ted Turner's sole tutelage, is an AT&T subsidiary. These interests present a growing chasm between accurate, impartial journalism and the interests of owners. Corresponding to the evolution of media ownership are, naturally enough, the increased demands to generate ever more revenues and assure the owner's political and economic interests.

So, we come to the present: the growing trend to demand curtailment of media activities on the premise that these are delivering "fake" news. As I have posited, this is a red herring. The real problem is that the media, as do many in the public, have come to believe that the First Amendment guarantee of free speech somehow gives broader preference to members of the media, the press, than to other members of the public. This is an utterly false premise. While the government may grant access to public forums to specific groups, such as the media for purposes of conducting press conferences, journalists enjoy the same rights to freedom of expression and are subjects to the same constraints thereon, as are the rest of us. Thus, relationships could be built between members of the media and government officials, on the basis of media's exclusive access to those officials, thereby giving media a "leg up," so to speak, on information.

This was all well and good, during the era when a television station, such as CBS, might report the news and then, separately and identifiably, have Walter Cronkite deliver an editorial opinion about some specific person or event. The alleged facts of a story might not always have been accurate, and the opinions oft controversial, but both were delivered with deliberation, decorum and civility. Print media operated similarly. This is no longer the case. As delineated above, news reporting has become so interwoven with opinion that fact is indistinguishable from fiction. Civility has all but been defeated. Instead, we see media personalities, more so on television, not just skewing information, but advocating uncivil conduct—to the extent of promoting violence to achieve specific political objectives and suppress alternative viewpoints.

The result is that we now see a push towards imposing licit restrictions on media's rights to freedom, rather than an exaltation of those rights. Among these, as was almost tested in court as regards Trump's efforts to ban CNN's Acosta from White House press conferences, due to Acosta's clear refusal to abide by the decorum thereof—is that the government has the right to limit the forums for free speech if there is a compelling interest in doing so—which may include keeping order. Rules of conduct, empowering the state to regulate media's conduct at press conferences will be imposed. Eventually, absent a shift in media's approach, other legal precedents may come into play. The First Amendment has been held to prohibit advocacy of the use of force or law violation where such advocacy is "directed to inciting or producing imminent lawless action and is likely to incite or produce such action." Threat against the lives of elected officials are also prohibited if deemed true threats, as opposed to political hyperbole. Proscriptions against "fighting words," such as epithets or personal abuse that are "no essential part of any exposition," may also be legitimately imposed. And, finally, public officials and figures may collect damages for defamation on evidence that the relevant statements were made with actual malice, or knowledge of their falsity or reckless disregard for their veracity. If these prospects seem unlikely, one would do well to pay heed to the violence that has arisen in the wake of some media commentaries and the reputational damage done to a number of public figures as a result of inadequate, or no, fact checking by media outlets. The US Supreme Court cases denoting the foregoing are, respectively, Brandenburg v. Ohio, 395 U.S. 444 (1969); Watts v. United States, 394 U.S. 705 (1969); Chaplinsky v. New Hampshire, 315 U.S. 568 (1942); and New York Times v. Sullivan, 376 U.S. 254 (1964). There are countless other cases. An additional anti-media weapon that will see deployment will come in the form of prosecutions for trading in classified information, or information that has been illegally obtained.

At present, it is certainly President Trump who is most publicly at odds with the media. However, notions of curtailment of hostile media by a variety of means, including federal licensing, have abounded within both parties in Congress for a number of years now. The true issue, then, comes to light—how to still the voices of opposition. Media, unfortunately by its own conduct is fomenting the possibility of its own demise.

The attitudes of media personalities have become so steeped in elitism that, it appears to me, they have forgone the concept of mortality. The stars of that sector have long relished salaries in the six, seven and even eight figures and the social stature they enjoy among pols and oligarchs alike. They have embedded themselves through galas such as the White House Correspondents Dinner and the DC party circuit to an extent that raises the question of whether there is any true desire, never mind the ability, to properly investigate the conduct of their perceived social peers. One wonders whether some of the hostility directed at Trump is that these elitists have become marginalized by his administration—no longer engaged in the love fests enjoyed with past presidents. One also wonders, while these same folks berate Trump's belligerence and often boorish behavior, why they now so desperately seek to emulate it.

If the media, as a whole, were to contemplate regaining its public relevance and, over the longer term, defusing its existential threats, it might, as has been suggested by Bob Woodward, lose its "smugness," and report facts without injecting emotional rhetoric, partisanship and opinions into its journalistic endeavors. My opinion is that this prospect is highly unlikely. Ironically, while repulsed at notions aimed at limiting the parameters of their rights to free speech, a plethora of mainstream media pundits adamantly advocate the suppression of free speech on the parts of their detractors—whether related to political views or climate change, and all that lies between. Now we even have Carl Bernstein, Woodward's former writing partner, suggesting that media edit White House press conferences, apparently because he views the rest of us as too ignorant to divine the truth of presidential utterances. Viewed deeply enough, much as is the case with the digital mafia, media has relinquished the role of monitoring and reporting on the social, economic and political pulse of our country, to instead assume the mantle of social engineering. In the case of social media, the consequences have been most dire. Aside from achieving, to an extent, the goal of engineering social mores, social media have caused the manifestation of increasing reactionaryism and psychological problems among its adherents. ⤙

CHAPTER 16

THE POPULARITY OF SOCIAL MEDIA CLEARLY DISPROVES DARWIN'S . . .

T he popularity of social media clearly disproves Darwin's theory of natural selection, that the fittest are destined to survive. The facts would instead suggest the prevalence of the herd, or even the hive, regardless of fitness, as the dominant factor in determining subsequent stages in evolution, or, if one prefers, devolution. As if dummied down educational curricula, television, excessive booze and legalized pot are not up to the task, social media, including smart phone apps and video games, which have become integrated into the sphere of social media, is morphing us into morons. Worse, it is adversely affecting our public's mental health, most assuredly amongst younger people.

Social media, generally owned by digital mafia entities like Google, Facebook and company, are platforms for digital communications through which users share information, ideas, personal data and links to other forms or formats of social media. Seemingly benign, at first blush, the utilization of social media presents a series of problems. The identities of users with whom one is communicating are uncertain; reliability of the information shared is generally assumed and little thought is given to the motives of the person or entity disseminating the information; the sources and recipients of shared personal data are also taken at face value; and the trails to other social media platforms, or groups within these, often exacerbate all of these issues by isolating users from broader spectra of ideas and information—thus defining a user's digital reality within shrinking parameters, much like the world created by Lewis Carroll, once Alice had gone down the rabbit hole or, more disturbingly, the worldview presented to North Korea's population by Rocket Boy and his predecessors. The common element of these latent, if not realized, conditions lies in the reality that the control of information, data and interactions can be used to create specific worldviews. And, there are troubling correspondent issues of consequence.

A significant facet of social media is its elimination of face to face interactions among people. This leads to a sense of detachment that fosters conduct that would normally not occur. The inability to read, in people's facial expressions and body language, reactions to digital output establishes an aura of unaccountability that is unavoidable in personal interactions. In addition, absent the context that is an inherent aspect of direct interpersonal conversation, reliance on digital communications is exponentially more prone to miscommunications and hence, misunderstandings. Though there are certain benefits to the employment of social media for mundane tasks, such as coordinating or organizing activities within families or among friends and acquaintances, the overarching effect suggests a decrease in responsibility and the erosion of civility on the part of users. This is even more pronounced when users participate in social media on a scale beyond that of the circle of actors that are personally known to them. These tend to gravitate towards group think, or mob mentality.

Studies of group mentality strongly suggest a correlative decrease in rational decision making. This is a matter of social psychology that was recognized outside the advent and influences of social media. People are driven to groups by any number of facts; however, most prevalent are loneliness and a desire to belong to a group. Joint research undertaken by the University of Exeter, in collaboration with researchers from Princeton University and the Sorbonne, published on December 17, 2014, in the journal *Interface,* concluded that group dynamics are such that individuals become prone to losing their instincts and personal beliefs in making decisions; that they are driven instead to decisions predicated upon the social information that is derived from the herd, or the group. This leads to "bad decision making" because the group's influence in abating individual decisions, based upon each member's values, leads to a collective lack of awareness regarding situational or environmental changes. Hence, the results indicated that groups evolved to be unresponsive to such changes because its participants "spend too much time copying one another and not making their own decisions." The researchers also concluded that this was the manifestation of a "classic evolutionary conflict between individual and collective interest[s]." This can lead to dire consequences, not only as to self-preservation of group members, but in terms of the effects of group or mob actions in response to something or when a directed at a specific objective.

Group members tend to experience a loss of self-awareness and personal identity, while feeling physically anonymous within the context of the group they are in. This leads to decreased inhibitions and the increased likelihood of engaging in behavior that would that would normally be aberrational to the affected individuals. The larger the group and the more physically anonymous its members feel, the greater the likelihood that its reactions or activities will push the boundaries of acceptability. In a charged setting, then, violence may become acceptable because of these criteria and an abated sense of responsibility because the entire group is embarked upon the same course of conduct. As noted by Tamara Avant, Psychology director at Southern University's Savannah, Georgia campus, in an interview with South Source in January, 2011, in addressing this topic, "... many people believe they cannot be held responsible for violent behavior when part of a mob because they perceive the violent action as the groups (e.g. "everyone's doing it"), rather than their own behavior ...

When people feel their behavior cannot be traced back to them, they are more likely to break social norms and engage in violence."

Unfortunately, social media provides sustenance to all of the conditions associated with group think and mob rule. Indeed, it does so on an unprecedented scale. Group mass, anonymity and loss of self-awareness, conjoined with blind faith in everything written, seen and heard are amplified through social media, and have provably and frequently resulted in the abandonment of all civility, the fomentation of mass hysteria and the employment of violence as a means to an end or to right a perceived wrong. As widely reported, in Mexico's cities of Pueblo, Hidalgo and Mexico City, mobs lynched and killed people wrongfully identified as kidnappers on social media. Likewise, in the same country, three young men were arrested for "stealing children," as a result of misinformation disseminated on social media. In India seven innocent men were lynched after hoax messages on WhatsApp accused them of kidnapping. In 2012, similar attacks, also grounded in social media, occurred in Indonesia and other countries throughout the world.

On a larger scale, social media, most frequently Facebook, have been linked to mass killings by groups. In Sri Lanka, for example, false information posted on Facebook led to prolonged, often fatal, violence between Buddhists and Muslims. As reported by *The New York Times* on April 21, 2018, "A reconstruction of Sri Lanka's descent into violence, based on interviews with officials, victims and ordinary users caught up in online anger, found that Facebook's newsfeed played a central role in nearly every step from rumor to killing." Facebook was also said to have ignored warnings of the latency for violence and refused to assist in any meaningful way. Facebook has also been held complicit in the posting of false information that led to the genocide mounted in largely Buddhist Myanmar against the Rohingya Muslim minority.

Domestically, social media have been employed to polarize people, most noticeably within the realms of sociocultural, economic and political issues, on the basis of false information and by stirring emotions before accurate information is even available. So too has it been used to incite violence by extremist groups such as the so-called Proud Boys and Antifa, idiots all of them, as well as pols on both sides of the aisle.

The overriding problem is that, on a mass scale, there is no real way to distinguish who is manipulating various groups and what their end game is. As put by Chamath Palihapitiya, a former Facebook executive, in addressing an audience at Stanford's Graduate School of Business, in 2017, "Imagine taking that to the extreme, where bad actors can now manipulate large swathes of people to do anything you [they] want. It's just a really bad state of affairs." Mr. Palihapitiya further pointed to the absence of civil discourse and cooperation, and the abundance of misinformation and mistruths, as being symptoms of social media impact. And, that this is "not an American problem—this is not about Russian ads. It is a global problem."

Manipulation of users through social media through the dissemination of false or misleading information is only one side of the coin. The flip side, as noted in the preceding chapter, is that through the introduction by social media platform, either of their own volition or at the behest of third parties, of algorithms that govern informational feeds on social media, the hosting entity may either stack the deck of results, thereby biasing the users perceptions, or censure the output in order to eliminate specifically identified results. Accordingly, some hashtag movement supporting a particular product, political position or denigrating a public figure will gain momentum in the digital world, while contradictory views are systemically eliminated. The notion of manipulating societal opinions is not altogether new and certainly predates the digital age. The tobacco industry infamously sought to do so through advertising and the presentation of false data regarding the the hazards of smoking, Pharmaceuticals have been accused of doing likewise over the years. The employment of propaganda by governments has been a tool of persuasion, on the basis facts, both real and false, for as long as there have been states. I once took a graduate class in political science at the University of Hawaii and recall the professor telling students that the art of swaying opinions, or public frustration management, euphemistically portrayed as "future modeling," inveigled public and private sector think tanks and university researchers in the practice of developing feints—creating areas of public focus—to divert attention away from other objectives. In this context, he proposed that the general public could never truly determine whether a grassroots movement, for example, was the result of spontaneity or the result of governmental or corporate machinations. Social media has simply expanded the scope and speed by which such undertakings are made possible.

Sadly, users of social media accept the realities presented through that medium and are ill-inclined to verify or debunk information received through other sources—more assuredly when it conforms to their inherent biases or things they would like to believe. An utterly ludicrous case in point, gleefully reported reported by the *Washington Post* on November 17, 2018, pointed to a Facebook site, started by Christopher Blair, as political satire. On that site, "America's Last Line of Defense," Blair and others posted stories that included California's institution of sharia (Islamic law) and Bill Clinton's emergence as a serial killer—all designed to poke fun at Conservative views. Incredibly, and in spite of a disclaimer that nothing on the site was true, it became popular with conservatives, who accepted all of the postings thereon as gospel.

Aside from the effects of social media on group think, the perception of user anonymity on these platforms, and the concomitant deterioration of inhibitions, has empowered individual users to escalate their behavior where this is aimed at doing bad things. Social media are increasingly used for cyber-bullying, child sex offenses, fraud and witness intimidation, live streaming criminal acts, including murders, as well as other crimes. This issue has been well documented by law enforcement agencies, globally, and has been publicly reported frequently over the course of the last decade.

As a byproduct to the negative influences of social media, it has become abundantly clear that its use harbingers mental health issues. Certainly it has become clear over the last two election cycles, in 2016 and 2018, that, as a general condition, public angst has risen dramatically. There are, however, more specific issues, most commonly among young people, that have risen to the forefront. The psychological consequences of cyber-bullying and "Facebook" depression were raised as concerns by the American Academy of Pediatrics as early as 2011. According to the Center for Disease Control (CDC), teen suicides have been increasing since 2010, after enjoying declines for the prior twenty years. Although the CDC did not explore causation, a number of reports strongly indicate a link between social media use and suicides.

One such study, undertaken by Jean Twenge, a psychology professor at San Diego State University, published in *Clinical Psychological Science* on November 14, 2017, indicated that the number of teens using digital devices, between 2009 and 2015, rose from 8 to 19 percent. Suicidal thoughts were 70 percent more likely to occur among these teens, than those whose device usage hovered at about one hour per day. Of some one-half million teens aged thirteen to eighteen surveyed in 2015, 36 percent reported indicia of depression or having either attempted suicide or experienced suicidal thoughts. Among females, that average rose to 45 percent. The causes of mental health issues among users are multiple, though often interconnected.

Among these are the addictive nature of social media and the tendency, in spite of being digitally connected to other people, of feelings of increased isolation, as compared to young adults who are less inclined to social media use. These are the findings of a number of studies published over the years in various journals, including *Medical News Today, The American Journal of Preventive Medicine* and *Enough is Enough* (EIE), an organization aimed at issues of Internet safety. A further contributing factor is depression that is caused by people comparing themselves to others on social media, such as Facebook. This was the finding made by the authors of a study entitled "Seeing Everyone Else's Highlight Reels: How Facebook Usage is Linked To Depressive Symptoms," published in the *Journal of Social and Clinical Psychology* in 2014 by Mai-Ly Steers, Robert E, Wickham and Linda K. Acitelli. More pressing is the issue of cyber-bullying. According to EIE, 95 percent of teens who have used social media have come across instances of cyber-bullying, while 33 percent have been victimized by such activity. Cyber-bullying does, of course, take numerous forms, ranging from physical threats of violence, to shaming and releasing a victim's personal information. Further inappropriate conduct, sexting, or transmitting messages of a blatantly and explicit sexual nature, are also in the mix. The ultimate problems with social media are its immediacy and anonymity, although the latter is a myth. Although true that recipients of communications have no real ability to ascertain the true identity of senders, this is not to say their identities are unknown. Every user's digital footprint and trail are recorded for posterity by both platform hosts and governments.

Although the notion that our privacy is thus invaded is reprehensible in every sense, the ramifications for younger people are latently devastating. Their online conduct is not only driven by the sense of security and anonymity, but is further denuded of inhibition by the naivety that is an inherent characteristic of youth. Imagine, then, the dismay of teens, who on reaching adulthood, find themselves in a job interview, to be met with stacks of data print-outs chronologizing their entire digital history—down to the minutest detail; every keystroke made and every utterance written. I have tried to warn my youngest of this eventuality, all to no avail. Yet this is the future faced by all of us.

The negative effect of social media on the public conscience, together with its mental health consequences, is unassailable. To an increasingly gullible society, there are additional venues for sopping up lousy ideas and information. Among them, given our infatuation with celebrity, are the worlds of sports and entertainment. ᴄᴏ

CHAPTER 17

COURT JESTERS
HAVE BECOME KINGS . . .

C ourt jesters have become kings and queens, elevated to this stature by a society that is ever more prone to adulate actors, athletes and pundits. Success in these endeavors is not dependent upon any particular knowledge of consequence beyond that necessary to their vocations. Nor is education a requisite. It does, however, insulate people from the realities faced by the rest of us, if for no other reasons than the scads of money showered upon those who rise to the top of their fields and, one might add, even mediocrity is amply rewarded. Nor are their social circles exemplars of economic diversity.

Yet, once publicly exalted, many of these folks are compelled to speak to all manner of deep subjects, perhaps in an effort to project gravitas to overcome the dearth thereof in their chosen careers as entertainers. This is no more than an iteration of spectator sports. Nor is it a new phenomenon. Entertainers have used their stardom to speak from the bully pulpit for eons. What is relatively new is the stridency and hysteria of the rhetoric and, above all, its lack of civility.

Presently, we have "Raging Bull," railing at President Trump, offering to "punch him in the face"—can you imagine the reek of the Ben-Gay infused sweat a-drip during that altercation—so incapable of articulating a comprehensive, objective assault, that his critique is reduced to epithets of the basest sort. Mr. "Bull" does own a number of investment properties in New York, suggesting, perhaps, that his vitriol may transcend political beliefs and is possibly directed at the consequences of Trump's tax legislation on related deductions.

Similarly, a largely minor actor, Tom Arnold, has spoken of committing violent acts against the president and we have had a comedienne,

Kathy Griffin, parading a photo-chopped image of herself holding President Trump's severed head. Other examples abound. The aging diva, Madonna, has expressed thoughts of "blowing up the white house;" rapper, Snoop Dogg, released a music video of himself shooting Trump in the head and, Peter Fonda tweeted that "We should rip Barron Trump from his mother's arms and put him in a cage with pedophiles and see if mother will stand up against the giant asshole she is married to." Barron Trump, the president's son, was twelve years old at the time. These are merely a handful of examples denoting the litany of like minded, moronic pronouncements blaring from the world of entertainment.

Whatever the motivations, criticism of politicians has long been the norm of celebrity rhetoric, as has campaigning for candidates and lending support to causes of one sort or another. The advocacy of un-adulterated violence to achieve a specific political goal, on the other hand, is relatively novel. And, although the bailiwick of leftist celebs for the moment, save for musician, Ted Nugent's infamously idiotic, violence laced diatribes against Hillary Clinton and then President Obama, the reality is that now unleashed, this genie will not gently return to the bottle.

The ultimate mischief of inciting violence is that it invites a like response. Sad enough in a banana republic or some other regime of absolutes, it is an outright threat of arson to the parchments that define a democracy. There is indeed mounting evidence that the es-pousal of violent means to achieve political ends by celebrities has found a corollary increase in acts, or threats, of violence against pub-lic officials from both political extremes. James Hodgkinson, a self professed supporter of progressive democrats, launched a rifle attack against GOP legislators playing baseball in 2017, wounding three legis-lators, of whom Steve Scalise, the house majority whip, was critically injured. Other Republican legislators, including Tom Garrett (VA), Martha McSally (AZ), David Kutsoff (TN) and Kevin Cramer (ND), have received threats of physical harm sufficient to warrant police and FBI involvement. More recently, thankfully deficient pipe bombs were mailed by a Trump zealot, Cesar Sayoc, to a number of high profile Democrats, including Barack Obama and Hillary Clinton, as well as several left of center media outlets. Any notion that there exists no nexus between these types of acts, which remain unabated, and the encouragement of violence by popular figures is nonsensical. The reality is that when people of public renown speak in these terms, it suggests an aura of credibility to the bad deeds contemplated by bad actors. The use of force then gains normalcy in political affairs.

Unfortunately, the involved celebs seems impervious to these turns of events, or at least their role therein. Among the scions of pop culture, we find a group that is not overly given to bouts of self-aware-ness—not only as to their culpability in setting the tone of acceptable political hyperbole, but equally so as to their hypocrisy. Clamoring for gun control, while marching around with gun toting bodyguards, we are meant to subscribe to and accept the difference between them and us because #celebritylivesmatter. While eschewing racism and biases based upon sexual orientation, both noble and justifiable endeavors, numbers of celebrities, including Snoop Dog, Kanye West, Kim Kardashian, Adele, Cameron Diaz, Jennifer Lawrence, as well as some pols, mostly Democrats and some Republicans, have supported projects mounted by Louis Farrakhan or endowed him with credi-bility through engagement. Farrakhan, leader of the Nation of Islam, is noteworthy only because he is as representative of racism and intol-erance as is David Duke, the self-styled, white supremacist. Farrakhan is arguably more dangerous because he enjoys a larger following than Duke. While issues of race are a necessary and meaningful aspect of American dialogue, the notion that some bigots are cause worthy, while others are not, is repugnant. Yet this dichotomy is a stark reality amongst a formidable number of celebs. The concept that racism is antithetical to combating racism lies well beyond them. This also seems to be true of misogynism, which seems to have gained wide acceptability if "artistically" expressed.

Almost unanimous, are the very public positions taken by celebs, particularly of the Hollywood variety, regarding the evils of racism, genocides, wars, totalitarianism, censorship, imperialism and the full gamut of related issues. Champions, they were, of all these causes until . . . until, the Peoples Republic of China (PRC), blatant practitioners of each of these sins, started investing in America's film industry. At this juncture, investors from the PRC, among them Dalian Wanda and Jack Ma's Alibaba Pictures, have significant stakes in Legendary Pictures, Paramount, Sony and Steven Spielberg's Amblin Pictures, as well as film distributors and cinema chains. These total in the billions of dollars.

The underlying motive behind these cash infusions, while certainly undertaken with the hope of profitability, is to promote the PRC's interests through what is referred to as the acquisition of "soft power." Soft power, in this context, is simply the employment of cultural and economic influence to establish positive public perceptions about the wielding entity. Less kindly, it is the use of propaganda to win over an enemy. And, although undertaken through the auspices of so-called private corporations, there really is no such animal in the PRC. All economic activity derived from coffers within the PRC is controlled by its government, the Communist Party. The long gone Senator Joseph McCarthy's delusions at long last come to life. Gone are the days of Richard Gere, the actor, working to forestall the genocidal aims of the PRC against the Tibetans. Now we have films that delight with the virtues of the PRC's largesse and global humanitarianism, such as *2012, The Martian,* and every recent film starring Jackie Chan. Indeed, one would be hard-pressed to find a single Hollywood production that paints the PRC or its government with even a scintilla of negativity.

And, we have have a plethora of new faces from the PRC in cinema, many of them excellent actors, though some tend to disappear without explanation into the political mists of the Middle Kingdom, sometimes, though not always, to re-merge as born again versions of themselves, re-educated and everythin', by golly. The clear consequence of all this is not just a limitation on the nature of US made films distributed within the PRC, but is rigid censorship of the scripts permitted to be filmed for American and other audiences, as well.

Thus having slithered under the doormat of the First Amendment, one would expect some challenge to the PRC's film industry endeavors, through exercise of that same right, on the part of Hollywood's normally righteously indignant. But, nary a peep is to be heard. One must suppose, then, that some causes are simply not worth the cost. Perhaps it is a matter of lucky happenstance that Hollywood did not arrive in time for the American Revolution. And, don't expect a rebirth of Richard Gere's career any time soon, save, perhaps, in the role of an extra, impaled on a Chinese warlord's spear.

Counted among the kingdom of celebrity are, of course, professional athletes. Paid exorbitant amounts of money, most notably players on the fields of football and courts of basketball, these sporting types have become institutionalized as the gladiators of American culture. Wrestlers, too, as well as boxers and mixed martial arts practitioners are well placed on the pyramid of lucre we have come to associate with professional sports. Other athletes, such as American soccer players, as opposed to their world-wide football playing counterparts, volleyball players, cyclists, and the like, seem to inhabit the mid tiers, while others, such as biathletes and their Olympian ilk, tend to obscurity, unless sufficiently marketed to an extent bestowing name recognition.

Some professional athletes are well educated or intellectually capable, parleying their relatively short careers into financial security that sees them though life. Others are dumb as toast. Some are avid self-promoters and others disappear into obscurity. There is a common thread among these professionals, as with many other entertainers, that speaks to the support of causes, oratorically and through monetary largesse, some driven in this by altruism and others by a need for tax deductions. And, as is the norm for celebrities, the world of sports is imbued with countless controversies. This has long been the case. From fixing fights to throwing games and doping, the American public has spent countless hours glued to television sets and sports pages, transfixed by the shenanigans of their heroes and antiheroes alike. The occasional fall of a gladiator, under such circumstances, is often accompanied by a sense of Schadenfreude; we take joy in watching the mighty fall from the comforts of our loungers and sofas. And, as spectators, we tune into televised talk shows to hear athletes hold forth and regardless of whether presented inanely or with gravity, we hang on their every word. Through sports, then, sports celebrities have access to the bully pulpit. Rightly or wrongly, this is a fact.

Against this backdrop has emerged a new controversy led, in large part, by Colin Kaepernick, a highly regarded football player. Kaepernick initiated a storm of controversy by refusing to stand, at the outset of games, for the national anthem—a tradition at football games, as with other events. Others have followed suit. Kaepernick's actions were motivated by the recent spate of largely unjustifiable police shootings of black men, mostly young, with few repercussions. In his words, "To me, this is bigger than football and it would be selfish on my part to look the other way. There are bodies in the street and people getting paid leave and getting away with murder." Kaepernick and several others have paid a price for this stance, though the former seems to have landed on his feet by winning a contract with Nike. Moreover, during his presently aborted football career, he earned more money than most of us will see in several lifetimes. Hence, his sacrifice is somewhat symbolic. The real issue, however, is that Kaepernick's failing lies in having chosen the wrong forum.

This is evidenced by lowered attendance at football games and a reduction in viewership of televised games. Team owners have sought to mitigate the issue, in an effort to maintain profitability. And throughout the celebrity world, the common rejoinder has has been that those fans abandoning the game must be racists. Similar accusations have mounted in the wake of television shows that, on delving into political issues, have lost audiences. Talk about missing the boat. People do not watch purported comedies on television, save perhaps for Saturday Night Live, or athletic events to be confronted with the harshness of life. They do so in order to escape their realities—to find solace in entertainment. What these audiences, largely poor or of the waning middle class, do not want is to be proselytized to during those fleeting moments of respite from their collective and ever mounting anxieties.

Athletes and the entertainment industry at large would do well to learn from the likes of Jackie Robinson, a true hero of the 20th century, whose travails, one might imagine, exceeded anything imagined by most Americans today. Robinson played baseball. On the field, and regardless of anything else, he played the game. In so doing, and due to his mien throughout, Mr. Robinson advanced the cause of anti-racism exponentially. And then he used his initial notoriety and ultimate fame to make a difference off the field—in advancing the cause of civil liberties.

Mr. Robinson was never a court jester. He was a king of his own making, perhaps more so, because that is not how he viewed himself. That said, returning to the present, while we may anoint those practicing within the collective field of entertainment as royalty, most are bound to remain as clowns until they develop an understanding of why we do so. Only then might one hope that celebs will exploit that stature, with grace and aplomb, to advance good causes, ever mindful of the time and place. In light of the generally elitist and condescending attitudes that seem to permeate the world of entertainment, this is highly unlikely—though perhaps the fault in the stars is ours, having exalted them for the wrong reasons in the first place.

Troubling though the cultural aspects of entertainment and its actors may be, these are but superficial facets of deeper societal issues that are exploited for ulterior purposes. These include the merger between politics and science. ᴄᴠᴐ

CHAPTER 18

THE POLITICIZATION
OF SCIENCE . . .

The politicization of science has befogged objective research in numerous areas of critical importance, though no where more so than the studies of climate change and other environmental disciplines. In fact, this phenomenon, now reaching its apex, has seen the supporters of particular, politically adopted pop science worldviews trumpet for vilification and public pillorying of any scientist, regardless of pedigree or depth of research, whose findings suggest even a hair's breadth of deviance therefrom. Even the suggestion of contrarian research in some fields has evoked emotionally charged reactions.

This is not to suggest a dearth of valid concerns regarding environmental issues, including climate change. Certainly the myriad of actually identifiable environmental risks demand resolution. Among these are so-called first world insistence on the use of plastics, which are not biodegradable and end up in our oceans and scattered across the landscape and, in developing countries, we still see an inability to to understand the virtues of select logging, in terms of both sustainability and long term economic prospects—these opt instead to adhere to the inefficient and devastating practice of large scale clear cutting. Moreover, where solutions have presented on the horizon, particularly regarding sustainable energy production and reductions in carbon emissions, the corporate welfare state we enjoy is geared more towards ensuring that inefficient, ostensibly private sector, behemoths remain dominant, by preventing light changes that could rock their financial stability, than it is to encouraging the crafting of sensible, cost effective solutions.

The overarching problems and controversies, particularly insofar as climate change is concerned, lie in first identifying the actual nature thereof and then crafting solutions to address proven determinations. Infusing the scientific labors necessary to both with politics is analogous to the Holy See's historic proscriptions against probing for knowledge contrary to its doctrines and self-interests. Undoubtedly, the zealotry accompanying politically adopted scientific theories speaks to the emergence of a religious movement, no more given to tolerance or open mindedness than its forebears. As with all religions, the risks lie in the fomentation of fear and conflict; the manipulation of the many by the few, for political and financial gains; and, above all, the consequences of being wrong. Applied to the case of climate change, the former two have clearly manifested, while the latter remains an open question.

The genesis of climate change, as a political issue, arose somewhat in the 1970s and more stridently in the 1980s as a clarion cry that the planet was warming and that humankind faced all manner of travesty, including extinction. Global warming, as it was coined, was said to be strictly the result of human activities. Carbon emissions and deforestation were identified as the mechanical attributes of that intervention. No mention was made of volcanic activity or other natural occurring events that affect earth's climes. A paucity of scientific evidence accompanied these pronouncements, leading proponents to lobby for collection of information.

The unfortunate truth is that the ensuant efforts were aimed at proving the theory by reverse engineering it, rather than arriving at some truth as to whether the presumption of global warming was even valid. As a result, we are now inundated with representations of global warming said to be predicated upon supporting data. And, as has frequently been the case, when the books are cooked in order to skew results in favor of the political thesis, debate is thwarted by emotional rhetoric. The US National Oceanic and Atmospheric Agency (NOAA) and the Australian Weather Bureau, as two examples, have been caught cheating on the data. We have reached a point where questioning of questionable conclusions is deemed criminal by the community depending upon them to forward their agendas. Adherents to the cause have sought to criminalize disagreement and eliminate the availability of any public forums, including media in all its forms, to anyone seeking to debate the validity of the data or conclusions drawn therefrom. The only concession wrested from these new age Inquisitors has been the re-characterization of the assumed problem as Global Climate Change, rather than Global Warming, although the underlying arguments remain the same.

The reality is that, in terms of general scientific knowledge, we know far less than we think we know, or better, what we presume to know is far outstripped by what we clearly do not. A recent example in the field of archaeology, published in Science during late 2018, was the discovery of stone cut tools and other artifacts in North Africa (Ain Boucheritt, Algeria), aged at about 2.4 million years, that exploded prior theories on modern human origins, thought for years to have been in East Africa. Exploration in other areas—physics, oceanography and natural sciences—to name a few, have likewise resulted in periodic and not infrequent resets of accepted paradigms. The case in climatology is no different.

There is, among those studying the earth's climate, general agreement about certain foundational questions related to historic climatic changes. First, that Milankovich cycles, regularly occurring shifts in the Earth's orbit around the sun and axial rotation, cause repeated cycles of alternating cold and warm periods, each lasting an average of about 80,000 years. This is derived from ice core samples taken in Antarctica, that allow a historical perspective of some 420,000 years.

Milankovich cycles are generally acknowledged, but not fully understood. General agreement also attaches to the fact that Earth's magnetic field affects its climate and that the magnetic field reverses several times every million years. There is some belief that we may be on the cusp of such a flip, north becoming south and vice-a-versa, as evidenced by the the escalating shift, over the last decade, of magnetic north. What this portends, other than something, has found no consensus. Similarly, there is a confluence of opinions related to the notion that solar activity impacts our climate, but not as to the severity or extent. Other natural phenomena, such as volcanic activity, are widely agreed to be of import to the issue. And, of course, the human factor is credited with being of consequence to environmental conditions. The professed impact of all of these variables is all over the map.

We are told that the planet is warming at an alarming rate; indeed, if one looks to the predictions of some two decades ago, the world's coastal cities would already be devastated by rising ocean levels. We are told that weather activity of every type, hurricanes, tornadoes, droughts, snowfalls and monsoons are harbingers of the coming planetary climatic apocalypse. On the other side of the board, we have predictions of ice ages and the ensuant likelihood of total crop failures throughout the northern hemisphere. Throughout, data denoting cyclical weather patterns seems to be ignored. Nor is there acknowledgment that we lack a full scientific understanding of things that influence climate changes. And, the recital of anecdotal evidence has become a preferred measure to rebut actual data that contradicts the political scientific view. In the latter instance, for example, the Northeast Snowfall Impact Scale (NESIS) developed by the National Weather Service to rank high impact snow storms in the northeastern US through the collection of relevant data, showed that between 2008 and 2017, the region suffered twenty-nine major impact winter storms;

while no prior ten year period experienced more than ten such storms. The response from the pol science crowd: this is proof of global warming. Everything I have read on the subject, over the last two decades, has brought me to the realization that we don't yet have a tinker's clue in hell what is going on. Nonetheless, voices of reason or skepticism are drowned in the mass hysteria that accompanies each new iteration of climate fear mongering. Quite naturally, this gives rise to the question of why.

To understand the present tenor of the climate debate, one would do well to examine the fact that environmentalism, as a movement, was not initiated by scientists. Its origins lie in politics, more precisely, in the emergence of the Green Party in Germany during the late 1970s. The party was formed by a combination of young idealists and pragmatic socialists. Among them was Hans Christian-Stroebele, a member of the Lawyer's Socialist Collective, who represented members of the Baader Meinhof Gang, also known as the Red Army Faction, a terrorist organization, as well as other radicals. Stroebele was convicted in 1983 of maintaining a communications network between imprisoned terrorists and their at large compatriots. Another founding member, Otto Schily, together with other party members, visited Muammar Qaddafi, the Libyan strongman, in 1982 to discuss removal of US military bases from Europe.

Throughout its original incarnation, the German Green Party, together with its then emerging fledgling counterparts throughout northern Europe, was infiltrated, or even co-opted to an extent, by the Stasi, the former East German Secret Police. In fact, though the significance was downplayed, a study commissioned by the German Green Party confirmed in 2018 that during 1980, fifteen to twenty of its members had cooperated closely with the Stasi, while hundreds more provided information to that spy organization. In another more recent twist, reports surfaced in Sweden that its Green Party had been infiltrated by Islamic radicals. While the Greens are still existent, though not particularly relevant, their objectives and underlying ideologies have morphed into our present environmental movements. The key aspect of Green Party politics, and that of its progeny, has been and remains a classically socialist agenda wrapped in the banner of environmental ideology.

The hallmark of all realpolitik aspirants is to don the cloak of an appealing ideology, particularly as to young people and the disenfranchised, in order to gain popular support and thereby the potential to realize their objectives. Historically, these ambitions have little to do with the scents deployed to attract bees. In the case of climate politics, every solution proffered entails expanding the role of governments into management of the private sector and individual lives; increasing taxation; expanding globalism as a means of wealth redistribution, in and of itself another form of taxation; employing globalism as a means of eroding national sovereignty; establishing a money making mechanism in the trade of carbon emissions and otherwise; and subsidizing alternative means of energy production and transportation. Every solution is promoted through fear and all are socialistic in execution. And worse, resolutions are crafted without an understanding of the problems they are meant to solve or regard for viable alternatives.

Should preparations for an imminent ice age begin, or ought we be finding ways to ameliorate the advent of rising oceans? Should we throw chemicals into the atmosphere to induce more rains or harden our shelters against microwaves in the event the off switch on our magnetic field is toggled? Sifting through all of the bullshit, the only truth that is readily apparent is that we haven't a clue. Do we trust the sharks swimming below the surface of climate ideology. I think not. Mistakes have already been made. Logging of beetle killed trees, in the tens of millions of acres, has been prohibited, as has all select logging of old growth trees, although there are now more forested acres in the US than there were 100 years ago. These are burning, spewing emissions into the atmosphere on a scale nobody wants to measure. We are striving to replace combustion engines with electric cars. Yet, the adverse footprint of these is never really addressed. From construction, through operation (charging electric cars through electric grids dependent on carbon fuels) and disposal, there is ample suggestion that the environmental impact of electric cars is not insubstantial. Mining of rare minerals necessary to battery production and the consequences of disposing of millions of used batteries is not part of the conversation. Nor are alternatives, such as hydrogen powered engines on the table. Is this because there are motives unaligned with the purported objectives of clean transportation at work here. Now we arrive at the real issue—money, and the further entrenchment of elitism at the expense of the middle class.

Enter the Ent. Not on foot, mind you; when Al Gore, self professed inventor of the Internet and the world's greatest climatologist, enters the room to preach, and preach he does, like a snake handler at a born again revival meeting, on global warming, rest assured he did not arrive at the airport on a commercial airplane. Nor did he travel from the airport to his hotel on a bus. Hopefully, when he leaves home, he turns down the heat for his pool, which, according to AP News and the National Center For Public Policy Research, consumed more electricity in 2006 than six average homes. At the same time Gore's utility bills totaled about $30,000 for the year. That was just for one of his several homes. He had substantial investments in oil companies, such as Occidental Petroleum, which has a less than sterling environmental record and received royalties from a mining company that has been cited for polluting waterways, while promoting his movie on the perils we all face because of global warming. He professes, in spite of all, to lead a carbon footprint free lifestyle. Perhaps he can be forgiven for this; the Ent is, after all, a mere pol and self-promoter extraordinaire, not a scientist. Gore is also well on the road to becoming a "carbon billionaire," with investments in carbon trading, bio-fuels, electric cars, Google and other high tech firms—a number of which enjoy governmental contracts, grants and tax subsidies. So, why does Gore matter. He doesn't really, not individually, in spite of being an utterly offensive, privileged twit, purporting to speak for the common person without having an inkling of what that means or having been asked to do so. Gore is contextually relevant to the "global warming" movement, however, in that he represents an indicia of the associated corruption and hypocrisy.

The institutional solutions to global warming that have been fashioned are well documented in United Nations' (UN) papers and, more tellingly, the Paris Accord, negotiated by some 196 nations at the UN Climate Change Conference in 2015. The US, under then President Obama, embraced the agreement and Trump, with much fanfare and subject to scathing commentary, withdrew the US from participation. The initial stated ambition of the accord is to reduce global temperatures to no more than 2 degrees Celsius above the average during the pre-industrial era, with the ultimate goal of holding these at 1.5 degrees. The agreement, made under the questionable assumption that we are dealing with global warming, employs three mechanisms to achieve the desired results.

The first, requires a reduction in so called greenhouse gas emissions on the basis of each country's determination of what that should be, with some caveats. Developed countries, most certainly the US, are expected to reduce their emissions at far greater proportions than other countries, regardless of their present relative contribution to greenhouse gas emissions. The US, for instance, was expected to reduce its emissions by a greater percentage than the PRC, even though the latter's emissions, as a percentage of all global emissions are by far the greatest. The underlying logic appears to be that countries that were at the vanguard of industrialization have contributed to emissions for a more protracted period of time than others and should, therefore, be punished for this. This is also the rationale behind the second major clause of the accord.

The Paris Accord further contemplates a transfer of wealth, payment, by developed nations to developing nations. The amount is to be some $100 billion dollars, and absent this condition, the developing nations threatened to abandon the discussions. The rationale behind this scheme, "climate finance" as it is called, is somewhat nebulous but seems predicated on the idea that developed nations owe an ecological debt to the others. More importantly, the payments are to be made in spite of no commitment on the part of recipients to reduce their greenhouse gas emissions or how the funds are to be expended. One suspects, in effort to match the lifestyles of their developed nation counterparts—an onslaught of private jet and limo orders—undoubtedly a boon to the developed countries manufacturing them. No offset is given in "repayment" of this "debt" for the past largesse, in form of investments and foreign aid, of developed nations. And, while developed nations are deemed culpable for not foreseeing the purported impact of their industrialization on the world's climate, their counterparts in the developing world, though avid consumers of the ensuant products, bear no responsibility. Put bluntly, the position seems to be "its not my fault we wanted a power plant so that we could have electricity—it's their fault for devising the means to do so and giving it to us." This argument is even more inane than a drunk driver blaming a distillery for getting cited. Obviously, the entire scheme is a crafty means of wealth transference, both in form of cash and in terms of debilitating the economic growth of already developed economies, while giving free rein to emergent economies to grow.

The third and equally interesting prong of the climate agreement ise the trading of emissions as commodities and carbon offsets. The first, most simply explained, and already a reality in the US and elsewhere, is that if my company, or country, exceeds its legal emissions, it can purchase carbon credits from another entity or country that will not reach its emissions limits. The seller may be any person, entity or country holding an emissions license, regardless of whether the seller is engaged in creating emissions as a function of their business. Carbon offsets are merely the agreement to do something in in order to to offset emissions. In other words, smoke a cigarette, plant a tree. The latter will be employed by the UN to offset its anticipated carbon dioxide emissions as a result the upcoming Climate Summit in Poland. According to the UN, not including the contribution of commercial airline seats and private jets, the 30,000 some odd attendees are expected to emit some 55,000 tons of carbon dioxide into the earth's atmosphere by virtue of their attendance.

Based upon US Environmental Protection Agency (EPA) standards, this is tantamount to driving 11,700 cars for a year and equals the annual emissions of 8,200 average US homes. No teleconferencing for these folks, but lest we judge them too harshly, the UN has agreed to pay the Polish government for the planting of some 6 million trees to offset these impact. These will be seedlings. This logic is infirm on several grounds; it assumes that Poland will plant the trees; it presupposes the extent of carbon dioxide emissions, rather than actual emissions; and it makes no sense.

If, as the political environmental movement, including the UN posit, we are faced with an emergency situation, can we wait the number of years it will take for the planted seedlings to offset the immediate release of over 55,000 tons of carbon dioxide. Perhaps things are not so dire. If, for example, Poland plants 6 million oak trees, a little over 2 million will survive. It takes about 20 years for an oak tree to mature. Once mature, those trees, assuming no disease or other forms of attrition, will sequester about 100,000 tons of carbon dioxide a year. This rides on the assumptions they will be planted, that they will never be harvested and that we have twenty years to wait. Fir trees will have less benefit per tree, and other species produce variable results, in any event. Yet, we are told, the problem is immediate; that we do not have the luxury of time.

In the meantime, urgency has compelled governments in developed countries to levy carbon taxes, ostensibly to pay their shares under the Paris Accords and develop an abatement in fossil fuel dependency. As with all sales taxes, these are levied against fuel and every stage of product development, manufacture, wholesale distribution and retailing, with the net effect of inflating consumer prices exponentially. The largest group of consumers in these countries are the so-designated middle classes and those of even less means. France is experiencing a violent tax payers revolt against these taxes which, as I write, in December of 2018, is spreading across Europe.

In the US, voters, even in Democrat strongholds like Washington State, have rejected carbon taxes. Nonetheless, our pols will keep trying. Democrat Florida Congressman Francis Rooney has introduced a national energy tax bill that can only be described as draconian in dimension. It proposes an escalating tax on Americans, commencing with a $15.00 per ton carbon tax that automatically increases by $10.00 annually, without further Congressional action. The IRS would be empowered to define carbon taxed items, which will include agricultural products, fuel, electricity, cars, transportation tickets, food packaging and so on. The bill also calls for empowering the US Customs and Border Protection to enforce the bill, together with the IRS. The revenues are not earmarked. Instead, under guise of an ideology, the income generated will go to grants, low interest loans and targeted contracts, for the benefit of corporate campaign supporters embarked on introducing alternate energies and transportation means, regardless of effectiveness, and to appease likely blocs of ever increasingly impoverished voters.

In net effect, the global warming initiatives are about money. None of this is meant to downplay the real challenges we face. Land fills are out of control, islands of plastics drift around our oceans and diseases, often mutations of earlier viruses and bacteria, are on the rise, to name but a few. And, there remains a pressing need to establish what climatic changes are occurring and how to address these.

There are, of course, other forms of pop science that seem to be running amok. Gene manipulation, stem cell research, cloning, designer pets and babies, anti-aging vehicles for the wealthy, growing possibly sentient brains in labs and creating new biological life forms to detect submarines are among numbers of emergent developments that seem to be trundling along, supported by politics, but lacking any underpinning in consequential research or ethical consideration. As in the case of climate change, these projects gain momentum in the political sphere despite a dearth of reliable information. And detractors, in keeping with so many other societal issues, are branded as politically incorrect. ∾

CHAPTER 19

A NATION WITHOUT
A SENSE OF HUMOR . . .

A nation without a sense of humor is doomed. Americans, though never renowned for enjoying the subtleties of nuanced humor did, once upon a time, fully enjoy the opportunity to laugh at themselves and others. This attribute of our culture has gone the way of the dodo bird. Crass comedy, perhaps suggestive of need for Freudian analysis of America's obsession with the genitalia of both sexes, given its puritanical roots, has always been an earmark of our culture. It has now moved to the forefront of what tickles us. This trend is accompanied by a burgeoning penchant for Schadenfreude—a somewhat perverse attraction to the misfortunes of others. And, throughout, minority witticisms have evolved a markedly singular attribute—the unilateral targeting of white people with overt bigotry, under the guise of comedy, while branding as racist any challenge to the practice.

Propelling the demise of maliciously targeted humor should garner no lament, but barring levity that seeks laughter as a form of mutual engagement and evermore allowing room to laugh at oneself is a mistake. Good humor is a necessary function of every culture, providing relief from life's travails and serving as a means of recognizing, or even celebrating, the differences between people without resort to maudlin rhetoric—itself given to an aura of insincerity. Banter has also functioned, in most traditions, as a rite of passage: educating young people in verbal artistry and developing in them a thickness of skin —teaching to dish it and take it and preparing them for those less humorous realities they are apt to encounter during the courses of their lives. The key distinguishing feature between ill-humored malice and that which is truly funny, lies in mutuality. The latter turns on a lack of cruelty and whether there lies as much acceptability in laughing at ourselves or having others laugh at us, as there is in laughing at others, in the context of a particular vein of humor. Sadly, Americans have lost this ability, succumbing instead to faux sensitivities that have our youth, as well as many adults, curled into fetal positions, cocoons in self proclaimed, or institutionally provided safe zones, bemoaning the very notion that anyone could make light of a world fraught with injustice, all at the hands of white folks, let alone hold frank discussions about the substantial issues, not just mere generational perceptions, we face as a nation. These are the snowflakes—emerged from decades of increasingly strident political correctness that have left us with generations of uneducated and hypersensitive idiots.

It has become politically incorrect to engage in any banter whatsoever involving ethnicity, culture, gender, sexual orientation, race, politics, religion, academic and athletic prowess or the myriad of other topics that used to be considered benign, fair game. In fact, the demise of humor in this country mirrors the curtailment of "permissible" public discourse. There are certain exceptions, of course. Misogyny is permissible in the context of rap music, an otherwise credible genre, most so when directed at real social issues. To decry the distinctly anti-feminist aspect of rap would be deemed racist. And generally, in the worlds of entertainment and marketing, the objectification of females continues, but has been spun as empowerment for women, heedless of the reality that the messages transmitted by these media are still about pimping sexuality. Misandry, general disdain for males, whether manifested as hatred, contempt or prejudicial attitudes towards men and boys, is evermore acceptable within the white population. And, the emasculation of the gender has become an express goal of new age social engineers. Women, scantily clad or encased in skin tight outfits, are paraded by Hollywood as the latest generation of Super Heroes, soon to be followed by protagonists of every imaginable sexual orientation or preference, and accompanied by efforts at empowering other minorities in cinematic achievements such as the *Black Panther,* credited with artistic worthiness in spite of celebrating the leader of a monarchical dictatorship. The latest manifestation of political correctness is the labeling of all whites as "privileged," and the advent of public self flagellation, or self-loathing, by white, so called Progressives. If I were the member of a racial minority group, I would be laughing my ass off. Yet, undoubtedly, this fashionable trend too will find its way into entertainment media's eye.

Noble as these may seem on the surface, capitalizing on the purported righting of social inequities and promoting empowerment issues by media are in actual fact counterproductive. When Hollywood's penchant for making money on politicized populism is coupled with with the entire premise of political correctness, and all that movement entails, the entirety can only lead to one outcome: the Balkanization of American society. There are several problems at play which suggest this. First, in seeking empowerment among the plethora of minority interests, preexisting and newly emerging, there is no interest in establishing equality among Americans in general, or even among these groups. Conversely, there is a drive to marginalize whites, in general, heterosexuality, women who opt to stay at home in order to raise children and European ethnic distinctions, as examples, in order to shift the balance of societal relevance towards those minority interests. The rationale appears to be that the former have not only enjoyed historical dominance, but are also to blame for the woes of the world.

Whether deliberately undertaken or as a matter of indifference, these efforts represent an assault on the historic sociocultural identities that distinguish between Americans of European descent. Instead, whites, as a race, are dehumanized by lumping all into one category, that of the vile "boogeyman." This is a dangerous turn of events. As a nation of immigrants, Americans have a long standing propensity for merging their origins with their national identity. Thus, we have Basque-Americans, Irish-Americans, Swedish-Americans, Japanese-Americans, Mexican-Americans, Italian-Americans and, the like whose pride stems not only in being American, but also lies in their roots. For African-Americans the story is somewhat different, though similar in net effect. The greatest harm done to slaves brought to this country, aside from the unconscionability of that practice, was the deliberate attempt to decimate their cultural heritages, which were as varied as the continent they were taken from. Nonetheless, distinctly rich and varied African-American traditions have evolved as an integral part of the cultural landscape.

Each of these traditions remain very much alive, whether adapted, morphed or evolved into a uniquely American variant, nationally and regionally—the sum and recognition of which are the very definition of Americanism. To denigrate or erase from the social consciousness the significance of even one of these groups, is a diminishment of our national identity as a whole and serves no purpose other than the fomentation of anger and resentment. It certainly does not somehow create equality or redress wrongs of the past or present.

Of further import is the irrefutable reality that there is no homogeneity among the minority groups whose interests are championed by our politically correct progressives. The entire movement is predicated upon a false premise: that racism, bigotry, prejudice and the discriminatory practices emanating from these are the exclusive domain of European descendants. Although patently absurd and suggestive of abject ignorance, both as to history and current events, this notion is the gravamen of the politically correct, or Progressive, position. This has led to equally ridiculous debates on such subjects as whether "reverse discrimination" is a real thing or if white people can actually be the victims of so called "hate crimes." The former is nonsense; there is only discrimination, no less vile when perpetrated by one group than by any another. And, as to the latter, any negative act against a person perpetrated on the basis of some form of prejudice is a hate crime. To attempt a distinction for one group or another is in and of itself a clear and undeniable act of bigotry. The sad reality is that just as there are bigoted whites, there are homophobic blacks, racist Japanese; misogynistic Hispanics and so on.

Ultimately, hatred and fear based upon the differences between people, be they questions of color, ethnicity, gender, sexual orientation, religion, perceived handicaps, wealth and the like are an integral characteristic of humans. It is a condition as long standing as the species itself and finds its genesis in several factors. Most obvious are fear based on ignorance and resentment rooted in jealousy. Less obvious, though far more insidious, is the capitalization on the differences between people, including ignorance and jealousy, by political and religious entities for the direct ends of gaining and maintaining power.

The manipulation of people's inherent emotional reaction to those of different persuasions for less than altruistic purposes is an old game of devastating consequence. Hitler, as is widely known, painted Jews, particularly as bankers, to be responsible for the economic plight of post World War I Germany, thus gaining popular support for his party and its objectives. Pogroms directed at religious minorities have been utilized by almost every religion and numerous political institutions to garner loyalty and create a common popular enemy. Among these are the systemic attacks on the minority Muslim Rohingya in Myanmar by political Buddhists; the Serbian displacement of Bosnian Muslims in the former Yugoslavia during the late 20th century; the ongoing Israeli removals of Palestinians in parts of Israel; the 1909 genocide perpetrated by the Islamic Ottoman Empire against Christian Armenians; and, of course, the Roman Catholic Church's historic and well documented assaults on non-conforming religious groups. Atrocities committed against other "different" groups are no less common. Members of the lesbian, gay, bisexual and transgender, or "LGBT," communities in Saudi Arabia, Pakistan, Iran and Somalia, for instance, may be executed. Fundamentalist Christians in this country and others, including in some African States, have advocated similar treatment. Countries in Asia and, most certainly, Russia are generally hostile to LGBT communities. Of interest, there are also instances of discord, based upon orientation, between those of relatively recently recognized groups, though these are not seemingly inspired by any institutional prerogative. Internecine warfare between various tribes in some African countries and among competing Islamic sects are commonplace, as is Xenophobia in most regions of the world. Blatant racism is alive and well globally. As an institutional problem, most surveys indicate that it is most prevalent in India; common throughout Asia; increasingly manifest in some European, African and Latin American countries; entrenched in Russia and the PRC; and has shifted from targeting blacks in South Africa to singling out whites.

The common thread here, as evidenced by the nature of the foregoing examples is that institutionalized discrimination against any minority requires a significant degree of popular support by the enfranchised. In every of these instances, that support is undertaken by marking the targeted group as some form of threat to the common well-being of the majority by the organized protagonists of the discriminatory policy in furtherance of their realpolitik objectives.

The other commonality is that popular support is made more likely by "group-think," which assures that when a mob gathers in a unified goal, regardless of the intellectual capacity of individual participants, its collective IQ drops to the lowest common denominator. Hence, people find themselves supporting and doing the unthinkable when stripped of their individuality. This is precisely the dynamic that drives lynch mobs.

This also the precise methodology deployed by the politically correct, newly coined as Progressives, and that will surely be retooled by their counterparts at the other extreme, should the former succeed in their endeavors. Fear mongering and the incitement of hatred can only have the effect of polarization and, if coupled with the potential onset of economic ills, will land us in an arena no different than that of Hitler's Germany, albeit with different boogeymen. Disguised as latter day Robin Hoods, promising to take all from the privileged and therewith provide redress to every manner of minority, the Progressives' true ambition is to bind and hold us in the thrall of a socialist experiment that will irrevocably bankrupt and enslave us—all of us—in a technocratic era that belies any return to any semblance of freedom. Underlying that objective is the age old aspiration to create in themselves a new political and economic elite.

The problems are aplenty. Most assuredly that the redistribution of wealth is fine—until there is no more wealth to be had. In short, as has been the case with all extremists—the premises for seeking power is subterfuge. This most certainly applies to the championing of civil rights through incitement of hatred and disenfranchisement.

The reality, often ignored by the politically correct, is that the United States stands alongside the Scandinavian countries, Belgium, Guatemala, Columbia, Brazil and Argentina in terms of institutional tolerance for minorities, due to the circumstances of having a diverse populace and the Constitutional shield that has constantly, albeit sometimes slowly, countered the effects of discrimination in the US. This does not mean to suggest that we do not have a problem with bigotry. However, as indicated by Pew Research in a survey conduct-ed in 2016, the majority of Americans believe that personal prejudices outweigh institutional discrimination against blacks in this country. Although not as resoundingly as non-blacks, black responses to the poll indicated that the majority felt this was the case. Are there still problems with institutionalized discrimination? Of course there are. Are there avenues of redress? There are. And this is what sets the US apart from so many other countries of the world. Are these always fair and quick enough? No, but they have proven to work more steadfastly than other options employed elsewhere.

Interestingly, according to Pew, the numbers of Americans who believe race to be an issue of concern in the US doubled during the Obama presidency and has continued to rise under Trump. The ques-tion arises, then, as to whether this is a matter of actual deterioration in race relations or the result of the idea being promoted for political gain. It is difficult to arrive at an answer; however, there is no doubt that the rising trend in polarization, by pols, will be met by a reac-tion. Put otherwise, if a white person is labeled a bigot by mere virtue of being of European descent, it must be expected that he or she will take umbrage at the allegation, take steps to protect their interests and, perhaps, challenge the originators of the charge as racist. The same principle applies to the back and forth between all groups and is suggestive of the notion that extremists do not offer viable solutions. Ultimately, there cannot and will not be any relational normalization between any groups, be they based upon race, ethnicity, gender, sexual orientation or what have you, through the disenfranchisement of any other group. And any effort to do so is in and of itself the very thing sought to be extinguished by these means. From a lay standpoint, if one accepts the premise that ignorance and jealousy lie at the heart of attitudes and beliefs that lead to discrimination, it seems likely that addressing these failings would go further in finding resolutions than will the exacerbation of divisiveness.

A final dilemma that attaches to the seemingly endless barrage of declarations of social injustices and finger pointing stemming from the politically correct through media, entertainment, and social media, is ennui. I will confess, for example, although I feel strongly about the evils of the Holocaust perpetrated against the Jews by the Nazis, as I do with regards to all genocides, I am becoming more numbed to that injustice than I am to the plight of other victims who are generally ignored. This is simply because I feel inundated, on a seemingly weekly basis, by reminders of the Jewish Holocaust, while no mention is ever made of others who suffered the same fate. Hence, the latter are fresh in my mind, their plight far more vivid, while the former are almost lost in the background of all of the noise we are subjected to.

In short, I find myself not caring anymore. And, much as daily broadcasts of the Vietnam war inured so many Americans to the horrors of that combat, I think that too much is too little, while less is more. That is, if we are to truly meant to care about the things we should be caring about. Applied in the context of the civil rights issues, regarding all of the minority interests at stake, discussed in the preceding paragraphs, and particularly where I, as a person of mostly European ancestry, am held to blame and admonished for taking some pride in my heritage and accomplishments, I am reaching the point where I no longer give a damn. Perhaps I have lost my sense of humor. If my sentiment is unique, it is largely irrelevant; however, if this is endemic to others in the same position, it is tragic.

With all of this said, the prospect of creating, though coercion, a minority blind society is highly unlikely. One can only hope that with time such a society will eventually evolve. In the interim, it is unfathomable why, instead, there is no cohesive effort to teach people to recognize the differences between all people and find the means to enjoy the cultures within our culture. Perhaps a lack of political expedience is to blame. And, although the domestic machinations of extremists present a threat to stability, the accompanying trend to dilute America's national identity is equally troubling. ✎

CHAPTER 20

NATIONALISM AND GLOBALISM
NEED NOT BE . . .

Nationalism and globalism need not be mutually exclusive. In fact, and contrary to the rhetoric presently bandied about by pols and multinational corporate sultans, nationalism is necessary for globalism to function efficiently and relatively peaceably.

This position contradicts that taken by the Trilateral Commission (not the conspiracy nut version) and other groups that have advocated large scale regional hegemony as the most appropriate vehicle for inducing wide spread global trade and minimization of conflicts. History has proven that thesis to be flat out wrong. In the simplest of terms, every instance in which one state has sought to dominate a collection of other states, the results have been dismal at best, catastrophic at worst. This was as true of the Roman Empire and subsequent iterations, among them the Habsburg and Ottoman Empires, the Soviet Union and Yugoslavia, as it is of modern Russia and the Peoples' Republic of China (PRC). In each of these instances, the subservient states have been nation states, or some semblance thereof.

The distinction between states and nation states is of the utmost importance. States are defined as political bodies capable of exerting their will over specific geographical areas, by force if necessary, and that do so. Nation states, while embodying the same attribute, generally have dominion only over a populace comprised of people with a common culture, be it comprised of language, traditions, religion history and customs, or any combination or variant of these. In sum, constituents of nation states share commonalities other than the government ruling them. Conversely, states lack the cohesive identity that is foundational to the raison d'etre of nation states. Also significant is that states encompassing a number of nations are commonly governed by people from the culture that first created the multinational state who invariably turn to supplanting the natural cohesiveness of subservient nations with artificial state identities. These conditions, quite naturally, set the stage for resentment of the governed towards their political rulers.

As applied in the Soviet Union, for example, which was governed by Russians and once by a Georgian, Stalin, in spite of its efforts to create a "Soviet" identity, even to the extent of relocating nationals throughout the Union, on its collapse, large numbers of people thusly displaced gravitated back to their nations of origin. Marshall Tito's efforts to create a Yugoslavian identity failed even more dismally. The demise of that state resulted in years of slaughter amongst former Yugoslavs, who had reverted to their former national identities as Serbs, Croats, Bosnians and Macedonians, as well as competing religious identities. The modern PRC has also embarked on creating a "Chinese" identity where none exists. Contrary to popular belief, a myth perpetuated by most Chinese Mandarin speaking Han dominated dynasties, including the present Communist Party, there is no homogeneous Chinese culture. Tibetans, Mongols, Uighurs, and some seventeen other groups found in China are not of the Han group, Moreover, among the dominant Han Chinese population found in the PRC, there are various subsets that belie the notion of other than a genetic commonality. These, such as the Hakka, enjoy differing languages, customs, diets, traditions and other cultural attributes that set them apart from the main. The formulas for creating a unitary identity in this multinational state, as fashioned by the PRC's governing party, has been draconian, to say the least. All are coercive and include ethnic cleansing, re-education, the modification of history and an absolute bar to any cultural practice, religious or otherwise, that contravenes the interests of the state, its political doctrine and the mores of its ruling class.

The common thread in the imposition of states' wills over multiple nations is that, over time, they implode from within. This is in part due to the inefficiency and corruption endemic to the governance of large state entities. Significant here, is that the artificial suppression of national identity provokes ongoing reactionaryism, in the form of resistance, that force the state to expend considerable resources to maintain its defining impetus—the continued control over its territories and constituents, even if by force. Exacerbating the latter is that while perhaps operating under the guise of ideology, the realpolitik purposes driving empire are simply not altruistic. Money, natural resources, labor, expanded borders to secure the perpetrating nation and power are the ultimate objectives. Thus is further motivation provided the disenfranchised, in the context of the multinational state, to resist the interests of their overlords. The British became well educated in these dynamics through the circumstances tolling the shrinkage of their Empire, near and wide, from Ireland to India, though violence and passive resistance. Nor had they lost that cognition in their retreat from colonialism, creating in their wake, arbitrary states comprised of multiple nations, all subject to the rule of a dominant group, under the express doctrine of "divide and conquer," the repercussions of which yet resound throughout Africa and the Middle East. An ironic, though largely irrelevant vestige of Britain's footprint in the US, is the propensity of our leaders to take great pains in establishing in their lineage a genealogical connection to British royalty. Good grief; we should pillory them.

Two additional exercises in regional hegemony abide, one deliberate and the other inadvertent. The first, the European Union (EU), assumes the model of creating a state among consenting nation states.

Theoretically designed to allow for the evolution of a European state by virtue of a common currency, open borders and the imposition of a binding, common regulatory scheme, while yet allowing some semblance of national autonomy, the EU is at the onset of crumbling. Nationalistic resistance to centralized governance is rising throughout Europe in direct proportion to the increases in power ceded to the European government by member states. Other factors are contributing to the EU's decay. These include the imposition of economic performance criteria by the EU, at the behest of generally northern European members, particularly Germany, on southern states. Immigration policies originating from EU government have had a direct and immediate impact upon the populations of EU member states This has resulted in negative economic consequences and rising political polarization. The imposition of economic criteria, based upon the northern European models, without regard for cultural implications has translated into a form of cultural imperialism: the notion that Greeks can and should adopt German practices, and the like. At the same time, immigration policies are an earmark of the globalist outlook of some modern European leaders, France's Emmanuel Macron and Germany's Angela Merkel, and are undertaken with ill regard for the burgeoning economic distress and identity crisis of their native middle classes. Germany now faces increased radicalism, left and right, while France is struggling with the "Yellow Vest" rebellion, both directly attributable to the embrace of interests outside the realm of domestic well-being. The EU's inability to fathom the importance of national identity within the constituencies of its member states will eventually prove fatal. In contrast, inter-European arrangements preceding the EU focused on free trade and the unfettered cross border movement of people, without impinging on sociopolitical and cultural sovereignty. These were widely accepted by people of the participating European nation states.

Although not by design, the United States is in the process of morphing from its intended embodiment as a nation state into a regional hegemonic regime. While this notion may raise some eyebrows, the supporting evidence is quite clear cut on several fronts. Geographically, the US covers a vast territory; its denizens representative of every possible racial, ethnic and cultural origin. All, save Native Americans, are the descendants of relatively recent immigrants who found their ways to this country by any number of means—migration, indentured servitude and slavery, or are immigrants themselves. In spite of the geographic and human diversity of the country, and adherence to often multiple cultural aspects associated with their roots, commonalities among her population persisted and developed into a uniquely American character. This is not to suggest homogeneity or even harmony are attributes of Americanism. They are not. Civil war, race riots, civil unrest, inequities and discord speak otherwise.

Nonetheless, bound by a common language; a sense of opportunity, real or imagined, of joining the ranks of the middle class and realizing the "American dream;" the hope suggested by a democratic, republican form of governance; and, perhaps, the subconscious realization that all are the same in being different, Americans have enjoyed a sense of national identity. Anecdotally, seems less a matter of belonging, than a sense of wanting to belong. An additional common thread has been a general belief in self reliance and appreciation of minimal governmental interference in the lives of ordinary people.

During the last several decades, increasingly so of late, the notions of assimilation and self reliance, on the part of inbound migrants, has abated. This has naught to do with the qualities of these recent immigrants. Instead, it is due to the politicization of immigration issues. Congressional delegates, in both houses, sworn to uphold the law, have encouraged migrants to bypass the legal avenues of immigration available to them and enter the US illegally. Enticements in the form of free services and funding through an already overburdened social safety net are offered, as are rights normally reserved for legal immigrants and citizens. Hence, large numbers of migrants arrive illegally and are encouraged to carry with them a sense of entitlement, rather than hope for the opportunity to develop independent means of success in their endeavors. Underlying the ideological front for this agenda are a desire to create larger "friendly" constituencies for the proponents of illegal migration and the fear of losing existent constituents by crafting laws easing the criteria for immigration. Critics of this scheme to foster "illegal immigration" are branded as racist for using the word "illegal" in this context. Absent is any rational explanation for continuing the practice. Thus, symbolism over substance prevails.

Coupled with this dilemma is the outright discouragement, by pols and progressive activists, of any requirement that immigrants, illegal or otherwise, be encouraged to assimilate. Again, any position to the contrary is immediately decried as "racist." Yet, a unifying identity is fundamental to maintaining a nation state. As aptly suggested by George Washington, incidentally a proponent of immigration, in a letter to John Adams on November 15, 1794 :

> "[T]he policy or advantage of [immigration] taking place in a body (I mean the settling of them in a body) may be much questioned; for, by so doing, they retain the Language, habits and principles (good or bad) which they bring with them. Whereas by an intermixture with our people, they, or their descendants, get assimilated to our customs, measures and laws: in a word, soon become one people."

Ignoring this basic proposition, recognized by most other countries, even Sweden, which requires certain degrees of assimilation, suggests a yen to design a factionalized society in lieu of fostering a common, national identity. Unremarkably, these turns of events have fostered resentment in several groups, including "old school," immigrants, underemployed minorities, beset descendant classes of "unprotected" ancestry and a middle class already assaulted by diminishing standards of living, increasing household costs and rising taxes.

Of further importance are the increasing centralization of power in Washington, DC, accompanied by increased tensions between states' rights and those subsumed by the federal government, the regional nature of our economy and the advent of geographical political polarization.

In essence, the sum of these conditions has led to the development of subsets within the country that are culturally, economically and politically distinct from one another. Accordingly, the United States is well on the road to becoming a state of nations instead of a nation state. It follows that the federal government will be faced with the prospect of more aggressively exercising its will over the multiple nations it governs, if it is to retain governance. Push back will come in the form of more frequent, legitimate and palpable urges of secession. Thus, we have a hegemony in the making, retarded only by the federal government's willingness to dole out money to its frustrated constituency—individuals, corporations, farmers and states. When the ability to continue the practice can no longer meet demand, as surely it must, factionalization along "national"lines will accelerate.

Quite frankly, if our national identity, if being American, is to wither away, I see no flaw, save in terms of geopolitical security, in seeing the replacement of the United States with a host of nation states. All hegemonies eventually fail to an orchestra of violence. It would be far better to see a negotiated, orderly and bloodless withdrawal of nations from the Union, than a series of civil wars. So too, would a group of autonomous nation states, associated by free trade, the open movement of people and mutual defense pacts be preferable to the emergence of a dysfunctional, techno-totalitarian state in form of the federal government. Seditious? Perhaps. It seems to me that loyalty is misplaced if not in support of the ideas behind our constitutional republic, rather than its errant government. More seriously, an event of this magnitude would likely see migrations, akin to those of the post Soviet era, of people towards areas in which they could find commonality with those already there. Recent demographics suggest this is already the case.

On to the modern perceptions of globalism. Modern globalism is the bailiwick of two distinct groups, the greedy and the mentally infirm. Among the first are global corporations. To these, globalism portends the means of further entrenching themselves as necessary economic attribute in their regions of operations. Consequences are of little concern, and indeed are to be unfettered by the interests of national concerns. The vehicles employed to achieve these ends generally take the form of international trade agreements that ignore the age old adage of business, that a bargain is well struck if all parties leave the table feeling sated. Instead, the trade agreements devised tend to unilateral corporate benefits and seek to rob the hosting nations of all legal redress for wrongs that might be committed by their corporate "invitees." Counted alongside this first group are those whose advocacy for globalism is directed at realizing a redistribution of wealth from developed countries to those in lesser stages of economic development. Their avenue of choice lies in the United Nations, through which unilaterally favorable treaties and pacts are crafted, under the guise of noble causes, such as the abatement of carbon emissions, that require no liability or sacrifice on the part of lesser developed states, while mandating all costs be borne by the developed countries, including the direct payment of money to the benefiting countries' coffers. The reality of both propositions, the corporate and the welfare states', is that very little economic benefit finds its way into the general populace. The former draw profits and resources to favorably secure and tax friendly venues, while the latter have proven a propensity for taking "redistributed" wealth, and anew redistributing it among the ruling elites.

Then there are the ideologues, acolytes of political globalists, whose adherence to notions of globalism are steeped in visions of an egalitarian world, governed by a benevolently inclined global government, perhaps akin to the United Nations or some other socialistic, Utopian model, possibly derived from the annals of science fiction. Though surely deserving of a "Kumbaya," moment, these naifs are hard pressed to understand that human evolution has not risen to this being even the remotest of possibilities. And, the notion of further empowering the UN is chilling. No greater example of bureaucratic and inefficient ineptitude has ever graced the planet, particularly insofar as the preservation of life is concerned; its failings in Yugoslavia and Rwanda mere examples. In the meantime, leaders of the idealists are bent on the decimation of the old, "new world order," of states and nation states, with an eye to achieving power in the new, "new world order," ambitions as old as politics.

All sides demonize nationalism as fascism, a la Hitler, Franco or Mussolini, out of ignorance or deliberate and wanton disregard for the actual nature of nationalism, which is no more than a descriptor of cohesion for the populations of nation states, states comprised of people with a common identity. In short, they mimic the arguments forwarded by the proponents of hegemony. Populism, no more than support for policies beneficial to internal economic security, is decried as antithetical to the "common" good. The vulnerability of these arguments is that hegemonic regimes have never succeeded over the long term. Accordingly, one cannot expect any success in a system of global governance. The weaknesses of hegemonies would simply magnify under the aegis of some regime of global proportion.

Returning now to the underlying thesis, and relying upon the previously presented characteristics of nationalism, globalism—as a model for interaction between states—is entirely possible, and desirable, where it does not represent a threat to the national autonomy or security of participant states. Conjunctively, there must lie an objective of achieving a modicum of economic equilibrium between global partners. This must entail each nation's willingness to negotiate on the basis of self-interest, with the will to impose tariffs on subsidized imports, most assuredly the cost of labor. Ultimately, efficiency will move to the fore, countries producing that to which they are most suited. It should be noted that national independence mandates the development of energy self sufficiency—achievable through development of alternatives to oil and natural gas—where neither are domestically had. So too, must there be mechanisms to restrain imperialistic or hegemonic ambitions, historically most effectively done through mutual defense treaties, along the lines of NATO, that do not move beyond the realm of that goal.

Criticism of models of governance, and international relations, would likely be of greater validity if directed at the impact of religions on regional and global stability, rather than the human desire for otherwise derived commonalities. ᶜᵃ

CHAPTER 21

IF RELIGION IS TO BE THE WELLSPRING OF HUMAN MORALITY . . .

If religion is to be the wellspring of our national morality, it is time to find a new fount. The problem is not one of a belief in God or religion, per se. And certainly morality, as a code of conduct in interpersonal relations, is a societal imperative. Unfortunately, the lines between morality and institutional religious doctrine are fuzzy and therein lies the rub. Doctrine tends to expand into additional requisites for conduct, including ritual, and each religion suggests a divine sense of superiority that allows and even encourages its adherents to treat those of other faiths, and those of none, differently than each other. This trait is as common to Buddhism and Hinduism as it is to Judaism, Christianity and Islam. It is, in fact, endemic to all organized religions. Hence, religious dogma more often than not breeds intolerance and thereby a duality of moralities; one applicable to those of the same belief and the other directed at everyone else. As such, absent within a state comprised of constituents sharing only a single religion, a unitary, religiously derived moral code cannot be uniformly applied unless coercively. This has, understandably, given rise to conflicts.

Now, there has been great debate, most assuredly of late, over whether religious wars or those undertaken by "atheists" have contributed most greatly to the violent demise of humans throughout history. On its face, the argument is a nonstarter. If one yields to the findings of Charles Phillips and Alan Axelrod, expressed in their well researched *Encyclopedia of Wars,* published in 2011 and which covers conflicts ranging from 8000 B.C./B.C.E. through 2003, and there is no reason not to, of some 1,763 wars fought during that time span, a mere 123, or barely 7 percent, were religious wars. According to Phillips and

Axelrod, these accounted for only some 2 percent of all war related fatalities. Counted among these wars were the Crusades, the European religious wars of the 16th and 17th centuries, the various Islamic wars and the Indian—Pakistani partition conflict. Thus, it is clear, that in relative terms, wars fought on behalf of God have been of minor consequence.

If, however, one adds to the mix conflicts which have arisen for other reasons, such as economics and the acquisition of territory, but which have found rationalization through moral superiority, the picture changes. The difference between these two types of conflicts is simply whether undertaken "for God," or justified by the rationale that "God is on our side," and add significantly to the human toll. Now we may include in these numbers the indigenous victims of European colonization of the Americas; the human cost of the Israeli-Palestinian conflict, the treatment of gaijin and other foreigners by the Japanese during WWII, the Ottoman purges of Armenians; and even Hitler's genocides against the Jews and Roma, as a small sampling of exemplars. All of this arises through the insertion of dual morality into the mindset of the protagonists in these misdeeds; the certainty that their moral code is divinely ordained as superior to that of their opponents, their actions, thereby, justified.

This leaves the matter of wars and other atrocities that are committed neither for God or in the name of God. As a practical matter there is no such thing. This, if once considers that the authors of these, by and large, the self-proclaimed atheist states, such as the former USSR and the present North Korea and PRC, are merely post-religious political entities that have undertaken to replace notions of God with the 'ideals" of the communist state. Religiously derived morality is then supplanted by state ordained ethos, which are no less inclined to moral duality as a form of rationalization than their forbears. Now we may include the casualties meted out by the Communist parties of the PRC, North Korea, the Khmer Rouge, the former Soviet Union and their ilk to the cost of religious morality. This done, and weighed together with the human toll exacted by other wars for and in the name of God, there is ample evidence that of the 1,763 wars cataloged by Phillips and Axelrod, most, if not all, and regardless of their root causes, have been accompanied by justifications based upon moral imperatives of a dualistic nature.

This dilemma was recognized by America's founders, who forged in their new republic a pantheistic tolerance of religion but, though the auspices of the establishment clause of the First Amendment to the United States Constitution, ratified in 1791, forbade the government from establishing a "state" religion. This, although the phrase is not specifically used in the Constitution, is the gravamen, both in terms of intent and subsequent judicial interpretation, of the separation between church and state doctrine. Thomas Jefferson wrote amply, though somewhat disdainfully, of his belief in religious tolerance and discarded the prospect of religious interference in the affairs of state Likewise, John Adams advocated a pantheistic outlook; however, he deeply mistrusted human motivations, seeing as a restraint to these, "a government of laws, and not of men." Although omitted in a subsequent treaty, then President Adams sought to remove religion as a factor in the Treaty of Tripoli, between the US and the Muslim ruler of Tripoli, signed by Adams in 1797, by including a clause stating that ". . . the United States of America is not in any sense founded on the Christian Religion . . ." It should be noted that while George Washington's position regarding the role of religious morality might negate these arguments, in actuality it buttresses them. Of the import of religion on national morality, in his farewell address of 1796, Washington suggested that ". . . reason and experience both forbid us to expect that national morality can prevail in exclusion of religious principle." However, in this sense, as the subsequent text of his speech assures, Washington was invoking a general spirit of religiosity, an admonition to do no harm, rather than advocating the doctrine of any one religion. Thus translated, George Washington's purpose lay in entreating the nation to avoid entanglement in foreign wars or even granting any favorable form of status to any one country, rather, treating each equitably, fairly and justly through commerce, regardless of such nation's internal ethos or third party imbroglios. Indeed, as he made clear in the same speech, Washington also abhorred the emergence of the political party system within the US, fearing the advent of dualistic moralities which he believed would cause domestic factionalization. Ultimately, the holy grail shared by these contemporaries of America's genesis, was an abiding understanding of the need to avoid the intolerance bred by competing moral dogmas. Their solution lay in seeding a unifying moral principle within the framework of the country's governance and society. At its heart, this proposition embodies no more than absolute tolerance coupled with an ethic to do no harm to others. Anything less represents an encroachment upon the individual liberty interests of anyone adversely affected, those interests a fundamental cornerstone of the classical liberal philosophy that gave rise to our republic.

Unfortunately, this tenet lies beyond the ken of most of our latter day politicians and constituents and has been all but abandoned. We have regressed at an exponentially accelerating rate towards a dark age of intolerance driven by the emergence of a virtual Babel of competing moralities—none of which pay even lip service to the moral principle of classical liberalism. The problem is both one of increasing intolerance by religious practitioners and the growing trend of governments, state and federal, to become entangled with religious institutions.

The Catholic church and its related charities received in excess of $1.6 billion dollars in contracts and grants from the federal government between 2012 and 2015. According to the Manhattan Institute, Catholic Charities USA, its largest charitable organization, receives about 65 percent of its funding from federal and state agencies. Although not an entirely new turn of events, it is noteworthy that government largesse towards religious organizations is a phenomenon of the latter 20th century and has markedly and steadily increased throughout the early 21st. For Catholic Charities USA, this has translated into an increase of government support from less than 25 percent of its budget in the 1960s to the present levels of over 65 percent. This equals the amounts given to some states by the federal government. Reconciliation between Congressional largesse and the Catholic Church's handling of child sex abuse cases has apparently never been an issue. The victims of these abuse cases were reported to the Vatican abuse summit, held in February, 2012, to number some 100,000, in the US alone, at that time. By 2010, other groups, including Lutheran Social Services and the Jewish Federations were also receiving the bulk of their funding from the federal government. These groups, as well as others affiliated with other institutional religions, including Islamic organizations, maintain offices in the nation's capital and expend considerable resources lobbying pols.

The full turn towards federal involvement in the funding of religious "charities," was undertaken by President George W. Bush when, in 2001, he established the White House based Faith Based Initiative. Aimed at contributing to religious charities and social service providers, and pandering largely to conservative Christians, the Initiative resulted in the federal expenditure of over $2 billion dollars a year to fund religious organizations. Likewise, about thirty-two governor's offices across the country established programs to finance religious charities. Support for the Bush League's ill-conceived foray into Iraq was heartily supported by his fundamentalist beneficiaries, who saw this as a form of support for Israel which, many held, would lead to the End of Days; a full blown middle eastern conflagration that would lead to the demise of half of Israel's Jews and the conversion to Christianity of the survivors. Bush, a self proclaimed devotee of conservative Christianity, embraced these views of religious superiority, as indeed he had in the wake of the attacks of September 11, 2001, when, during the course of addressing the nation he, for all intents and purposes, alienated the Muslim population by inferring in Islam a general proclivity for violent fundamentalism—save, of course for the Saudi royals, with whom his family enjoyed business relationships. One consequence of this approach, which was institutionalized by the Bush administration, was the re-characterization of all Palestinians as religiously driven terrorists, rather than nationalists seeking an autonomous state. Another, resulting from the power vacuum in the aftermath of Saddam Hussein's demise, was the rise of the Sunni Wahhabist ISIS, or Daesh, and its bloody effort to establish a permanent, fundamentalist state in Iraq and Syria.

Bush's successor, Barack Obama, in spite of election promises to the contrary, expanded the scope of the Faith Based Initiatives during his tenure at the White House. Funding, though somewhat nebulous, appears to have been maintained at at least the same levels as during the Bush League era, but now encompassed additional religious organizations. President Obama did somewhat abate the US's foreign policy long tradition of unilateral support for Israel, largely predicated upon a perceived Judaeo-Christian moral imperative and, of course, tremendous lobbying efforts, coupled with substantial campaign expenditures. For this, he was labeled as having "anti-Semitic" tendencies, as is anyone who disagrees with Israeli policy as a matter of principle rather than prejudice. The term is in and of itself ludicrous, given that where properly applied it must also encompass Arab Christians and and Muslims, and certainly speaks to moral duality. Nonetheless, Obama did not help himself in this regard; his faith based funding extended to the likes of Louis Farrakhan's Nation of Islam, which received almost a half million dollars between 2009 and 2018, and can only be described as a vehicle for abjectly racist and anti-Jewish zealotry. Nor has President Trump helped matters. While there is little rational argument to be had against his concern that allowing immigration from countries where circumstances hamper security vetting, the problem arises that Trump's position has religious undertones, rather than the secular rationale that is desperately called for. This is exemplified by references to Christian morality and superiority given during his inaugural address. According to Trump, after making biblical references, ". . . most importantly, we will be protected by God." At first blush, these words appear relatively innocuous, but in the context of having been delivered to a nation of people whose beliefs may not be biblically derived, and rhetoric related to wiping fundamentalist Muslims from the face of the planet, the undertone becomes somewhat troubling.

In essence, the secular intentions of the scheme of governance devised at the outset have ceded to promotion of competing value systems by virtue of political influences. The federal government now funds, directly and indirectly and at unprecedented levels, faith based schools and universities of various denominations, including those that are Catholic, Baptist Jewish and Muslim. Churches, Temples and Mosques receive monies as do their various charities. At least one federal prison is oriented towards Jewish inmates; the Otisville Federal Correctional Institution, located in New York state, the future home of former Trump attorney, Michael Cohen, allows for Jewish religious observances and provides inmates with access to kosher foods and Rabbis. And, Nation of Islam's federal funding is aimed at prison outreach activities.

In every instance, the public narrative offered in support of government largesse is based upon the pressing need for charitable action. This is total nonsense. In reality, Americans privately donate some $300 billion dollars a year to various charities of their choosing. Thus, while significant in terms of federal expenditures of public money, its $2 billion dollar annual contribution can hardly be deemed necessary. Moreover, government spending here is derived from money that is mandated of taxpayers. This somewhat belies the notion of charity, which generally connotes a voluntary act. Thus does government, if only in this manner, force its religiously driven moral imperatives upon people who might be otherwise inclined. A gay person then forced to contribute to an anti-gay rights religious organization, as a mere example of many.

Aside from presidential religious bents, an examination of the Congressional religious make-up may also offer some clue as to federal de-secularization. According to a Pew Research poll conducted of Congressional members on January, 2019, those identifying as Christians of all denominations, particularly Catholics and Protestants, and Jews are over represented in Congress relative to the affiliations of adult Americans. Some 88.2 percent identified as Christians, compared to 71 percent of the adult population that does so and 6.4 percent as Jewish, compared to a population percentage of 2. Other religions are generally represented in Congress in accord with the numbers of adherents within the general population, save one group that is grossly underrepresented. These are people who consider themselves atheists, agnostic or unaffiliated with any particular faith. Comprising some 23 percent of all American adults, their Congressional presence comprises only 0.2 percent; a lone Senator, Kyrsten Sinema, from Arizona. Religiously speaking, as exemplified by budgetary allocations for religious groups and their political interests, dominance seems well in the hands of those sharing a Judaeo-Christian moral base. Thus we have moral duality in the operation of government; the ethos of one group superseding that of the rest. Interestingly, in times past, when the vast majority of Americans identified as Christians, secularism was more likely in that the common ethos was a given. Diversification of religious doctrines, together with a growing trend towards the abandonment of institutional religions has had a polarizing effect—entrenching those imbued of traditional dogma against those becoming indifferent to such organizations and yet others, a growing group, whose embrace is of the later order of religion—the notion of the Progressive State. The latter represents no less a religion than its traditional forebears or contemporaries, the communist or socialist state. Masquerading under the guise of a truly secular outlook, one need only challenge the tenets of this movement, however fleetingly, to become aware of the religious fervor and intolerance that accompanies. Communism, ideal Socialism and their latest iteration, Progressivism, share with religion a number of unifying characteristics; all are based upon emotional irrationality and seek to impose, by any means, their own version of morality. All promote ignorance due to an inherent inability to withstand rationale scrutiny, and each is inclined to increasing intolerance in proportion to the growth of their constituencies. Taken as a whole, people are the opiate of all of these religions; the more ignorant the flock, the more boisterous the shepherd. And none take to heart the notions of doing no harm and allowing personal individual liberty interests to prevail. Were this not sufficient to raise alarm, we now have the onset of yet newer religions to contend with. ∞

CHAPTER 22

ARTIFICIAL INTELLIGENCE, ALTERED STATES AND ALIENS . . .

Artificial Intelligence, Aliens and Altered States are at the forefront of the budding religions our society must learn to navigate. Unfortunately, we are utterly inadequate to the task. The problem lies in humanity's proclivity to make and embrace technological advances without fostering the cerebral wherewithall to comprehend, never mind manage, its long range societal consequences. We are primates who have progressed from employing sticks and stones as tools to abet our labors to deploying technologies with the theoretical purpose of avoiding such mundanities. And, all the while, we have remained monkeys. The result, that as much as our technology may afford us lives of leisure, it also presents more than adequate means of destroying them. These dichotomies abound. We have nuclear energy and medicine and we have nuclear weapons. We have security and nigh unimaginable ease of communications and we have a totalitarian surveillance state. And now we hover on the brink of even greater advances that are embraced, at least by their advocates, with religious fervor.

First and foremost is artificial intelligence or AI as it is commonly referred to. The late renowned physicist Stephen Hawking suggested quite vigorously that the advent of AI would likely be marked as humankind's greatest achievement and its last. Grasping this sentiment requires an understanding of what AI is and what it is not. AI is not the plethora of algorithms that are programmed to track our communications, shopping patterns, website visits and the like in order to gather data about us for sale to advertisers and governments. These are common enough, and though becoming evermore capable of "learning" to divine patterns of conduct and otherwise improve performance of their intended tasks, are not truly intelligent in the context Hawking was referring to. Nor do the technologies behind self-driving cars and other modes of transport, albeit becoming increasingly self-aware in the context of their surroundings and growing capabilities in reacting to environmental circumstances, rise to this threshold. The same is true of other machines, such as chess playing computers, which are devoted to mastery of a single task. That said, self-operating machines and those that can learn to improve their efficiency, though not endowed of true AI, can become dangerous to people because they lack awareness of environmental circumstances outside of those necessary to performance of their specific tasks. Hence, as exemplified in a recent case, robots employed to fill orders in a warehouse risked harming firefighters responding to a blaze at the facility because, operating autonomously and powered by batteries, these machines simply continued in their programmed duties, oblivious to the risks posed to firefighters, who were forced to dodge the machines. Although there were no injuries or fatalities to humans in that instance, there have been cases of both. Similar problems have arisen with self-driving cars, not programmed to anticipate the litany of possible reactions to a particular situation by other cars driven by humans, not machines. Yet, and spite of popular labeling, none of these machines are "intelligent;" their shortcomings resolvable by tweaking their operating systems and programs. True AI is something more than the machines we see today.

The AI referred to by Stephen Hawking and others, such as Elon Musk, are perhaps best described as artificial entities that are completely self-aware, are capable of cognizance similar to that of humans and are self-directing, acquiring knowledge about everything and applying that information as a matter of principle to any task or goal. They would, in essence, be capable of rational thought, albeit from a digital perspective. Alan Turing, the noted mathematician, posited in the 1950s that if a machine could pass the "imitation game," whereby an evaluator could not distinguish between a human and a machine, based upon a natural conversation between the two, then the machine would have reached intelligent behavior equivalent to that of humans. The obvious flaw in this is that it presupposes humanity in a machine capable of thought equivalent to that of humans. This in turn relies upon the notion that a machine can not escape all of the parameters of its original programming. Otherwise, the question arises, why would communicating with a human be relevant and, even if it were, what interests would a machine intelligence share with a human that would suggest any need for a natural conversation to be had. Beyond Turing's criteria, the threshold for AI is reached upon achieving "singularity," the term applied to that eventual future when artificial intelligence surpasses that of humans. It is to this hypothetical event that concerns regarding the development of AI are directed. Given the fact that great resources are being expended on realizing that moment, together with the growing belief in its possibility, or even likelihood, there are ample reasons to fear the emergence of technological singularity. Well in advance of the concerns expressed by Hawking and Musk, in 1993, computer scientist Vernor Vinge argued that the realization of singularity would cause the end of the human race because, once achieved, the intelligence so endowed would make such rapid, quantum leaps in technologies that humans would be left bereft of the means to cope with these. The prospect of human extinction in the face of AI connotes a future envisioned by countless science fiction novels and films, such as *Terminator,* in which great wars are fought between machines and humans. This vision is highly unlikely because it attributes human qualities to AI, such as malice, and assumes an existential necessity on the part of machines that have attained singularity to engage in a war of survival. Neither makes any sense.

Once having surpassed human intellect, AI would likely continue on the mission that gave rise to its genesis: to learn and apply its acquired knowledge to learn more. Its ancillary functions would be devoted to ensuring that purpose. Thus, an AI would develop further technologies to promote its purpose, and it would do so, not from a human standpoint, but as a self aware entity defining its own needs of self preservation, efficiency and expansion. Its course would diverge from that of humankind because its demands would not be based upon human criteria. Humans, rather than becoming objects of enmity, would simply be irrelevant. So too would our aesthetics become obsolete. Just as humans terraformed Earth, according to their needs, forests into fields and fields into coal mines, and dream of conforming Mars to our survival requisites, an AI would transform our planet into an environment best suited to its purposes. For instance, it might see logic in the elimination of salt water and oxygen in order to ameliorate their corrosive effects, seeking efficiency in friction reduction by replacing the atmosphere with a vacuum, countering the effects of gravity to facilitate space exploration or, even, moving the earth into an orbit further removed from the sun to more efficiently cool itself and the machinery within its purview. In every event, it is more than plausible that a planetary environment most suited to AI would be hostile to humans and every other form of biological life.

Human reaction to such turns of events will vary, but most likely is that we will succumb with a whimper not a bang. By the time technological singularity arrives, we will be further along in our intellectual regression to the stone ages; our entire survival infrastructure, be it military defense, the transmission of electricity, the supply of water and access to information will be even more dependent on a grid operated by advanced technology which would, of course fall under immediate control of AI. So too would every tidbit of information about each of us. Our ability to respond to technological advances would be woefully inadequate, as would our efforts to adapt—the pace of technology by then far outstripping any evolutionary or intuitive prowess our species enjoys. We might try to communicate with whatever form the manifestation of AI might take, but face the risk that this would be as ineffective as ants asking us to stop knocking over their hills because if ants do have a language, we are surely unaware of it. Nor, if we are honest about it, do we care. We are busy doing bigger and better things, like trying to develop AI. However, although ants hold no truck with us, having developed on a separate evolutionary track, AI would be cognizant of our existence because of the role played by our species in its development and as the originators of its initializing information or data sets. The salient inquiry should be, would this mean anything to an exponentially expanding intelligence. Would it be intellectually drawn to a species that expended some II million years evolving to its present state, a leap that might take an AI mere weeks, hours or even minutes. And if, into its cognition, an AI were to synthesize some characteristics of its originators, what would these be. Given the breadth of its knowledge of our history, it might see compassion, for instance, as a mere curiosity, paling in comparison to the overarching bloody mindedness of people embarked on realizing their objectives. Or, were it to have a sense of humor, it might see us as amusements, deigning to keep at least a few of us around to that end, or as living relics, a present reminder of the frailties of biological life forms; holding us in capsules, with pumped in air and intravenous feeding tubes. All told, it is certain that if our species is permitted to survive subsequent to the advent of a singularity, AI would become the central object of a new religion: those of its creators replaced by that of its dependents.

Perhaps the most interesting question one should explore, is where our species reached its apex by abandoning general intellectual pursuits in favor of developing technological advances, what would represent nirvana to an intelligent machine?

The more readily attained holy grail of modernity is altered states. One might think, at first blush, that this is somehow directed at the legalization of pot, genetically imbued with unprecedented levels of THC, sweeping the country. And while, to some, the notion of thusly altered mental states is somewhat of a religion, it is neither new or particularly noteworthy. Morons and escapists have always abounded. Altered states, in the context at hand, relates to the concept of enhancing humans, physically and mentally, through robotics and genetics. The aim is said to be future generations of super humans, endowed with historical physical powers, access to information through interconnection with the internet, or some form thereof, and unprecedented longevity.

Elon Musk and others have posited quite forcefully that transformation of our species into genetically improved, internet wired cyborgs of enhanced longevity is going to be humankind's sole defense against the advent of technological singularity, or true AI. This notion is blatantly infantile, given the ramifications of AI and the fact that it would be in control of what we now term the internet and everything else that is digitally connected. Variations on the theme include exploration of technology that would allow downloading of one's self into a virtual reality platform, thereby achieving a form of immortality. In reality, these movement towards altered states are the playground of the super wealthy, particularly in technological fields, bent on creating in themselves an enhanced caste or an uber class, if you will. The attributes sought, if successful, then paving the way for a ruling class that will claim literal superiority to its subjects.

That the technology developed in pursuit of these ideas will have a collateral effect on the general populace, regardless of targeted success, seems certain. Genetic engineering is on the brink of leading to designer children, theoretically free of disease prone genes and is likely to lead to the induced evolution of a "master race." Gene therapy has already been employed to deal with specific infirmities and will increasingly be aimed at this end. The question, magnified exponentially by the infirmities of our health care system, is whether these benefits will accrue to the fortunes of the average person; in short, whether they will be affordable. The present system, as would the socialist healthcare paradigm envisioned by the Progressive movement, render this prospect highly unlikely—unless, for the insured, a cost benefit analysis suggests otherwise. It is safe to assume that therapies engineered towards longevity will not be commonly affordable unless there is a looming dearth of labor or expertise in a certain field that would lend economic justification towards making the technology available to fill that need. The advent of direct cerebral connectivity with the digital world will surely be available to, if not eventually mandatory for, everyone, though probably with varying degrees of "access." Most important in this manifestation of the future will be direct access to individual data, such as thoughts, activities and location. An individual's access to the net will be limited through censorship that belies any sense of a reality other than what is spoon fed directly to the brain. Further, there is no reason to doubt that connection, in this sense, would allow for digitally induced "reeducation" or, for the resistant, the termination of brain activity. If this seems the stuff of science fiction, think again. All of the necessary technologies are very much in post conceptual stages.

Finally, a word about aliens. The efforts to search out extraterrestrial life forms that are capable of communication and traveling to our small planet have intensified of late. There are, quite naturally, all manner of romantic connotations attached to the concept of first contact with such beings or life forms. Some scientists and scholars, among them Stephen Hawking, have suggested that a modicum of caution ought to be applied in these endeavors. Their reasoning, quite simply, that any alien entities capable of extending into our environs will be technologically, and likely intellectually, superior to us. Much as Europeans presented an immediate threat to indigents on landing on America's shores, one suspects that the dichotomy in technological superiority, if nothing else, between alien entities and humans will be an issue. Indeed, it could well present even more of an existential threat, likely akin to that posed by the passage of a singularity leading to Artificial Intelligence. As to the intellectual chasm such an encounter might present, who knows. Our abilities tend to species-centrism which have left us fully bereft of any ability to understand the measure of intelligence in other earthbound species. This suggests an utter inadequacy were our efforts of understanding directed at something otherworldly. Hence, if successful in meeting an alien species, one suspects, in light of our proclivities when faced with the unknown and the fears generated thereby, the eventuality of yet another new religion.

Woven throughout the foregoing scenarios are two commonalities. The first, that each represents the prospect of a new religion, whether by demand, borne of fear, or a matter of perceived necessity. The second is that our foray into each of these realms has been arbitrarily forced upon society a a whole. Debate regarding merits and latent risks are limited to what can only be described as an elite sliver of the populace. There is very little public debate over the issues these avenues present. This in spite of the fact that all are funded in some form by the American taxpayer. Congress, ostensibly tasked with representing its constituency, is by and large silent on these fields of research. Certainly it has been the standard that technological developments arise in the normal course of events without a requisite for any preceding public consensus. However, we are at the cusp, and beyond, of developing technologies of unprecedented relative consequence, save perhaps splitting of the atom. And, while debate regarding the development of the atomic bomb may have been generally limited to those who understood it, there was at least sufficient classical knowledge among the participants to engender a lively discussion based not just upon science, but also on philosophy, including the application of ethos.

This approach has long been abandoned in the realms of science and technology. Moving forward with advances is now predicated strictly upon ambition and countered, on rare occasion, by squeaks of religious outrage. Yet a debate is called for. The ramifications of realizing any one of the ambitions at issue are sufficient to irrevocably alter the human landscape. That such discourse will emerge is highly unlikely. As a society, it lies beyond our radar, never mind our ken. ∽

CHAPTER 23

THE DEMISE
OF OUR SOCIETY. . .

The demise of our society is marked by a burgeoning lack of civility, the abasement of mutual respect, an inability to empathize and a proclivity for navel contemplation, under the guise of self-improvement, but in reality not more than a form of self adulation. By definition, then, we are well on the path to becoming a nation of narcissists with sociopathic tendencies. On top of all this, we are dumb as sticks, embracing ignorance with dogmatic fervor, and are in abysmal physical condition.

The demise of civility in American society is readily apparent. Discourse has become impossible and the nation is polarizing politically. Indeed, this seems to be the only thing that can be agreed upon by everyone. Informed dialogue has ceded to name calling, emotional rhetoric, hate mongering and the justification of violence against those who hold opposing, or merely different, points of view. Nor is this trend restricted to street rabble. It has become the norm within all of our institutions, from Congress to the media. Left to this course, and if the economy falters yet further, the disintegration of our civil society will be indistinguishable from the uncivil chaos that has preceded the rise of most tyrannies, be it Lenin's Soviet Union, Hitler's Nazism, Mao's Peoples Republic or Castro's Cuba. Then, as now, friendships were rent asunder, marriages collapsed, families were torn apart, neighbors estranged and strangers bared their teeth for no more than a presumption of disagreement.

In our world, we have also lost the little niceties of civility. Words once associated with good manners are no longer a part of our daily lexicon; "please" and "thank you," as obsolete as offering aid to strangers or dipping one's lights to warn oncoming traffic of a radar trap around the next bend. Hell, we don't even hit the low beams to avoid blinding oncoming traffic. We crowd the loading gates at airports and eat like pigs at troughs in restaurants. And in most cases, the customer, once exalted, has been transformed into a burdensome nuisance. Examples abound to an extent it must suffice to simply say that we have become flat out rude. In essence, we have succumbed to notions of the ultimate I: the zealously held and acted upon belief that only I matter, with everyone else presenting an inconvenience.

And yet, addicted to an endless cycle of pharmaceuticals, celebrity news, digital devices and the virtual reality that most informational media has become, we profess, indignantly if challenged, to care. And what do we care about. Ostensibly, causes. Racism, poverty, LGBT rights, animal rights, climate change and anything else that suggests culpability on the part of the United States and affords opportunity to blame someone.

These domestic causes share several attributes. They are all safe; the rights to take them up and craft remedies are constitutionally protected. Nor can these be characterized as having grassroots origins, having been crafted by political entities to garner popular support to attain a shift in power dynamics under the guise of ideology. Where peers of one political realm or another share responsibility for actual misdeeds, such as the Democrats' support for the Bush League war on Iraq or Republican involvement in further bankrupting the country, no cause comes to the front. And even the ideology of youth, though not to be entirely discounted, is marred by a lack of critical thinking and even more so, by questionable motivations. Ideology appears to have become merely another facet of self promotion: a means of fleshing out our flow of perennial "selfies," literal and figurative digital postings, all aimed at painting the perceptions we seek others to have of us.

"Coolness," then, dictates causes. Thus, we have selective causes; those that are popular and those that are not, with the latter to be ignored.

And, as to the causes that do abide, we are not driven by any interest in researching these of our volition. Instead, we accept that which is fed us, by mainstream and social media, and refuse to accept the possibility that these might be misleading or entirely false. We accept allegations of criminal conduct and take great delight in pillaging the accused, stripping them of their livelihoods and reputations in wanton disregard for the processes of law, due process, they are entitled to. This is most true where accusations of sexual misconduct are leveled. From Michael Jackson to Kevin Spacey and R. Kelly to Harvey Weinstein, public convictions are rendered even before investigations are completed. Facts, whatever they turn out to be, are mere inconvenient truths that stand no chance against the onslaught of societal blood lust; societal judgments no less draconian than those rendered during the dark ages of The Inquisition.

Hate crimes, another example, have come to the forefront of criticism of the Trump administration, the president critiqued for his responsibility in fostering an unprecedented rise in such acts. Hate crimes, for whatever reason perpetrated, are heinous and should not be tolerated. However, the statistical evidence presents a showing that such crimes are well below historical averages and are perhaps holding relatively even.

At their nadir in 2014, while President Obama held office, with 6,727 victims reported, the victims of such crimes had risen to 7,615 by 2016, Obama's last full year in office. The number of victims rose again, to 8,493, during Trumps first year in office, during which the largest number of law enforcement agencies ever, some 16,140, provided data to the Federal Bureau of Investigation (FBI), which compiles annual hate crimes statistics. It is this data that is cited by the media. On the face of this data, there does appear to have been a jump in hate crimes between Obama's last year and Trump's first. In 2016, 7,615 victims of hate crimes were reported. In 2017, that number had risen to 8,493. Of note, however, and leading to a difference in the numbers of victims of hate crimes is the fact that in 2016, 15,254 law enforcement agencies provided data to the FBI. By 2017, that number had risen to 16,149. The dictates of logic suggest that with an additional 895 agencies contributing data, an increase of 5.86 percent, in 2017 there must be an additional 446 victims, a correlative increase of 5.86 percent, of reported hate crimes in 2017, At minimum, then that number would 8,061 and, if used as a baseline, and adjusting for the increase in the number of law enforcement agencies providing data, there were an additional 432 victims in 2017, representing an increase over 2016 of 5.67 percent. This is within 2 percentage points of the increases in hate crime victim numbers under Obama during the prior two years. Victims of hate crimes did decline under the Obama administration between 2007 and 2014, though less significantly than might appear, again based upon the number of agencies providing data to the FBI. More importantly, and never having been made an issue by the media, is that during the Clinton Administration, with between 11,300 and 12,200 agencies reporting data, the numbers of hate crime victims ranged between 11,039 and 9,924. Under Bush, such victims numbered 12,016 in 2001, eventually dropping to 9,641 in 2008. Again, adjusting for the lesser numbers of data contributing agencies, these figures are likely higher. Also worth noting, and without demeaning the relevance of reported hate crimes, and bearing in mind that these are under reported, counted victims presently represented some 0.0026 percent of the US population. As a matter of priorities, the question now arises: Are hate crimes of more significance than other issues, or are they matters of political expedience. Were they not the latter, one supposes, charges for victimizing people on the basis of hatred would be leveled at a far greater array of public personae then Trump.

Unfortunately, the pursuit of any cause, say humanitarianism, for example, becomes an exercise in hypocrisy when done selectively. Hence, we have so-called Progressives unwilling to raise the specter of inhumane conditions in Venezuela because the Maduro regime represents their avowed ambitions; some Democrats and most Republicans turning a blind eye to the Palestinian human crisis lest Israel take offense; and a re-characterization of racism to preclude its applicability to some, while touting it as an outrage as to others, all to establish politically convenient truths. These inconsistencies, their evolvement and institution as societal mores, point to an actual rejection of the morality which has traditionally underpinned just causes. This suggests a form of pragmatism, in the choice of ideals, that is certainly narcissistic and somewhat sociopathic.

It is also sad. Causes we should embrace have become entertainment. Marie Colvin, the renowned journalist who was assassinated by order of the Syrian government for reporting on its President Bashar Assad's blitzkrieg against some 28,000 civilians in Homs in 2012, spent a career attempting to convey the atrocities of war, particularly as to non-combatants, to her readership. Her reporting, if the measure of public outrage is any measure, fell on deaf ears. Her story, now the subject of a movie, A Private War, will, no doubt, enthrall movie goers, as war movies are wont to do, especially when viewed from the comforts of our living rooms or cinemas, but will not provide the genesis of a cause. Thomas Goltz, a lesser known, though no less formidable journalist, wrote extensively of the devastation wrought by the Russians in Chechnya and about other conflicts. He remains relatively obscure to the general public and his stories by and large ignored, in spite of his sacrifices, which were not inconsiderable. These and other wars that have targeted civilians in Ukraine, Iraq, the Peoples Republic of China (PRC), Myanmar, Philippines, Somalia, Nigeria, South Sudan, Northern Mali, Libya, Yemen, Afghanistan and Venezuela, to name but some, continue. The collective death tolls number in the hundreds of thousands. ISIS, or Daesh, alone slaughtered some 33,000 civilians, injured another 41,000 and kidnapped 11,000 more between 2002 and 2015, according to the University of Maryland's National Consortium for the Study of Terrorism and Response to Terrorism. Yet no causes arise. At the moment, India and Pakistan are on the brink of an escalating armed conflict over Kashmir. This has elicited a response: a flurry of " #nowar" tweets on Twitter, undoubtedly launched from sofas and armchairs, which will surely serve to resolve the issue.

After WWII, American soldiers were welcomed home as heroes. In the wake of the Vietnam war, returning soldiers, although most had been drafted, were reviled. If nothing else, the public was certainly aware of them and where they had been. Since 2000, at a minimum 20,000 American soldiers have been deployed to do battle in Afghanistan, Iraq, Syria and other countries at any given time. Upon their return, whether in body bags or because their rotation is up, they are not greeted by anyone, save relatives and acquaintances. Most Americans seem blithely unaware of these combat oriented deployments. This, in spite of the fact that of the estimated 500,000 total casualties in Afghanistan, Pakistan and Iraq, between 2001 and 2015, according to the Congressional Research Service and the Watson Institute of Brown University, 6,951 US soldiers were killed, 53,700 were wounded, including 1,645 having at least one limb amputated, and 300,000 suffered traumatic brain injuries. Further, 566 humanitarian aid workers were killed, as were 362 journalists, including Marie Colvin. Clearly, there are no causes here. In fact, nobody cares—not about civilian casualties, not the journalists who have been killed in their efforts to keep the world informed, nor the aid workers dying in war zones or the soldiers we have sent into harm's way.

America's military leaders are predicting with increasing certainty the prospect of an armed conflict with the PRC, Russia or both. To meet this concern, military training has shifted accordingly, even within National Guard units. A survey of active duty members of the military, conducted by the *Military Times* in 2018, suggested that the rank and file resoundingly share in their leadership's assessment. Nonetheless, within the general population there is no understanding of the fact that the PRC and Russia are repressive regimes, the former a totalitarian state, the latter an oligarchy, and that neither holds benevolent ambitions in the global arena. Both have notably increased arms production and have become increasingly hostile to neighboring countries. Both have engaged in bouts of cyber-warfare and espionage, as well as disinformation campaigns, all with significant consequences. And, short of overt declarations of war, both have unequivocally made their respective intentions clear. Yet, the only public pause for concern, perhaps eliciting a cause oriented response, would be if the PRC were to to force us into withdrawals by ceasing delivery of its cheap wares, digital and otherwise, or if Russia were to digitally "kill" the internet. Then, to some Americans, it would be our fault, not theirs.

In sum, it is inarguable that when it comes to "just" causes, the general trend lies in indifference to the risky and politically unsexy. Societal indifference, of course, denotes a lack of empathy, or even sympathy, and bespeaks of a narcissistic commune.

In the meanwhile, glued to our digital worlds, awash in smugness and sanctimony, each of us fully is convinced of our righteousness and contribution to just causes, by merely thinking about them. One singular manifestation of this form of self-indulgences is that we have become obese. Quite literally. Our gluttony has emerged as two crises, one as to our overall societal health and the other a matter of national security.

Obesity is generally defined as weighing more than 20 percent of one's ideal weight. The Centers for Disease Control (CDC) calculate obesity in terms of one's having a Body Mass Index (BMI) of thirty or more. Almost 70 percent of all Americans are overweight, with 40 percent of adults and 18 percent of children, aged two through sixteen, considered obese. This, according to government health agencies, such as the CDC, which further peg the direct annual medical costs of obesity at about $190.2 billion dollars. Excluded from these numbers is any account for other related economic costs, such as work absences due to illnesses attributable to being overweight. The cost of obesity outstrips the medical costs of healthcare for smokers, which are about $170 billion dollars per year. The CDC and others have declared obesity to be a national healthcare crisis.

The US military reports significantly lower rates of obesity than those found in the civilian sector, estimating that about 7.8 percent of active duty members are obese. As reported by the *Army Times,* on October 9, 2018, the real problem for services branches lies in recruitment. Army recruiters report that of all reasons for disqualifying prospective soldiers, the majority, 31 percent, are rejected due to obesity. According to the Pentagon, there are very real concerns about meeting military recruitment necessities as a result. Retired Lieutenant General Sam Ebbeson, quoted by the *Army Times,* and iterating the sentiments of a master sergeant at Fort Dix he had encountered, posited that "... fat people don't make good soldiers. They're a weak link in the chain, and they get themselves and others killed."

Conversely, our society has a different take. Airlines should make larger seats available, at no cost to the overweight, and the mere suggestion that national obesity is an issue demanding some response is characterized as "fat shaming," a recently coined example of "hate" speech. There is a missed opportunity to develop a new cause here; Trump, who is beyond rotund, could readily be blamed for furthering the epidemic of obesity sweeping the country.

Coupled with all of this, is an abiding belief in entitlements. Moving beyond the bipartisan systems of social security, unemployment benefits and individual and corporate welfare systems, we now see increasing gravitation towards postulations by Progressives that we are all entitled to receive government checks if we elect not to work. The wealthy will pay, though we have no better definition of who that is than we do of the economic middle class, while the rest of us will be freed to cavort at will. Indulging our digital addictions, getting fatter and, of course, dreaming up new causes. One must assume, given that they are not idiots, that the super wealthy must be forcibly confined, forbidding them from leaving the country or transferring their funds. Of course, one wonders, why they would continue generating wealth under such conditions. Naturally enough, there is a Plan B. According to Congresswoman Ocasio-Cortez, stalwart of the Progressive movement, a dearth of funding for these and other projects is simply remedied by the government. It need only print more money. Ignorance of basic economics among the elected is not a new concept and these concepts would be laughable, were it not for the fact that they are gaining traction in our society. In this sense, populist leaders are not to be feared. Populist ideas are.

It is an unassailable truth that where lies an inability to reason, engendered by ignorance, emotional rhetoric will lead the charge into oblivion. In the case of modern American society, ignorance has led to a narcissistic culture that is oblivious to the consequences of its intellectual turpitude and discardment of its civility. ⌘

CHAPTER 24

EDUCATION IS
THE CORNERSTONE . . .

E ducation is the cornerstone of every great civilization and most assuredly of democracies. And, as with any great edifice, removal of the cornerstone will see its collapse. In this country, there are two educational maladies. Our illiteracy rates are an embarrassment and the literate are largely uneducated, lacking in the breadth and depth of generalized knowledge necessary to the application of critical thinking.

Literacy rates, as with many statistical representations, are measured in several ways, but are generally applied to people's ability to function, both in reading and in writing. In this country, based upon surveys reported by a variety of sources, including the the US Department of Education and the national Institute for Literacy, some 32 million adult Americans, or 14 percent of the adult population, can not read. A further 40 to 44 million adults, representing 20 to 23 percent of all adult, read at basic or below basis levels. Of these, 30 million are unable to comprehend written material normally taught to fifth graders in public schools. The reading abilities of an additional 63 million adults hovers between sixth and eighth grade levels. Among young people, it is estimated that about 19 percent of high school children are functionally illiterate on graduating from the twelfth grade. As with adults, among young people, the degrees of proficiency beyond that tend towards the lower strata of abilities. Ultimately, only 11 to 12 percent of of the US population is deemed sufficiently literate to be declared proficient. According to UNESCO, the US ranks sixteenth among developed countries, in terms of literacy, while other organizations, such as Worldatlas, an on-line geographical website, ranks the US literacy rates as 125th of 197 countries world wide. This said, and of the utmost significance, there is a direct nexus between illiteracy, on the one hand, and crime and poverty on the other.

In 2014, the Federal Bureau of Prisons and other researchers reported that 70 percent of all adult prisoners in the US were either functionally illiterate or were ranked in the lowest tiers of literacy. Interestingly, inmates availing themselves of literacy programs whilst incarcerated enjoyed a 27 percent recidivism rate, while 60 percent of those who did not participate in such programs re-offended upon being released. Among juvenile offenders, the illiteracy rate was found to be a staggering 85 percent. Similar statistics apply to persons dependent upon pubic assistance for their survival. Logically, there is also a direct correlation between literacy levels and incomes; the more literate one is, the greater one's earnings. Problems also abound in our knowledge of math and science, as well as in having a basic understanding of personal finances, which fall well below the standards enjoyed by other developed countries. A 2013 report issued by the Organization for Economic Cooperation and Development offered the chilling conclusion that Americans ranked well below the global average in educationally induced skills and at almost the bottom of reading, math and technological capabilities among developed countries.

Blame for illiteracy and other educational lapses of our public schools have been assigned any number of causes. No discussion has been mounted to suggest that this is a matter of deliberate institutionalization. Yet, this is precisely the problem. In the same manner as poverty, ignorance has become institutionalized. The result, an educational caste system designed with two goals in mind, satiation of predicted demands for specific fields of employment and sowing of a docile populace inclined towards acceptance of, as well as dependency upon, the machinations of government. Credence to a contrary hypothesis could stand were our public school educational shortcomings a relatively new phenomenon to which our bureaucracies had not yet had time to react. Unfortunately, this is not the case.

Our educational decay has been decades in the making, though, it must be said, that the history of education in America has been generally mediocre. The only good news is that during the last 120 years we have seen the elimination of religiosity from public school curricula, increased enrollment, access to schools for minorities and desegregation. The bad news is that academic standards have been lowered, albeit incrementally, over the years. Standardized proficiency tests have systemically been adjusted to ensure higher pass rates and some states are considering lowering the threshold for grading. North Carolina, for example, is contemplating lowering its failing grade score from 60 to 39 percent.

Subject matter in public school has also seen dilution of content. Courses have evolved to embrace the tenets of political correctness. World history, save WWII, the plight of native Americans in the wake of European settlement, slavery—to the extent this vile practice was practiced in the US—geography and the like have vanished from the landscape of education. The context of past and present events is blatantly ignored. Civics are not commonly taught. The result is that most Americans—save, ironically, naturalized citizens, who are required to to test in civics—have no clue as to the basic functions of government, the separation of powers scheme or the rights enumerated in the Amendments to the Constitution. By way of example, The Freedom Forum Institute's most recent "State Of The First Amendment" survey resulted in a single respondent listing all five 1st Amendment rights. Forty percent of those surveyed could name none. Worse, given the current demands for change voiced by our youth, only 2 percent knew of the Amendment's provision for the right to petition the government. In contrast, these rights were well understood by civil rights activists during the 1960s and 1970s, who depended upon them. Though in an ironic twist, it was this latter generation that fostered the laissez faire culture in education that has contributed to its academic dilution. However, problems in education predate those events.

During colonial times, throughout the American revolution and for a period of time thereafter, schooling was undertaken in the home, local schools and by some, through tutors. Thomas Jefferson, for example, started school at age five and at age nine was enrolled in a local Presbyterian school where he studied the natural world as well as Latin, Greek and French. On turning thirteen, Jefferson was tutored for two years in science, history and the classics, after which he enrolled at the College of William and Mary, in Virginia, where he continued his studies, but added to these math and philosophy. John Adams shared a similar educational experience. Before entering Harvard, at age sixteen, where he studied the Classics in Greek and Latin, Adams, as of the age of six, attended a local, coeducational "Dame School," and shortly thereafter attended Braintree Latin School. His studies at Braintree included Latin, logic and rhetoric, and he remained there until commencing at Harvard. While not everyone shared in the extent of education enjoyed by Jefferson and Adams, attendance at small local private schools and home schooling were, by and large, generally employed to educate youth. And, although many of the schools attended were imbued with religious overtones, these nonetheless instilled discipline in learning and produced students well versed in the so-called "three Rs," reading, writing and arithmetic, as well as more general knowledge related to history.

This system largely prevailed until the Civil War era, when governmentally funded and controlled schools moved to the fore of educational responsibility. The changes invoked by this turn of events was not drastic. Schools yet continued with similar curriculae and were greatly influenced by their locality. Through this period, college was an elitist pursuit, with most students focusing on the means of making a living upon completion of their studies. While most students did not attend high school, the level of education through middle school was formidable as compared to present times. By the early 20th century, public schools accounted for about 90 percent of all students, the rest attending private schools, a ratio still valid through the present day. In the same era, pressure from industry and labor unions led to the institution of federal educational standards which were expressly designed to meet the anticipated labor and production needs of an industrializing country. During the course of the 20th century, again, quite overtly, public education shifted from the teaching of general knowledge, together with skill sets, to molding good citizens. And, not just citizenry in general, but good American citizens, ready to meet the demands of the country's needs for general labor, trades and professions. Hence, the demise of critical thinking as an aspect of education.

The devolution of teaching knowledge, and how to apply it, has since then been accompanied by the overarching theme of good citizenship, a political paradigm that is evermore shifting, and intrusions into traditionally family held responsibilities, such as the teaching of morality. In addition, without parental consent, or even public debate, most public schools now mandate the utilization of Google programs which, as has become readily apparent, vacuum up the data associated with every student doing so. One consequence of these policies was a deterioration among students of all races and ethnicities of Scholastic Aptitude Test scores by the late 1980s and early 90s, used for university admissions purposes, which has subsequently been remedied, from time to time, by degrading testing standards. Another, is that the qualitative chasm between private and public school education markedly widened.

Disparities within the public school sector are well recognized, affecting minorities and the impoverished by denuding education through insufficient funding. The dichotomy between public and private schools, however, presents a far starker contrast between elitism and commonality. Private schools, originally dominated by religious institutions, particularly Catholic, but now increasingly the purview of non-religious entities, historically maintained standards of education well beyond that offered in the public domain. Evidence of this lies in the fact that 90 percent of the students accepted into ivy league colleges are graduates of private, so called "feeder" schools. These schools maintained a connection to the classics, certainly demanded high degrees of literacy, foreign language proficiency and offered broad, knowledge based curricula. Critical thinking—the ability to apply reason to information, based upon amassed knowledge and an understanding of historical context, to draw conclusions as to its viability—was mandatory at many, if not most. This was true even of those with a religious bent. Jesuit schools, for instance, have long been held in high esteem for precisely these reasons.

Of late, however, many of these elite schools, though still a bar above public institutions, perhaps mostly so in terms of literacy and the opportunities they afford, have succumbed to the foibles adopted by their public counterparts. Critical thinking, as a key element of private education has ceded to the politicization of education. Much vaunted schools, including some offering the esteemed International Baccalaureate, are fully staffed by left leaning and, more frequently, so-called Progressive liberals; the notion that a diversity of philosophies, opinions and beliefs might engender healthy debate and the application of critical thinking having been deliberately ceded to indoctrination and intolerance for competing world views.

"Excellence in Education," or some such buzz phrase has replaced critical thinking as the averred mission of most of these schools. Nor do many any longer require foreign language proficiency, an understanding of the classics or philosophy or the study of world history and geography; these topics are now relegated to the world of "old white males," and deemed meritless.

Universities, public and private, are likewise infected. Worse yet, many serve as incubators of the disease coursing through our educational system. These have long served as breeding grounds for the intolerance that is sweeping the country. Political correctness and, of late, so-called "trigger words," symptoms of injecting partisan politics into the sphere of academia, has all but terminated legitimate debate on social, political, cultural and economic issues. Events, past and present, may no longer be contextually questioned. The who, why, what, where and when aspects of scholarly inquiry have been supplanted by dogmatic judgments rendered in a vacuum of relevant circumstances. There is an unpalatable arrogance associated with this approach to teaching. One wonders of the academics, comfortably ensconced in an ivory tower, replete with the comforts provided by tenure, whether context could suggest that as a child of the past, they might have worked as slavers, sacrificed a child or eaten a heart to placate a deity. Or in an alternative, though very real, modern world, would they hack a neighbor to pieces with a machete for belonging to another tribe or religion, buy slaves in a Libyan market, torture a monk, for being a monk, or eat some creature on the brink of extinction to fend off starvation.

In our present culture of higher education, the ultimate hypocrisy lies not so much in judging the past, as it does in failing to see the possibility of ourselves in that past or, for that matter, in the present, elsewhere in the world. Where there are no processed foods; no light bulbs; no running water or toilets; no internet; no legal rights; no guarantees of success; no shelters; no safe havens on campuses, because there are no schools; and no security from crime. A place and time where there are no "snowflakes" because the sun is far too hot, metaphorically speaking.

Thus are the circumstances underlying, surrounding and giving rise to events given short shrift. Objectively driven critical thinking has been replaced with subjective criticism. Acceptable thought and speech is defined arbitrarily. And the results? First and foremost, ignorance. Then, good ideas, if unaligned with the dominant political paradigm, are suppressed. And worst, bad ideas, which should be held to the flame of honest and objective debate, are instead left to fester and grow in the dark. Problematically, bad ideas are simply another facet of the beliefs controlling academia today. Both are soaked in deliberate ignorance, intolerance and a totalitarian worldview that can not abide scrutiny.

Small wonder then, that the graduates spewed from these institutions of higher learning, if electing education as a career, permeate public and private schools with a corrosive culture of academic corruption, rather than planting the seeds of curiosity and a desire for the honest intellectual pursuit of ideas. Many are schooled in the administration of rules, the promotion of political agendas and as bureaucratic functionaries, rather than the subjects they are meant to teach. Indeed, all that is required as qualification is a degree in education, not in specific academic disciplines, such as math and history. Some private schools require more but, as a matter of personal experience, the margins between public and private school requirements are shrinking. Anecdotally, as a matter of personal experience and because no measure of proficiency is required or, for that matter, scrutinized, there is every indication that the literacy rates among educators is in decline. This is not an issue. All that is required is proficiency sufficient to follow course outlines that are mandated from on high and brook no deviation. Learning by rote, as a tool for instilling mental discipline, has been replaced by teaching by rote.

What then of the import of institutions of higher education. Public universities, as do public schools, fulfill the role of social conditioning and training students to become proficient at their chosen fields. More is not required. Philosophical mores and ethics have become irrelevant, even in medicine, where the Hippocratic oath has been relegated to obscurity on grounds of being deemed archaic. Ivy league schools continue to serve their functions of promoting elitism by fostering connections and networking opportunities not readily available to outsiders. As bulwarks against intellectual corruption, their walls have crumbled. They serve primarily to issue successive generations of masters. The notion of entitlements, at least for some, permeate both public and private universities. All of the foregoing belies the role of education in maintaining the tenets of democracy. As best put by John Adams, America's second president:

"Government is nothing more than the combined force of society or the united power of the multitude for the peace, order, safety, good, and happiness of the people. . . . There is no king or queen bee distinguished from all the others by size or figure or beauty and variety of colors in the human hive. No man has yet produced any revelation from heaven in his favor, any divine communication to govern his fellow men. Nature throws us all into the world equal and alike. . . . The preservation of liberty depends upon the intellectual and moral character of the people. As long as

knowledge and virtue are diffused generally among
the body of a nation it is impossible they should be
enslaved . . ."

One suspects that Adams would be mortified at the state of our
educational system today. So too would he take umbrage, as should we
all, at the increasing unavailability of access to higher education, not
due to any dearth of universities, but attributable to the costs of attendance. Adams, after all, as written in a letter to Mathew Robinson, Jr.,
on March 23, 1786, proposed that ". . . education and knowledge must
become so general as to raise the lower ranks of society nearer to the
higher. The education of a nation instead of being confined to a few
schools and universities for the instruction of the few, must become
the national care and expense for the formation of the many."

This has certainly not become the case. Although state schools do
generally offer lower tuition to in-state students, the overall costs have
become prohibitive. Most students, absent scholarships or the good
fortune of family resources, are required to borrow money to pay the
costs of tuition, housing and food, then graduating with debt loads in
the tens of thousands of dollars. And while incurring debt for graduate school makes some degree of sense, given there is a likelihood of
earning salaries sufficient to meet the debt load as well as the costs of
living, the same is not true of undergraduate students. The unfortunate reality is that upon graduating, undergraduates are not endowed
with the leverage to demand salaries far beyond those earned by high
school graduates. Thus, these students are ever more likely put in
positions of being unable to meet the financial strains of the debt
service associated with student loans, while yet sustaining themselves.

According to the Federal Reserve, moving into 2019, some 45 million students in the US, owe over $1.56 trillion dollars in student debt.

Sixty-nine percent of the class of 2018 graduated with an average debt of $29,800. An additional 14 percent had their university costs paid by parents through federal Parent Plus loans, which averaged $35,600 per student. The present cumulative student loan debt is more than 500 billion above the nation's credit card debt. Of the gross amounts in student loans, some 11.5 percent are in default. Others are in periods of deferment or grace before payments become due. Although federal student loans tend to be lower, though not the lowest interest rates charged by the federal government, private student loan interest rates reached rates of over 14 percent during the fall of 2018. In 2018, federal student loan annual interest rates ranged from just over 5 percent to over 7 percent, depending upon the type of loan and whether for undergraduate or graduate school enrollments.

In net effect, the quality of education, or lack thereof, and its associated costs most severely impact the impoverished and the middle class, the latter rapidly joining the ranks of the former. Loss of a meaningful education results, and has resulted, in an inadequate understanding of the basic governing and economic principles of our republic. This circumstance is aggravated by manipulation of those tenets by pols and elitists to an extent that their meaning and intent are entirely subverted—transmogrified into a dystopian interpretation of democracy, the likes of which well exceed the depiction rendered by George Orwell in his book, *1984*. Hence, "Big Brother" will provide for all. This begs the question of who will provide for "Big Brother." The middle class has traditionally underwritten the operations of stable governments and, most assuredly in a democracy, political stability is incumbent upon the economic well-being of the majority of its constituents, the middle class. Should that economic class diminish into a minority position and its financial security fall under threat, the nature of democracy must, as a matter of certainty, succumb to political uncertainty and, ultimately, a different form of governance. ᴄᴧ

CHAPTER 25

MARGINALIZATION OF
THE MIDDLE CLASS . . .

Marginalization of the middle class has become endemic to America's political landscape. Though lip service is paid to this group of constituents by pols from both sides of the aisle, there has arisen a complete misunderstanding of its economic dimensions and the role of this class in maintaining the stability of the republic.

The middle class has been utterly disenfranchised, politically, economically and even socially, by corporate America, our politicians, media and warring factions of extremists whose only common thread is an abiding intolerance for any world view other than their own. The middle class, once referred to as America's silent majority, has provably now become a minority. In reaction, as a whole, its voice was found in formidable fashion during the last general elections in 2016, which led to the presidency of Donald Trump, and again during the 2018 mid term elections, which clearly signified increased polarization of the electorate and a shift towards non-traditional support for more radical candidates.

Those voting for Trump were immediately met with confusion and scorn, labeled by pundits and pols alike as racists, fascists, white supremacists, ignorant hillbillies and, in the case of women, too weak willed to know their own minds. Underlying this emotional rhetoric, even now, over two years later, is an abject inability to fathom what motivated Trump's supporters.

Trump was, by and large, elected by middle class voters. As a demographic, it is impossible to view the middle class in stereotypical terms, though its constituents share one deep commonality of critical importance. It is a class defined economically as those income earners bracketing the mid range of overall earnings. This, in turn, has traditionally tended its membership towards political moderation, in the interest of maintaining economic stability. Hence, historically, the centrist politics of the middle class has been foundational to the success of every democracy; the caveat being that it must also comprise a majority of the electorate. Against this backdrop, there are three crucial factors worth noting.

The first, that it is insufficient to merely categorize the middle class through some arbitrary, immovable determination of what constitutes its defining range of income. Understanding the middle class in political terms necessitates periodically recalculating its economic status. This is particularly germane at the lower strata because financial erosion, resulting from the real rate of inflation, that is to say the decline in purchasing power of a dollar without a correlating increase in incomes, devolves that segment of the middle class into poverty. Hence, the middle class is subject to shrinkage.

This shrinkage, the second aspect of middle class dynamics requiring thought, is of critical importance. It has manifested in the US for some time, largely affecting young couples with children, wage earners and the growing number of elderly people, particularly those whose retirement benefits inadequately meet the real rate of inflation. At this juncture, I think it safe to say, shrinkage of the middle class has sufficiently deflated its numbers to allow characterization of the class as a distinct minority. The descent from the sphere of financial sufficiency into the realm of inadequacy has obvious political consequences; not only in form of reactions by those directly affected, but through the fear of others in the class, sensing a looming risk of sliding into the abyss. These are signaled by departure from an innate centrist oriented desire to maintain political stability, as assurance of continued economic security, towards more radical tendencies, borne of a desire to regain or maintain a sense financial security. Operationally, then, when the status quo is threatened, the middle class, as a political constituency, shifts from relative passivity, often ear marked by political ennui, into reactionary participation in the electoral process. Ultimately, the consequence of political inertia in addressing rising dissatisfaction within the middle class results in its factionalization.

Finally, of equal significance, if not more so, any assumptions of middle class cohesiveness are wildly misplaced. Although the class operates as an organic whole in striving to maintain economic security through political stability, this is a coincidental objective, not the result of sociopolitical cohesion. Indeed, the inherent commonality of the middle class, as an entirety, is basically economic. Otherwise, its composition depicts a mosaic of races, ethnicities, genders, sexual orientations, cultures, religions, educational levels, interests, ages and, yes, political affiliations, or a lack thereof, all of whom derive their incomes from a myriad of activities. The class counts amongst its constituents blue and white collar workers, tradespeople, professionals, farmers and, the self-employed, comprised of small and medium sized business owners. Given this diversity, it should come as no surprise that political factionalization of the middle class, under conditions of extreme economic duress is not random, but is the manifestation of the pre-existant fault lines that underlie it in all but economic terms.

These factors are certainly germane to America's present economic and political circumstances. Neither Congress nor the executive branch have undertaken a realistic reassessment or redefinition of the economic middle class in decades. Instead, the economic health of the middle class has become fictionalized, in positive terms, by officialdom, to an abjectly ridiculous extent. Viewed through the federal government's take on reality, for example, a couple with two children, collectively earning $60,000 per annum, are solidly within the framework of the middle class and are taxed accordingly. In truth, and under the best of circumstances, that couple is living a zero sum game. And, this is based upon assumptions that nothing untoward requires unforeseen expenditures and that they are qualified for subsidization under the Affordable Healthcare Act, or that healthcare is an employment benefit.

On a need based assessment, the annual cost of living, consisting of housing, food, transportation, child care, healthcare, sundry necessities and taxes, for an urban family of four is at minimum about $60,000 per year, but averages well in excess of that amount. This is according to figures released by The Economic Policy Institute in early 2018. Present inflation is driving that number upward. Contemporaneously, the average annual urban household income is about $58,000. The dichotomy between incomes and living expenses in rural areas is even more dire. Moreover, across the board, household debt is at an all time high, savings at their nadir and, underemployment a burgeoning reality. Exacerbating these circumstances are the unmeasured ramifications of the so called Affordable Healthcare Act, affectionately dubbed Obamacare, which has decimated those of us in the middle class who do not qualify for some form of subsidy or employment benefits. In my case, for example, the monthly premiums for our family of five are a staggering $28,800 a year, accompanied by an annual deductible of $10,000. Small wonder, then, that relatively objective organizations, such as Pew Research, have declared the middle class to be shrinking at an alarming rate. This prognosis is supported by the US Census Bureau's figures which showed in 2016 that 43.1 percent of households in the US earned less than $50,000 per year; some 17 percent took in between $50,000 and $74,900, and the balance in excess of the latter figure, though only a small margin of households exceeded earnings of $100,000.

Given the foregoing, the Trump phenomena should be of no surprise, even to our political elite, the One Per centers and the ever indomitable Fourth Estate, the media. Shrinkage of the middle class leads to venting of its frustrations and fears through increasingly radical participation in political processes. A seemingly enthusiastic Trump and his somewhat more recalcitrant Republican cohorts promised a golden era in form of restoration of the middle class which, in the wake of Obama's frontal assault on the middle class' well being, and the utter neglect imposed on it by prior administrations, resonated with this increasingly disenfranchised constituency. Make no mistake about it, Trump's bombastic rhetoric, without exceptions, pierced the core of legitimate middle class angst—that the bottom was falling out of its economic security.

More specifically, curtailing immigration as a means of diminishing the labor pool during a period of high unemployment; reforming taxation of the middle class, in order to ensure a higher degree of retained, disposable income; restructuring corporate taxes in order to kick-start the economy and decrease unemployment; eliminating the Obamacare mandate requiring the purchase of health insurance; and imposing tariffs on imports, at least to a degree matching the subsidies provided by their countries of origin, were the issues that ultimately, though barely, carried the day. As an aside, one suspects that had a somewhat more regal or presidential personage campaigned on a platform constructed of these planks, the margin would have been dramatically greater. Ultimately, and regardless of the degree of victory, the outcomes of the 2016 elections did not establish a mandate for the Republican Party or President Trump. To the contrary, both were elected as a reaction to economic conditions at the time and neither will stem the hemorrhaging of middle class economic malaise. This failing was evidenced by the 2018 mid term elections, which shifted support towards the opposite end of the political spectrum.

Critics of this position will, quite expectedly, point to the institution of numerous political promises made by Trump and company. And, at first blush, they would not necessarily be mistaken. However, they would be missing the mark. Immigration laws are being enforced somewhat more rigorously. Tax reform has been implemented. Unemployment is down. Although Obamacare is still very much with us, the mandate is in abeyance. And, the threat of tariffs looms large while trade agreements are being renegotiated. The question remains, have any of these changes bolstered the net income and wealth of the middle class. The answer is a resounding no. In fact, middle class circumstances are only worsening.

While unemployment has ebbed markedly to historic lows, net incomes have not met the real and rising rate of inflation. Marginal gains realized by the middle class through tax reforms have translated into rising State taxes and inflation, not to mention an increase of some 25 percent in health insurance premiums, the sum of which exceeds any tax reform benefits. Furthermore, tax reform did not bring current the defining range of middle class incomes; hence, the reality that the lower echelon continue to face decline while the upper strata, still archaically characterized as exceeding the scope of middle class income, are penalized by limitations on deductions under the guise that these are aimed at the wealthy. Finally, while trade sanctions and negotiations offer some trickle down benefits, in form of increased employment opportunities, these ultimately benefit large corporations who, now faced with the prospect of increased domestic market share, are bound to maintain caps on wages in order to maintain affordability within that market, achieve competitiveness overseas and increase net revenues. Small manufacturers, on the other hand, face the dilemma of rising prices on foreign sourced components and domestic unavailability, as well as rising prices for necessary materials on the home front. It remains to be seen whether jobs created by this myriad of small and medium sized entities will eventually decline as a result.

Compounding these problems is the myth that our economy is driven by principles of free market capitalism, the perceived root of all evil when things go awry. In truth, we operate within in a highly structured command economy managed through an alliance of government and large corporate interests. A true free market economic system is contrary to our current policies of corporate protectionism, rewarding inefficiency and incompetence, and notions that some corporate entities are "too big to fail." Nor would it countenance enactment of laws to create captive markets and otherwise circumvent the concepts of competitiveness. Germane to the issue of middle class economics is the fact that the sandbox we play in has evolved to institutionalize erasure of financial gains of the middle class, through taxation and controlled inflation, to the extent that its frustrations are still manageable. The latter, save when it runs amok where mismanaged, is of course, a profit oriented mechanism, while the former drives funding of state coffers in order to redistribute wealth sufficient to manage the needs, and therefrom derived frustrations, of the growing number of people unable to fully do so for themselves. The inherent, systemic miscalculation in all of this is that the increasing burden on the middle class is evermore out of sync with its actual size and concomitant representative wealth. Essentially, in robbing Peter to pay Paul, the invariable outcome is that Peter becomes Paul and therein lies the crux of the problem.

Further, along this vein, one cannot overlook that incompetence and greed permeate management of our economy, as has been evidenced by the federal government's intervention to "save" large private sector entities and a national debt that has breached all barriers of sanity or fiscal responsibility.

Nor can a blind eye be turned on the fact that, by virtue of technology, the middle class, as the largest consumers thereof, have been converted into commodities, their personal data harvested, sold, bought and resold by and between private tech companies, as well as government. This has culminated in the absolute destruction of individual privacy interests, constitutionally protected and otherwise. A burgeoning factor in middle class reactionaryism, then, compounding fears over economic well-being, lies in increasing insecurity regarding privacy issues.

Relative to the issues of malfeasance in directing our economy and the theft of privacy, it is worth noting that Trump, the Republicans and Democrats are in lock step. They have done nothing. Under all, the US debt has escalated, more sweetheart deals have been inked between government and corporate behemoths and privacy issues receive token consideration. Overshadowing all of this, of course, is the federal government's unprecedented and unfettered collection of data on its citizenry under the guise of national security.

Further frustration and fomentation of public unease lies in mainstream media's overt conversion from dissemination of objective information to partisanship. This has sown confusion and mistrust. People are unable to distinguish between "real" and "fake" news, and most are time barred from delving into the internet morass to find primary or other reliable sources to corroborate or debunk media's representations.

The unabated decline of middle class institutional confidence will culminate in its factionalization into two general categories, the first engendering a shift to more radical viewpoints such as those of

Bernie Sanders, Alexandria Ocasio-Cortez and others of the so-called Progressive movement, lured by promises of enhanced forms of free cheese. Others will lean to right wing extremism for solutions. And neither will tolerate the other because the unease of financial insecurity gives rise to fear which, in turn, breeds mistrust and hatred. The second group, those who are not inclined to either form of extremism, will simply stay at home during subsequent election cycles. Thus, future determinations of governance will be left to the active factions of radicalized middle class members, together with those already bent on extremist left and right wing politics—a truly frightening proposition. When this will occur remains to be seen, although the trend has begun. At present Trump enjoys a marginal 47-50 percent approval rate, though this may be fueled, in part, by the efforts of the Federal Bureau of Investigation and the Democrat controlled house of representatives to oust Trump, seen by many to be aimed at usurpation of the electoral process through unfair, political partisanship. Further, there remains residual hope among his constituents that the Trump effect will yet translate into economic relief. Nonetheless, the 2018 mid term election results clearly indicate that a shift is in the offing. The election of a Democrat majority to the House of Representatives in Congress is one harbinger of this, while the inclusion of more than a few Progressives within that group is even more telling.

Political platforms once thought laughable are moving to the fore. Socialism, and not of the relatively benign European persuasion, is being debated within the Democrat party as a viable direction for the country. Advocates for such political and economic governance have made clear that, if successful, they will brook no democratic processes that might counter their vision. Freedom of speech and choices has been overtly threatened by elected pols, who appear to envision some form of green-techno-totalitarian replacement for democracy. For

Progressives, none of whom in office have displayed even a scintilla of understanding related to economics or constitutional processes, an agenda replete with fear mongering, emotional rhetoric and impossible promises, provides the path to power. Lets be clear; they suggest a Green-New Deal, requiring the elimination of all nuclear and fossil fuel power sources. All aircraft are to be replaced with trains. Gas and diesel engines are to be illegal. Every standing structure in the US is to be replaced or modified to "green" standards. Any person who wants to work for the federal government will be hired and any person who elects not to work shall be entitled to a federal paycheck. Independent estimates of the overall, short term, costs of these programs, are $100 trillion dollars. When asked about these costs, Representative Ocasio-Cortez, a Progressive leader in Congress, suggested the federal government could simply print more money. Like they did in Venezuela, perhaps, where the annual inflation rate has reached a million percent.

At first blush, one might dismiss these ideas; Americans would never embrace this modern form of Stalinism. Incredibly, however, they are gaining traction. Invariably, young people are drawn like moths to flames towards notions of radical idealism. This has always been the case. And, as always, they are yet unaware that political ideology is generally the sales pitch of realpolitik practitioners. More concerning is the attraction such promises, assuredly those offering financial security, however impractical, have to the poor and the lower strata of the middle class that find themselves impoverished or moving in that direction. This is a harbinger of the transition from a majority to a minority position of the economic middle class. Angry at their deteriorating circumstances, the adversely affected will explore radical alternatives, if for no other reason than to maintain or regain financial security.

Mainstream Democrats and Republicans seem unable or unwilling to sense this shift in the economic dynamics of their now fading constituencies. Accordingly, they offer no viable solutions to the resultant discontent. This inaction will result in the demise of the middle class as a reliable, mainstream political bloc. In fact, this trend has begun. And, if left unchecked, we will see the end of our democracy which, despite all its flaws and foibles, still represents the best of all alternatives. ∽

CHAPTER 26

SOLUTIONS ABOUND . . .

Solutions abound to the problems facing our nation. They must. After all, as Otto von Bismarck is said to have suggested, "... there is a special providence for drunkards, fools and the United States of America." But, time is running short. The United States lies confronted with sea changes politically, economically, socially and technologically. We face internal conflicts and increasing prospects of war. Our government and people are awash in mounting debt. With each successive generation, the sense of meaning and responsibility that attaches to every democracy diminishes further within the American psyche, whose frailties stand exposed in the face of educational decay and the ennui of its constituents. There is an urgency for national debate. One that is steeped in the tradition of objective reality and critical thinking, not navel contemplating narcissism brewed in emotional rhetoric. Our discussion must, above all else, be honest and culminate in our resolve to make changes. To reaffirm the democratic principles of our republic.

The notion of national debate is perhaps more aptly phrased as debate within our nation, within families, communities, towns, cities and states. Nor should it be limited to mere oratory. This debate must be accompanied by appropriate individual and collective actions. Our country has heard from the fringes. Now it is time for the voiceless, the once silent majority to move to the fore. And, if it can be said that our leaders are mere reflections of ourselves, we must modify the images they mimic and then hold them accountable if they then fail to see us or hear us. This means too, that we must be prepared to resume the responsibilities and self reliance required of the beneficiaries of every democracy. The question remains, of course, just what the solutions we fashion should look like.

It would be hubris for any one person to arbitrarily define a set of finite solutions to the maladies that ail the nation; the problems are complex and, as stated, require discussion. The following, then, are thrown into the fray as merely a sampling of the plethora of possibilities.

First and foremost, the dictates of logic suggest that absent addressing educational shortcomings in this country, the likelihood of resolving any other issues is marginal. Further, in addition to providing qualitative schooling, there is a pressing need to ensure that this is made readily available to all students, regardless of their demographics, be these racial, ethnic or economic. This is the only sensible avenue for replacing institutionalized poverty and negating the adverse consequences it has entrenched. Educational is furthermore the frontline weapon against racism and, one would hope, would harbinger the onset of a color blind meritocracy. To attain these objectives, our schools should be striving for absolute, real literacy rates and providing tools that breed critical thinking.

Unlike the expectations of their counterparts in less benevolent regimes, good citizens in a democracy are those who understand their system of governance, the basis of their economies and are sufficiently knowledgeable to rationally and objectively arrive at independent conclusions related to all that is of consequence. With this objective in mind, curriculae should include English, math, science, geography, economics, technology, arts and a demand for proficiency in a globally relevant foreign language, such as Spanish or Mandarin. World history ought to be mandatory and presented with an eye to teaching its events contextually, rather than in terms of equities or conjuring blame. The end objective, here, is to seek avoidance of history's mistakes and the propensity we humans have for repeating them. The past need not be prologue. So too does instruction in civics warrant inclusion in our curriculae. A free society cannot prevail absent an understanding of the functions of its governance together with the individual rights and obligations necessary to both perpetuate the democratic state and curtail its ever latent propensity for overreaching. As a finality, engendering in our children the ability to apply critical thought processes to all they learn and do, coupled with some comprehension of ethos, suggests the subject of perhaps greatest import: philosophy. Study of this discipline would sate the pressing need to imbue in our society the skill to apply acquired knowledge and experiences. Else we are left with no more than competent mechanics, following instruction manuals devised by others to lead us through the courses of life. These are oft designed with ulterior ambitions in mind.

We should also consider instituting a two tracked educational system designed to allow students the choice, once a certain level of academic achievement has been realized, to opt for either an academic or technical course of study. The latter would encompass choices to gain proficiency in any of the traditional or emerging trades. On graduating from high school, those having elected academics as their realms of endeavor would move on to universities while students having elected a trade could move forward to more comprehensive study of their chosen fields, culminating in formal apprenticeships. There are two basic rationales supporting this approach. The first is that there is every indication that academic standards in the US have been systemically degraded in order to increase the numbers of high school graduates. As pointed out in the previous chapter addressing education, the actual literacy rates of graduating students belie the quality of education underlying the much touted 84 percent high school graduation rate. A bifurcated educational system would allow the elevation of academic standards by eliminating the need to create statistics that include those who are ill inclined to academics. An alternative educational track embracing vocational education and training would further serve to assure skill sets for those not inclined to academics, including those who would otherwise drop out of school. These young people are presently left to their own devices, with some dependent on the service industry for survival, while others are informally, and most often inadequately, taught trades through anecdotal by others who preceded them in this course. A great number find themselves enmeshed in the criminal legal system, then moving on to join others in reliance on some form of public assistance.

Regardless of the track chosen by students, their educational tenure within either of these proposed fields fields, through university or apprenticeship, as the case may be, should not be subject to any financial limitations. Education in both instances should be free, both to combat future demands on our social welfare system and, more importantly, to combat inequities of every type. Indeed, education, whether vocational, with an academic foundation, or purely academic, is essential to the function of democracy, where not, as is the present case, crafted as the institutionalized propagation of ignorance, and thus ought to be considered an inalienable right.

As footnotes to confronting the problems endemic to our educational system, while sports are obviously of paramount importance, it seems ludicrous to expend disproportionate amounts of money on school athletic programs, vis a vis the financing of academic programs and scholarships, given the comparative societal contributions one could expect from the myriad of students who would benefit from access to academia, as compared to the one in however many thousands that might have the physical prowess to graduate to professional sports. In reality, athletic games require no more than an open field or a simple gym, shorts, sneakers and t-shirts. More than that serves no purposes other than to breed a group of students with elitist views, oftentimes to the extent of dismissing the rules of societal conduct, particularly among males as to females, and fostering a false sense of competence among educational bureaucrats. So too, ought we reconsider having schools supplant our obligations, as parents, to imbue our children with senses of values, morality and civility. While teachers may be moral, or immoral, as the case may be, the institutions they serve are neither. It is ridiculous to cede responsibility for these aspects of child rearing to schools. These are mere proxies for the State, which, by its very nature, will formulate agendas designed to further its amoral interests in self-perpetuation. Thus, absent our overarching influences, we see, within each successive generation, a propensity for malleability meant to seed a socially engineered populace molded to accept governance justified by artificially contrived truths and mores.

Akin to the alternate reality presented in the film, *The Matrix,* the dilution of critical thinking in education and the cancerous growth of institutional values has led us, as a society, to unquestioningly accept the pap we are fed by pols, pundits, "news" organizations, social media and the tech industry as gospel. We are induced to accept the absurd as paradigms. And, we have succumbed to Placebocracy; our worst fears are preyed upon and solutions then proffered to manage our frustrations, all the while we are encouraged to ignore the realities that confront us. Thus, we are to believe that Saddam Hussein needed to be removed because Iraq possessed weapons of mass destruction and had abetted Al Qaeda in conducting the attacks of September 11, 2001. That market capitalism is synonymous with government protectionism, bailouts, and welfare for select corporations. That Free trade really is. That the only corrupt politician that has ever held a federal office is Donald Trump. That our national debt is irrelevant and if government needs more money, it can simply print it. That we can take trains to Europe. That individual privacy rights do not matter, if one has nothing to hide or unless you are Jeff Bezos. That opinions are facts. That we need Facebook, Twitter, Amazon and Google to regulate our news so that we are not misinformed. That Google is promoting democracy by helping the People's Republic of China impose blanket, informational censorship. That the sky is falling. That there really is a war against drugs. That all Republicans are bigots and all Democrats socialists. That only whites can be racist. That we are educated. That institutionalized poverty management will cure poverty. That America does not have an elitist system. That everyone on television is smarter than we are. That there are better systems than democracy. That white males are responsible for all evils in the world. And, that we, as individuals really do matter. Really. These are but some random samples. This book is amply replete with a panapoly of further instances of the nonsense we are repeatedly inundated with—to the point where, frighteningly, more of us are becoming believers.

These diversions are readily overcome by treating them as the placebos and false flag issues they truly are. We need to reject pols telling us what we want to hear or creating straw men to gain political support; corporate monoliths, most assuredly in the high tech sector, lulling us into acceptance of a new reality wherein we both subsidize them and accept their dominion over our lives; and media, supplanting journalism with social engineering through information manipulation, under the guise of purported fact dissemination, all the while simply furthering the interests of their increasingly monopolistic masters. We need to make abundantly clear that we have reached a point where public frustration management through these devices will not suffice. We must demand that the failure to address the problems facing our nation, particularly those of the shrinking middle and burgeoning poverty, be remedied.

The heart of ordinary people's ability to invoke change lies in our dual roles as constituents and consumers. It is a powerful position if employed collectively, though dangerous if driven by symbolism, rather than substance; by blind, reactionary emotionalism instead of reasoned logic founded on critical thinking; or if bereft of specific objectives. The key is to overcome the inherent tendency we have to act in our perceived immediate individual self-interests without contemplating the consequences of success. Instead, we, as a society, need to take the longer view of advocating systemic changes that will serve our long term interests without adverse effect. It would further behoove us to drive issues and not allow these to be formulated from the top down. This is critical to eliminating the contrivance of controversies that deliberately manipulate our choices while ignoring or misconstruing what really ails us. The starting point lies in politics and, rather than in party affiliations, should be a question of individual candidate qualifications and non-party associations and obligations.

Every successful political candidate, from a local to the national level, is required to take an oath of office that demands fealty to the United States Constitution and its Amendments, commonly referred to as the Bill of Rights. Yet, in word and action, there is clearly a disconnect among most elected pols between this pledge and even the remotest understanding of what this document, the holy grail of our republic, actually embodies. Indeed, one might venture that most have never read it. Sitting and aspiring pols must be challenged on their knowledge and willingness to safeguard our principles of governance and the the rights we enjoy that they are bound to protect if elected. This is applicable not only to rule making for government agencies, such as the NSA, CIA and FBI, but is equally pertinent to their continence of violations of our civil rights by private entities, whether acting in quasi governmental functions or operating on their own.

Any pol unwilling to expressly denounce and actively prevent dilution of our Constitution for any reason should be denied office, or if an incumbent, voted into oblivion.

The same holds true for a willingness to adhere to the rule of law. Congress has developed a propensity for encouraging violations of law, as is the case regarding illegal immigration, for example, rather than risking the latent political repercussions of enacting legislation to legalize such conduct. Congress then relies upon the judiciary to craft remedies for which Congress then can deny culpability. Not only is this a form of abject cowardice, it is also a cynical view that fails to consider the long term effect of this tactic which further politicizes the desirable independence of the judiciary, encourages partisan application of the law by the executive branch and ultimately robs constituents of their right to approve or reject acts of their elected members to the bodies of Congress. Ultimately, this ploy undermines our separation of powers scheme and its consequent requisite for the rule of law. In every instant a pol abstains from undertaking his or her legislative duty, they should simply be ousted in any election that follows.

Participation in the elections process has become increasingly bound to a candidate's ability to raise money from corporate donors, in return for supplicating to the demands of their lobbyists, and has thereby become an elitist endeavor. This is in large part due to the United States Supreme Court determination that corporations and their lobbyists enjoy the same First Amendment protections as individuals in our political processes. Without belaboring the foibles underlying these rulings, it is sufficient to know that this does not translate into an obligation of any pol to accept such contributions or succumb to the wishes of lobbyists. This opens the door for two avenues of response by any electorate. The first, to reject any candidate who accepts such contributions, whether directly or through political action committees, or PACs, as they are known. And, the second, to boycott the products of corporate donors to candidates or PACs. If a PAC is unwilling to reveal its corporate donors, rejection of a candidate accepting funding from that PAC is the simplest response. Campaign donor information must, as a matter of law, be made public and be generally, readily available on line. This tactic should send clear messages to existing pols of our unwillingness to accept the status quo and should lead to the eventual emergence of candidates unimpaired by a dearth of finances and questionable alliances. In the interim, if it appears there are no "clean" candidates, voters have the power to either boycott elections or conduct a write-in campaign.

Any politician extolling or denigrating our economy by characterizing it as "market capitalistic" system ought to be rejected out of hand for either disingenuousness or stupidity. The same applies to anyone claiming to be engaged in the great debate of whether we are on the road to "socialism." This is a true red herring. In truth, the United States has never had a market economy. Indeed, it is already socialistic. The notion of a market system requires no more of government than the establishment and maintenance of a level economic playing field for all private, economic endeavors; the ebb and flow of success and failure governed solely by efficiency, competitiveness and competence. It is belied by artificially established concentrated control over the factors of production, government protectionism and bail-outs of specific corporate entities, inequitable tax treatment and subsidization of some corporations, favoritism in rule making and rigged bidding processes by government and revolving doors between the private and public sectors for high end employment opportunities. Indeed, we would perhaps be wise to encourage abandonment of our corporate welfare oriented economy by voting out of office any pol that has or does support those aspects of our economy and, further, boycotting the corporate and large agricultural recipients of such taxpayer largesse. This would encourage the emergence of a wave of entrepreneurship unfettered by unfair competitive advantages created by government. Economic efficiency, job creation and new ideas would undoubtedly ensue.

"Free trade," is another buzz phrase that should elicit candidate rejection. Trade agreements bearing this moniker serve several real purposes, those of creating a protectionist environment for some US corporations, the institution of economic imperialism and providing a market venue for certain countries whose exports are the result of forced labor. To be truly "free," and meriting political support, thusly labeled trade agreements should provide for the free, cross-border flow of all goods, services and labor. It would tax imports to the United States at the value of any subsidy, regardless of form, as a sub-sidy tax, provided by the exporting country and would illegalize the importation of anything that benefits from forced labor. Goods from the People's Republic of China, for instance, would be barred for that reason alone.

A properly formulated free trade agreement would serve well to resolve the immigration crisis along our southern border. The migra-tion of illegals entering the United States from Mexico is driven by poverty and a dearth of viable economic opportunities for the people of Mexico and, by extension, parts of Central America. The simplest of solutions would entail allowing these people entry into the United States, after undergoing criminal background checks, and document-ing them to work in the country on a two tiered system. At one level, if they elect to avail themselves of the social services available in the United States, they would be taxed accordingly. Declination of this op-tion would result in lesser, or even no, taxation. Once documented, these people could move back and forth between the two countries at will. The ultimate goal being to see repatriation of incomes generated thereby back to Mexico, with the end purpose of allowing the development in Mexico of an increasing middle class. It seems likely, given the pride of her people and the richness of its culture, that such opportunity would see the return of many people to Mexico and the development of small, entrepreneurial enterprises. Such an agreement could well be accompanied by an undertaking to allow US participation in monitoring Mexico's ports of entry in order to screen out terrorists and potential third-party illegal migrants seeking entry into the United States. Conjunctively, there would be no duties imposed on any legal goods and services moving in either direction across the border. Equally important, is that all rights and protections, whether of ownership or otherwise, granted by the United States to persons migrating in this manner must be reciprocated by Mexico with respect to American citizens.

Free trade is also the portal through which nation states, by definition nationalistic, are open to embrace globalism. This form of globalism would not be one defined by hegemony or some other form of imperialism. Instead, as was to some extent the model for the Hanseatic League, a trade and defense pact among various Baltic city states, lasting from the late 12th century through the mid 15th century, there is no reason that nation states cannot develop free trade and mutual defense accords without interfering in each other's internal affairs. In fact, earlier incarnations of the European Union (EU) mimicked this model. An EU model fashioned along the lines of true, inter-nation free trade, as described on the preceding section, mutual security agreements and nothing more, would likely have avoided its present turmoil, caused by the creation of a centralized government, dominated by Germany and France, with the ultimate intent of creating a state comprised of all the member nations. Small wonder then, that there has been a backlash. Europe's masters have sought to create a strictly European identity, including creation of cultural standards, that seek to eradicate centuries of cohesion among people, many of whom, such as the Basques, are already subsets within of existent, member nation states. And, quite naturally, the standards sought by the EU are far more attuned to the norms found in its most powerful states. As with every historical effort towards hegemony, this is one step too far. The drive to create an overbearing, centralized political system, together with the imposition of uniform "standards," is precisely the action that incites reactionaryism and xenophobia among people who would otherwise not be so inclined. This is equally applicable to historic efforts in the US to impose a white, Anglo-Saxon, protestant state identity upon her population, rather than devising a less destructive means of governing as a state comprised of multiple nations. The key is to develop a common thread that binds constituents, without seeking to strip them of their cultural heritage. It simply does not work. Not regionally and certainly not globally.

A further issue of trade demanding our attention is one of empowering those states with whom we are at risk of conflict by providing them with unfettered access to our technologies and markets. The People's Republic of China (PRC) is foremost among these. As consumers, we have the power to boycott goods and services imported from those countries. On a personal note, I have chosen to avoid purchasing anything made in the PRC since 1984, when it became readily apparent that we were on a collision course with that country's regime. Avoiding such purchases will force one, in some instances, to spend more money for certain items. And, in other instances, it may prove impossible, where components made in the PRC, in automobiles, for example, are such an integral part of every like product that it becomes impossible to avoid them. Nonetheless, one can be largely successful.

There is a growing availability of clothes, electronic devices, appliances, dishes, furnishings, tools and cellphones that are not made in the PRC. A good percentage of every dollar we spend on wares manufactured in the PRC is apportioned to its government which, in turn, uses this money to suppress its population, presently with Google's help, and construct a military that is being utilized to bolster the PRC's imperialist ambitions. The same is true of the technology we sell the PRC and that which it steals. In addition, it has become evident that digital technology imported by us from the PRC is inundated with backdoor accesses that allow for the gathering of intelligence and carry the risk of deliberate infrastructure disruption. Absent our money, these ambitions could, to some extent, be held in abeyance. Our trade with the PRC is a Trojan horse that represents the greatest possible external threat we face as a nation. Trump's trade negotiations with the PRC altogether miss this point, as have similar negotiations and agreements instituted by past presidents, beginning with Richard Nixon. Aside from our power in the marketplace, this is an issue that must be politicized from the ground up, not only as to the PRC, but in generally in our relation with foreign states. It has become the norm for elected officials, most markedly in the Senate and the White House, to personally capitalize on the foreign relations they develop while holding office. This was assuredly the case with little Bush vis-a-vis Saudi Arabia, the Clintons as to Russia, Diane Feinstein relative to the PRC and appears to be in the offing with Donald Trump, given his relations with Saudi Arabia and quite possibly a number of other countries. Some form of legislation barring elected officials from deriving financial benefits from foreign companies and governments for a period of time after holding office should be enacted. Similarly, former bureaucrats, most assuredly in the intelligence arenas, should lose their access to classified information on leaving office We, as constituents, must demand that our pols take steps to limit foreign state influences in the development of our policies, foreign and domestic. And, our trade agreements must take into account the humanitarian records and military ambitions of the countries involved. The present culture of prioritizing short term greed over long term strategies, designed to assure our national security, must be reversed by holding pols accountable through the political processes we enjoy.

Our wars on drugs and terror also open doors to political accountability. The drug war is easily won. Any financial institution, such as Rabo Bank, Wells Fargo and the multitude of others that have been caught laundering the proceeds of illegal drug trafficking should not merely be fined a small percentage of the amounts laundered, as has been the case to date. Instead, if American, they should be shut down and, if foreign, their rights to do business, directly or indirectly, terminated. In both instances, their executives should be prosecuted to the full extent of the law. Any legal drug manufacturer or distributor found culpable in profiteering in the illicit trade of opiates should face termination of their FDA certifications. And again, their executives brought up on charges. Finally, foreign policy considerations, whether political or derived of the intelligence community's machinations to raise covert funding, must be eliminated from any determination of whether or not to vigorously pursue prosecution of drug traffickers, whether institutional or cartel affiliated. The reality is that if in the considerations of financial institutions, pharmaceuticals and foreign governments, the risks far outweigh the latent benefits of illegal activity, the latter will be curtailed. If not, banks and pharmaceuticals are replaceable and foreign governments may be leveraged by other means, such as trade limitations and other sanctions. The present thesis, that we alone are responsible for the drug trade because of our demand for illicit substances, though not entirely invalid, is largely an indication that we lack the political will to attack the core problems of supply and money laundering. This is likely because of the billions upon billions of dollars at stake. Any notion that some percentage of these amounts do not trickle into the hands of pols and policy makers is laughable. This said, any politician not willing to tackle the drug trade along these or similar lines is not fit to hold office.

The war on terror is more complex. However, under the guise of that conflict, our law enforcement and intelligence communities have successfully terminated every constitutionally protected privacy right of every American. They have done so directly and through their respective proxies, such as Google, AT&T and Amazon. Interestingly, as a side note, the NSA has suggested it abandon its blanket surveillance of Americans, but has not offered to terminate third party contracts for that purpose. These activities, largely condoned by Congress, present an existentialist threat to our democracy, not only through abasement of our rights, but though the chilling prospect that such surveillance of elected officials by bureaucrats will inevitably lead to the implementation of political policy by those bureaucrats through coercion and political manipulation. We have already witnessed two glimpses of this. In the first, the CIA was caught digitally spying on at least one US Senator, Diane Feinstein. The most recent case appears to be one where the FBI and NSA surveilled the Trump campaign and post election transition team in efforts to discredit the now sitting president. Regardless of one's sentiments regarding Trump, this should raise alarms with anyone with an interest in preserving our republic. At this juncture, we will likely never ascertain which of our elected officials have been compromised in their abilities to conduct their offices without being blackmailed as the result of third party possession of information adverse to their interests. From a constituent standpoint, every voter should demand of those running for office that they not only legislate existing blanket, warrantless surveillance out of existence, but that they criminalize any such surveillance, whether conducted by government agencies or third-party contractors. If they refuse, they should be denied the opportunity to regain or hold office.

In the process of developing a surveillance society, we have become not only fodder for tech companies such as Google, Amazon, AT&T and Facebook with respect to the sale of our personal data to government entities, but that information has become a commodity for sale on the open marketplace. While other governments, most certainly the European Union, have begin to tackle the privacy issues at stake, our Congress has remained silent, the finances of its members and contractual relationships of government so completely intertwined with techno totalitarian inclined corporate entities, that any form of regulation will ultimately be meaningless. Recourse is, of course available. The obvious, an iteration of the thread set out above, is to leverage pols with the threat of withheld votes, absent their implementation of meaningful curtailment of this aspect of the private sector. More powerful, would be to re-establish ourselves as voluntary consumers of the products and services offered by high tech, rather than the mere commodities we have become to these entities. Multiple potential examples abide. Every major car manufacturer has admitted to collecting data related to conversations within new vehicles, music listening choices, locations visited and the like, and then selling this information. A consumer boycott of just one brand, say General Motors, accompanied with the demand that the enabling technology not be included in new vehicles unless asked for as an option, would turn the tide on this issue. The same would apply to purveyors of "smart" home implements and appliances, telephones and other digitally driven devices. A unified boycott of any one of the most insidious offenders, Google, Amazon, Facebook or Twitter and their ilk, if held for a mere thirty days, would deeply resonate throughout the industry and invoke the prospect for change in how our data is accumulated and distributed.

Google is particularly nefarious in that it has burrowed its way into most school systems around the country, positioning itself to collect data on our children without parental knowledge, never mind consent. School districts provide Google as a search engine on school computers and students conduct research and write papers through the auspices of Google technology. Local governments further employ the digital technology offered by high tech firms to conduct their affairs, including tracking real estate and other tran actions undertaken by their constituents. Again, the public is largely unaware that these practices entitle the tech providers to collect the data thusly managed. The same is true of medical and dental providers, retailers and any other entities that employ digital, on-line technology to manage files. Our responses, on local levels, should be aimed at a requisite that any contractual undertakings between tech providers, such as Google, and local schools, government, retailers and medical providers, be tailored to protect our privacy interests and those of our children. Were enough momentum gained by leveraging locally accountable businesses, schools and bureaucracies, throughout the country, the adhesion contracts presently employed by Google and its cohorts in providing their services would be replaced with contracts that are actually negotiated with the interests of students, constituents and consumers in mind.

The aim is not necessarily to rid ourselves of techno-totalitarian corporations. They have, in terms of some of their services, become far too enmeshed with the conduct of our affairs, commercially and otherwise. Instead, the ultimate purpose of calling these entities to task is to re-empower consumers; to offer us the choice of opting into these data collection and surveillance schemes, rather than have us fulfill the roles of mere commodities.

On a final note, given that the services at issue have become necessities in order for us to function in our society, and that these are largely carved up into monopolistic areas of technology, our efforts to sway legislators should perhaps also focus on treating these entities as utilities and quasi governmental agencies, thus empowering the State to both regulate their conduct and prosecute their executives if our civil liberties are impinged upon.

The 1st Amendment to the United States Constitution is under assault. Ironically, media, social media, elected officials and academia are most culpable in this affront to one of our most cherished rights. So called "traditional" media, no longer content with reporting news and distinguishing this from editorial commentary, now thrives to shape public opinion by spewing emotional, opinion laden rhetoric, under the guise of news, to an extent the public is rapidly losing faith in its trustworthiness. From the cruel evisceration of the Ramsey family, on the death of their child, Jon Bonet, to the completely negative coverage of President Trump, objective reporting has been utterly discarded, even in the face of evidence that information disseminated is outright false. While this has been a mounting problem, it has never been more so than during the course of the Trump presidency, which has consistently endured more than 90 percent negative coverage, even when certain of its accomplishments have had generally positive effects. In addition, media has embarked on a course of censorship, stifling news, views and opinions that contradict a particular outlet's political stances. For media, this turn to polarizing, extremist partisanship and active advocacy is dangerous because it will open the door to its eventual treatment as something other than the independent purveyors of news. The lines between specific political blocs and individuals in media have become so blurred, that one can easily envision a future whereby outlets are subjected to campaign laws. Lawsuits for mischaracterization of people and events will also become more common, and it is only a matter of time before plaintiffs in such cases begin prevailing. This will most certainly become the reality if such cases overcome First Amendment legal challenges and are decided by jurors comprised of lay people who have increasingly lost faith in media as an institution. Finally, as has been somewhat tested by Trump, government will increasingly curtail media access to briefings and information. Be forewarned, this is not an anomalous issue birthed of Trump's election. It has become the new norm and will not weather the polarization of America that media is encouraging. From media's perspective, the solution lies in fostering a return to traditional journalism and ensuring that editorial content is expressly identified. Media must be again willing to fully disseminate information and views without judgment, leaving it to consumers to determine the import thereof. As a matter of its survival, it would behoove media to seek re-institution of the Fairness Doctrine—the requisite to present balanced points of view, particularly as to issues relevant to public opinion. From a consumer standpoint, until media makes these changes, we would be wise to check multiple sources of information and always, where possible, delve into primary sources, rather than trusting media to be accurate and provide context. Again, the power of boycott could be employed, if only against one media outlet, say Fox or CNN, for a relatively short period of time. A loss of viewership would, in turn, affect advertising revenues.

Social media managers, most of whom are large tech companies, Facebook, Google and the like, together with elected pols and academia, are increasingly advocating for censorship, under the banner of combating "hate" and "politically incorrect" speech. Such designated forms of speech, at this juncture, apart from the obvious, such as neo Nazi nonsense, includes discussions that question a number of new political paradigms, ranging from climate change to whether a person accused of sexual misconduct or rape is entitled to a defense to abortion and whether non-whites can be racist. This is frightening stuff because it presumes that someone is entitled to be the final arbiter of defining what is allowable speech. It is further troublesome in that censorship, of any kind, and certainly by the hands large techno-totalitarian companies, is representative of an effort to engineer a society into unquestionable acceptance of designed mores. Equally unsettling is that the suppression of any ideas, most assuredly dangerous ones, removes any prospects of open debate and drives these to fester, unchecked, in the minds of those who hold them, until they are acted upon, often with dire consequences. Moreover, proponents of censorship fail to recognize that shifting extremist political tides will not serve to abate the notion of censorship, rather these may well usher in an entirely new set of defining characteristics for disallowed speech. All said, the truth of the matter is that a democracy that is unable to withstand the open and free expression of ideas, regardless of how reprehensible or inane, is probably doomed anyway. Against this backdrop, any pol supporting the suppression of free speech, in any form, save those few exceptions carved out by the Supreme Court, or voting in favor of subsiding thusly inclined academic institutions, or any legislation with the same objective, should be denied our votes. It is their sworn task to preserve the integrity of the First Amendment, not subvert it. As consumers, we again are armed with the power of withholding the use and support of any entity, be it social media or a school, that would curtail freedom of expression.

Open, honest and, most importantly, civil discourse are paramount to our union's survival as a democracy. This notion becomes more pressing as we delve into a future fraught with the risks posed by artificial intelligence, latent alien encounters and the prospect of further enhancing the elite through genetic engineering. As individuals, even acting in concert, we have very little influence over these and other emerging technological issues, save through political processes. Hence, we must use these. Not to forestall change, but to demand it be reasoned, well thought out and undertaken with care for the long terms consequences for us and our progeny. Such advances should require the establishment of a broad societal consensus, rather than see development behind closed doors, whether public or private.

As a society we have much to do. In truth, we are a mess. We lament Donald Trump's lack of civility, yet fail to recognize he is not its cause, his conduct a mere product of an endemic societal problem. We seek to hold others accountable, but not ourselves. We have become snowflakes, bereft of any ability or inclination towards self-reliance. We have taken to hiding behind our digital devices, rather than dealing with real people and situations. We allow ourselves to be manipulated because we are too lazy to think for ourselves. We demand to be tended to, from cradle to grave, and have become fat and stupid. In short, we have morphed from being a society of hunters into a herd fit for little more than the role of prey. Clawing out of this state of affairs will be far more difficult than the effort it took to get here.

In the first instance, there is a desperate need to regain our self-respect, individually and as a society. As thoroughly posited above, instituting educational reforms to develop in us a penchant for critical thinking is perhaps the most important long term response to our present dilemmas. A return to the practice of holding ourselves accountable for our actions and becoming self-reliant, assuming responsibility for ourselves and our families, financially and otherwise, is called for. So too is an understanding that the array of so-called entitlements through which our pols entice us to support them have reached a point of unsustainability. In essence, government has no money, absent that which it takes from taxpayers to pay for these programs or borrows. Unfortunately, the donor pool is shrinking, while our national debt expands exponentially.

While we may curtail the excesses of government, by seeking an increased modicum of independence from our codependent relationship with the state, there is a concomitant requisite that we rein in our own excesses, as consumers, in an effort to reduce household debt and increase savings. Our society has been trained to incur debt. And we do so oblivious to the fact that our expenditures on technology, which are excessive, at best, are used to enslave us, while the material purchases we make are designed to become archaic, even as we pay for them, and lose at least a third of their value by the time we get them home or into our garages. We are encouraged to borrow, and keep borrowing, from college through the cemetery plots we buy in our twilight years. If we are late on a credit card payment, the interest rates soar to twenty and some annual percentages, in spite of the fact that the issuing banks pay next to nothing when they borrow the funds to re-lend us. We need to stop these patterns and redefine those things that are of importance to us.

We need to relieve the daily stress that we subject ourselves to over technology and materialism and, as the adage goes, take the time to "smell the roses." We will regain our self respect by holding ourselves accountable, becoming self reliant and shedding the role of commodities that has been assigned us. If we can accomplish these things, the way lies paved towards regaining our civility. And, if we can be civil, then we can develop the empathy towards others, that seems lost to us, and revisit the almost forgotten notions of mutual respect. Perhaps we may graduate from contemplating our navels to engaging with the real world we have abandoned. Might we then notice the plight of returning war vets and the families of those who will not, to the poverty stricken around the country and the war devastated millions around the world. Dip the light if we see a speed trap. Open the door for an elderly person. Treat customers as if we really do appreciate them. Offer a modicum of politeness to wait staff that serve us. Stop for a stranded motorist. Take our children into the woods. Have them experience the natural world. And, read. Read. Read. We might even temper our use of the phrase "fuck you," now so oft verbalized, signaled, or at least thought, at the forefront of so many of our interactions with strangers, those who annoy us, however mildly, or anyone who might ask something of us, however slight. If we choose to insist on an opportunity to shout that expression from some rooftop, then lets save it for the pols that treat us like idiots, the bankers that hold us hostage, the techno-totalitarian twerps that run amok with our freedoms and want to manipulate us, the welfare corporations that bleed us while their hands are held out on Capital Hill and in the salons of the White House and anyone that tells us the rain is falling when we can clearly see the sun is shining. After all, we'll be damned if we need any one of them.

There is more we do not need. As the next election cycle commences, and has been the case for decades, pols and pundits alike, from all strata of the political spectrum. remember the middle class. They woo and cajole us with hollow rhetoric and empty promises. Mostly, they bait us like mice, with the lure of free cheese. Government checks for everyone, government jobs for everyone, tax cuts (an old favorite), raises of the minimum wage, free healthcare for all, a choo-choo train to Europe, more jobs, more free trade, walls to the north of us, walls to the south and here we are, stuck in the middle with them. If pressed, not a single one of them, Republican, Democrat, Neo-Liberal,

Progressive, Conservative or Neo-Conservative, could accurately define the middle class. None should be elected absent a willingness to develop an accurate understanding of the middle class and the nature of the problems we all face. We do not need another round of pols paying lip service to the middle class to then turn around and further legislate us into oblivion.

The first step is to require of candidates the acknowledgment that the middle class is not a a specific, cohesive segment of the electorate that can be defined as "blue collar," workers, farmers or some other occupationally characterized group. The middle class must instead be recognized politically as a segment of our society that is bound solely by a specific range of incomes. The insertion of occupational groupings accomplish no more than divisiveness—pitting one sphere of the middle class against others on the basis of false premises. In truth, and as they are affected by legislation, most certainly insofar as taxation is concerned, there is absolutely no distinction made between tradespeople, unionized employees, professionals, teachers, small business owners and others, so long as their incomes fall within the parameters that define them economically. Thusly are plumbers, teachers, longshoremen and automobile factory employees treated as are most lawyers, accountants and small business owners. The ultimate problem facing the middle class, and which pols and pundits alike refuse to address, is that as an economic bloc, it has not been redefined for decades. The result is that the lower tiers of the middle class are sliding into poverty, while the upper tiers are still taxed as if wealthy. Concomitantly, the truly wealthy are taxed insufficiently. This is not to suggest an income tax scheme that penalizes wealth. Rather, those provisions of the tax code that serve only those of the highest means in eliminating latent tax liabilities should be completely eliminated. Moreover, a compelling argument arises that the complexities of the

tax code inequitably favor the super wealthy; its translation only possible at the hands of lawyers and accountants—services unaffordable
for the average American.

This leads to the second demand that must be made of candidates:
a commitment to overhaul the tax code to take present and future realities into account. For example, anyone earning less a year than the
amount it costs to provide for essential needs should be taxed at a marginal rate, if at all. Those income earners are not in the middle class.
They are flat out poor. Based upon the realities faced in 2018, then,
a household of four, living on earnings less than the average cost of
living for that year, over $60,000 per year, should be re-categorized as
poverty stricken and, frankly, should face no income taxes. And even
this seems inadequate because it provides no allowance for other than
basic necessities. There are, in this scenario, no margins for expenditures beyond these. Once redefined, the taxation of income should be
adjusted annually on the basis of the real rate of inflation, the annual
decline in purchasing power of the dollar, not the fictitious inflation
rates presently relied upon by government. Less pressing, though not
less significant, is a need to adjust the upper tiers of middle class
income taxes. As to the entirety, taxation must take into account annual reductions in disposable incomes, where incomes are a constant.

We often hear the lament from pols that allowing for deductions,
often coined as "benefits," means that many people in the middle
classes pay insufficient taxes. These are not benefits. Income earners
are entitled to every penny earned. We submit to taxation as part of our
social contract, to provide funding to the governments that are meant
to serve us, trusting them to expend these monies on our behalves
for the common good. A careful reading of the government's annual
budget, coupled with the unfathomable public debt it has amassed,
offer the unquestionable conclusion that government has abused

this bargain beyond all reason. It has breached the public trust that is necessary to its continuance. Furthermore, as the largest bloc of consumers in the country, the middle class, and indeed, those facing poverty, pay a litany of taxes most are unaware of on every item purchased, including food, clothing, fuel, utilities, housing, automobiles and the like. At present, Trump and the Democrats are contemplating a $2 trillion dollar, so called, infrastructure agreement, that would be funded by increasing fuel and other "hidden" taxes and increasing the national debt. This is almost egregious as the Progressive notion of spending exponentially more tax payer money to guarantee government incomes to everyone, convert every structure in America in to "greenness" and ban the sources of our energy without an alternative, viable plan on hand. Perhaps, then, it is time to press our pols to fully explain their ambitions, expressly inform us of the consequences to us, of their largesse with our money, justify their budget abuses and demand that they publish the true extent of existent taxes on the things we buy—the taxes on production, wholesaling, retailing, all transportation, labor at all stages and so on—all of which are passed on to the consumer. They will undoubtedly balk. Nonetheless, the time has come to demand an accounting, as well as accountability.

So too, must we be suspicious of promises to lower income taxes, increase minimum wages and give everyone a government check. The problem with lowering income taxes has been, as it is with Trump's execution of this notion, that it is a shell game. The ultimate question to ask in this regard is, if taxes are lowered, thereby reducing government income, how can the government be spending more money. The answer is threefold. One, if there is a perception that consumers have more disposable income, large corporations and banks kick up inflation by raising prices and interest rates, particularly on credit card debt. As a by-product, this does marginally increase government tax revenues from these entities. The next, is that what government gives overtly, it takes back covertly, through increases in other taxes. And finally, if corporate tax breaks result in job creations, as has been the case in terms of Trump's tax scheme, the income tax revenue stream increases as the result of taxes on wages of the previously unemployed. The net effect of all of this, is that retained earnings simply do not rise. Indeed, if one factors artificially created inflation into the mix, they fall.

Minimum wage increases, while seemingly noble, are of similar effect and more. The increased cost of labor, mostly impacting the service industry and small businesses, would result in consumer price inflation, not only to cover the direct costs thereof, but also the additional taxes on labor that would have to be paid by employers. For small businesses, such as independent bookstores and cafes, an arbitrary requisite to raise wages could well result in mass closures if these are too high. Such enterprises often operate on slim margins and are already facing the challenges posed by large chains, which enjoy greater, volume based purchasing power for their supplies, thereby reducing their overhead. Measured against the inflationary effects and increased taxes on mandated raises, one wonders whether the ensuant net disposable would actually rise or, if so, whether this would be significant. It seems more logical to lower the tax bracket for minimum wage earners, to allow greater retention of present earnings. Moreover, the present tax structure requires employers to pay taxes on tips that are recorded through credit card transactions. In the service industry, this has resulted in employers refusing to allow such tips. Tips, which are an expression of customer satisfaction, should simply not be taxed. One suspects that service industry employees would reap more benefits in this manner, than through the introduction of an increased minimum wage.

As for the burgeoning promises among aspiring pols to constituents of free, monthly government checks, as with all free cheese programs, something for nothing is all well and fine, until there is nothing left to give because there is no one left to take it from. Accompanying suggestions include forcing the most wealthy Americans to foot the bill, which would be effective only as long as it took them to relocate to more favorable tax environs. Or, as suggested by some Progressives, we can always print more money. The nexus between this solution and hyperinflation, along the lines experienced by post WWI Germany, Argentina and, at present, Venezuela, is completely lost on the morons offering this idea; their knowledge of history and economics an abysmal reflection of an educational system desperate for repair. In this context, think wheelbarrows of money to buy one loaf of bread. To every political proponent of these promises, we must imagine all of the long term consequences of their proposals to buy our votes and and challenge each and every one of them on the efficacy of their rhetoric.

On another score, some Americans have gained a perceived benefit through the Affordable Healthcare Act, or Obamacare. None more so than medical providers, pharmaceuticals and the insurance industry. Some 30 million people, mostly of the middle class, who neither qualify for subsidies or work for employers that subsidize or pay insurance premiums on their behalves, are unable to afford insurance premiums which, for a family of four can run to over $2,000 per month, with a $10,000 deductible. Others, who pay nothing, abuse the system to an extent that it is overloaded and driving up premiums for those who pay something. The system is rife with fraud. One suspects that providers are bilking the system by over treating and over prescribing medications. Certainly, there are myriads of people that utilize creative tax accounting to qualify for federal subsidies of otherwise unaffordable insurance premiums. The system will prove unsustainable over the long term. It is inequitable and unaffordable. There are but two solutions, both of which should be put to sitting and prospective lawmakers.

The most genuine and palatable is to abandon the present system and generally get rid of health insurance, save by government devise in form of a social safety net for those who are truly in need. Medical providers and pharmaceuticals thusly cut adrift would find themselves in a competitive marketplace. Most assuredly, the costs of medical services would be reduced dramatically, as would prices for medicines. Easily envisioned is the likelihood of doctors making house calls for competitive and affordable rates. Conversely, if we lack the daring to experiment with market economics in this not insignificant economic sector, then the creation of a captive marketplace for medical insurance demands the implementation of caps and controls over provider charges, pharmaceutical pricing and insurance premiums, which must then be predicated, not on spreading costs or risk assessments, but scaled upon people's individual capacity to pay. In either event, some concise policies are called for of our political establishment. Perhaps this should be done conjunctively to a call for members of Congress to fully subject themselves to all of the same laws they expect us to abide by. With luck, we would see the passage of fewer laws, in general, or even the repeal of redundant or archaic legislation.

And, perhaps this should represent the ultimate demand of our political representatives in the House and Senate: to spend less time holding self-aggrandizing hearings and enacting new laws, to concentrate instead on fixing the laws and systems we already have in place. To act substantively instead of continuing on this ever increasingly failed course of attempting to manage our frustrations through the implementation of placebos that only make matters worse. These have simply failed to address the actual problems our nation and her people face.

The approaches to resolving issues that we should be concerned about, that are set out within these preceding pages, certainly do not present an exhaustive list of possibilities. Nor are they intended to be exclusive of competing ideas. Their sole purpose is to promote discussion and debate and, foremost, to have us develop a sense of the problems we face and the urgency in seeking resolutions to these. ᵔᵔ

CONCLUSION

I started writing this book during the early summer of 2018 and find myself now, at the end of October, 2019, penning its conclusion. Unfortunately, the events of the intervening fifteen months have served to not only confirm its content, but further suggest that America's institutionalized dysfunctions are becoming evermore indelible.

Some pundits have finally tumbled to the possibility that President Trump's tweets are not quite as random as once thought, and are calling for investigations into the possibility that these might be linked to insider trading. Congress, holding true to the precepts of Placebocracy, has embarked on a course seeking to impeach Trump, thereby further fueling the political polarization already gripping the country, while forestalling any efforts to address the national debt, the real economic crisis' facing their constituents or any other matters of substance.

The obvious remedy for any alleged misconduct on the part of the president, of course, would be to let the voters decide. As for Trump's greatest offense, perhaps it is that he has become an open and abject caricature of the heretofore, though less overt, norms of American political behavior. And in this, contrary to my earlier assertion, he does gain relevance. Trump's legacy, then, to expose, through his ineptness at conducting himself with any modicum of finesse or discretion, the machinations of America's political system. So too has the venerability of our federal law enforcement and intelligence bureaucracies called into question. Moreover, President Trump, oft skewered for his bumbling throughout the realm of foreign affairs has, inadvertently, of course, laid bare the secret of America's long standing foreign policies; we have none, save to the extent that these can be manipulated for the economic gains of our politicians, their friends and relations. In every other sense, I am not swayed from maintaining that Trump remains irrelevant; a manifestation of the underlying problems that ail this country.

Other events have also given rise to the credence of the assertions made in this book. Russia and the People's Republic of China have gained exponentially increasing influence throughout Latin America, the Middle East and Africa. America's high tech industries have expanded the scope of their interests. On such instance is Facebook's present endeavor to create and manage a new digital currency.

And finally, most troubling, are the indicia that Americans are trending ever more sharply towards polarization. According to poll results released on October 23, 2019, by Georgetown University's Georgetown Institute of Politics and Public Service, a majority of Americans, of all persuasions, races, locations and party affiliations, believe that the country's political, racial and class divisions are worsening. Additionally, on a scale of 0-100, with 100 representing the United States being on "the edge of civil war," the response of average voters came to a mean score of 67.23.

All said, if there is a message in this book it is that if we fail to come to terms with our malaise and craft the cures we need, there is every reason to fear our slide into a chasm of increasing intolerance and deteriorating individual liberty interests that will harbinger the onset of a very different kind of republic. Given the fleeting historical instances of democracy, the demise of our democracy will undoubtedly ring the death knell of this distinctly western concept. The emergence of unaligned historical philosophies from other parts of the world, converged with the unfettered technological wherewithall that abounds, certainly will forbid its reemergence.

Hope, if we are to circumvent such a future, lies in our willingness to confront the detrimental circumstances we face, and our resolve in fashioning a renaissance of the principles underlying a free society. Were we to embark on such a course, there is every reason to believe that we may yet steer clear of the shoals encountered by our predecessors, the Greeks and the Romans among them, in navigating this grand experiment, democracy. ∽

Acknowledgments

W riting a book, particularly a work of nonfiction, is a lonely ordeal. Acquisition of the underlying knowledge, experiences and ideas is not. These are a process of osmosis, dependent, in great part, upon the people one encounters; the absorption, analysis and assimilation, where apropos, of their offerings is a latent aspect of critical thinking. Thus, teachers, friends, acquaintances and colleagues have played a significant role in the development of the ideas I have presented in this work.

Chief among these are Arthur E. Ross, JD, Lt. Col. Gayle Gardner (USAF) and Lt. General Edgar Doleman (US Army), all now deceased and who gave immeasurably to their country, both in times of conflict and peace; Rory Soares Toomey, Lt. Col. Paul Stankiewicz (USAF, ret.), Hawaii Pacific University Professors Greg Gaydos, Ph.D and Paul Vonnahme, Ph.D, champions of critical thought, and then Dean Gordon Jones, Ph.D, for affording me the opportunity to fast track my degree in International Studies by waiving course load restrictions and encouraging one on one directed studies opportunities; and, Professors Amy Bushaw, JD and Bernie Vail, JD, of Lewis and Clark Law School and an international law seminar leader from Mercy Corps, whose name I have simply forgotten—my deepest apologies, all of whom held open minds and presented challenges during debates related to international law.

Thanks as well to Chris and Sabrina Lee, Ian Kellet and Gigi Aelbers, Dave Templeton, and Steve Jennings. And further thanks and appreciation to our new friends in Sonoita, all of whom have made us feel welcome in our safe haven in the Sonoran Desert. There are countless others, people I know and those I have spoken to in passing, whose contributions have been invaluable, and my appreciation goes to all of these as well.

Once written, a book needs the attention of others. Hence, I am indebted to Hanna Hartwig, whose frustration at editing a book she only partly agreed with often tempted her to toss the entire manuscript in the air—this urge tempered only by her fears that she would never be able to reassemble it in any meaningful order—due to a technical problem, since resolved, the pagination was entirely in Roman numerals; Jennifer McMillion for an exemplary editing job; Kathy Springmeyer, Director of Publications at Sweetgrass Books, for her patience and understanding in answering all of my questions and getting the book through the printing process and to the marketplace; Brian Feinblum and the folks at Finn Partners for their more than able public relations work; and, James Bennett of James Bennett design, not only for his work in crafting a terrific book jacket, but for taking the time, not part of his contract, to discuss the myriad of subjects covered in this book and found elsewhere.

The creation of a book requires multiple virtues, among them, patience, kindness, tolerance, computer literacy and faith in the process. I have none of these. Instead, these were readily supplied by my family. My thanks and love, then, to Hanna Hartwig, Guthrie Devine, Curran Devine, Thor Hartwig and, most assuredly, to my wife, partner and best friend, Angela Hartwig, without whom there would have been no more than a crumpled mass of papers to show for my efforts. Without you, this book would not have been written. ༀ

Recommended Reading
(A Partial List) / Bibliography

Baker, Russ. *Family of Secrets: The Bush Dynasty, America's Secret Government, and the Hidden History of the Last Fifty Years*. New York: Bloomsbury Press, 2009.

Barrat, James. *Our Final Invention: Artificial Intelligence and the End of the Human Era.* New York: Thomas Dunne Books, St. Martin's Press, 2013.

Bastiat, Frédéric. *"The Law," "The State," and Other Political Writings, 1843-1850 (The Collected Works of Frederic Bastiat).* Edited by Jacques de Guenin. Translated by Jane Willems and Michel Willems. Foreword by Pascal Salin. Indianapolis: Liberty Fund, Inc., 2012.

Bismarck, Otto von. *Bismarck: The Man and the Statesman, Vols. I and II.* New York: Cosimo Classics, 2007.

Booker, Christopher. *The Global Warming Disaster.* London: Continuum International Publishing Group, 2009.

Bradbury, Ray. *Fahrenheit 451.* Introduction by Neil Gaiman. Trade Paperback Edition. New York: Simon & Schuster, 2018.

Bullough, Oliver. *Moneyland: The Inside Story of the Crooks and Kleptocrats Who Rule the World.* New York: St. Martin's Press, 2009.

Cervantes, Miguel de. *Don Quixote.* Translation by Edith Grossman. Introduction by Harold Bloom. New York: HarperCollins Publishers, 2003.

Chappell, Vere, ed. *The Cambridge Companion to Locke.* Cambridge: Cambridge University Press, 1994.

Clausewitz, Carl von. *On War,* Indexed Edition. Edited and Translated by Michael Howard and Peter Paret. Introductory Essays by Peter Paret, Michael Howard, and Bernard Brodie. Commentary by Bernard Brodie. Princeton: Princeton University Press, 1984.

Colvin, Marie. *On The Front Line.* New York: Harper Press/HarperCollins Publishers, 2012.

Ebenstein, Lanny, ed. *The Indispensable Milton Friedman: Essays on Politics and Economics.* Washington, D.C.: Regnery Publishing, Inc., 2012.

Foer, Franklin. *World without Mind: The Existential Threat of Big Tech.* New York: Penguin Press, 2017.

Foner, Eric. *Tom Paine and Revolutionary America.* New York: Oxford University Press, 1976.

Ford, Martin. *Rise of the Robots: Technology and the Threat of a Jobless Future.* New York: Basic Books, 2015.

Gibbon, Edward. *The History of the Decline and Fall of the Roman Empire:* Abridged. Edited by David Womersley. London: Penguin Group, 2000.

Goltz, Thomas. *Chechnya Diary: A War Correspondent's Story of Surviving the War in Chechnya.* New York: Thomas Dunne Books, 2003.

Greenwald, Glenn. *No Place to Hide: Edward Snowden, the NSA, and the U.S. Surveillance State.* New York: Picador/Henry Holt and Company, 2015.

Harari, Yuval Noah. *Sapiens: A Brief History of Humankind.* London: Harvill Secker, 2014.

Harreld, Donald J., ed. *A Companion to the Hanseatic League.* Boston: Koninklijke Brill NV, 2015.

Harvey, Phil and Conyers, Lisa. *The Human Cost of Welfare: How the System Hurts the People It's Supposed to Help.* Foreword by Jonathan Rauch. Santa Barbara: ABC-CLIO, LLC, 2016.

Hayek, F.A. *The Constitution of Liberty.* Edited by Bruce Caldwell. Chicago: The University of Chicago Press, 2011.

Hobbes, Thomas. *Leviathon:* Revised Student Edition (Cambridge Texts in the History of Political Thought). Edited by Richard Tuck. Cambridge: Cambridge University Press, 1996.

Humboldt, Wilhelm von. *The Sphere and Duties of Government.* Mansfield Centre: Martino Publishing, 2014.

Huxley, Aldous. *Brave New World.* New York: HarperCollins Publishers, 1932.

Irving, Washington. *George Washington: A Biography.* Edited by Charles Neider. New York: Da Capo Press, 1994.

Isikoff, Michael and Corn, David. *Hubris: The Inside Story of Spin, Scandal, and the Selling of the Iraq War.* New York: Crown Publishing Group, 2006.

Johnston, David Cay. *Free Lunch: How the Wealthiest Americans Enrich Themselves at Government Expense and Stick You with the Bill.* New York: Portfolio/Penguin Group, 2007.

Keynes, John Maynard. *The Essential Keynes.* Edited with a Foreword by Robert Skidelsky. New York: Penguin Books, 2015.

Kneller, George F. *Introduction to the Philosophy of Education.* New York: Macmillan, 1971.

Koehler, Benedikt. *Early Islam and the Birth of Capitalism.* London: Lexington Books, 2014.

Kozol, Jonathan. *Savage Inequalities: Children in America's Schools.* New York: Broadway Paperbacks/Crown Publishers, Inc., 1991.

Lao-Tzu. *Tao Te Ching.* Indianapolis: Hackett Publishing Company, Inc., 1993.

Lord, Carnes. *Aristotle's Politics,* Second Edition. Translation, Introduction, Notes, and Glossary by Carnes Lord. Chicago: The University of Chicago Press, 2013.

Lukianoff, Greg and Haidt, Jonathan. *The Coddling of the American Mind: How Good Intentions and Bad Ideas Are Setting Up a Generation for Failure.* New York: Penguin Press, 2018.

Machiavelli, Niccolò. *The Prince:* Second Edition. Chicago: The University of Chicago Press, 2010.

MacRitchie, Finlay. *The Need for Critical Thinking and the Scientific Method.* New York: CRC Press/Taylor and Francis Group, 2018.

Malone, Dumas. *Jefferson and His Time:* 6 Volumes. Charlottesville: University of Virginia Press, 1948-81.

Martin, Thomas R. *Ancient Greece: From Prehistoric to Hellenistic Times.* New Haven: Yale University Press, 1996.

Marx, Karl. *Capital: A Critique of Political Economy (Vol. I: The Process of Capitalist Production).* Samuel Moore and Edward Aveling, trans. Frederick Engels, ed. Revised and amplified according to the 4th German ed. by Ernest Untermann. Chicago: Charles H. Kerr and Co., 1909.

McCullough, David. *John Adams.* New York: Simon & Schuster, 2001.

McCullough, David. *1776.* New York: Simon & Schuster, 2005.

McLean, Bethany and Nocera, Joe. *All the Devils Are Here: A Hidden History of the Financial Crisis.* New York: Penguin Group, 2010.

McNamee, Roger. *Zucked: Waking Up to the Facebook Catastrophe.* New York: Penguin Press, 2019.

Mises, Ludwig von. *Liberalism: The Classical Tradition.* Preface by Bettina Bien Greaves. Foreword by Louis M. Spadaro. Preface to English Language Edition by Ludwig von Mises. Auburn: Mises Institute, 2018.

Moghaddam, Fathali M. *Threat to Democracy: The Appeal of Authoritarianism in an Age of Uncertainty.* Washington, D.C.: American Psychological Association, 2019.

Neitzsche, Friedrich. *Beyond Good and Evil.* Revised Edition. New York: Penguin Classics, 2003.

Orwell, George. *1984.* New York: Signet Classics, 1950.

Paul, Ron. *50 Essential Issues That Affect Our Freedom.* New York: Grand Central Publishing, 2012.

Perkins, John. *Confessions of an Economic Hit Man.* New York: Plume, Penguin Group, 2006.

Pillsbury, Michael. *Hundred Year Marathon: China's Secret Strategy to Replace America as the Global Superpower.* New York: St. Martin's Press, 2015.

Rousseau, Jean Jacques. *The Social Contract and Discourses.* Translated with an Introduction by G. D. H. Cole. London and Toronto: J. M. Dent and Sons, 1923.

Schweizer, Peter. *Secret Empires: How the American Political Class Hides Corruption and Enriches Family and Friends.* New York: HarperCollins Publishers, 2018.

Schweizer, Peter. *Extortion: How Politicians Extract Your Money, Buy Votes, and Line Their Own Pockets.* New York: Houghton Mifflin Harcourt Publishing Company, 2013.

Shakespeare, William. *The Complete Works of William Shakespeare.* Introduction by Michael A. Cramer, PhD. San Diego: Canterbury Classics/ Baker & Taylor Publishing Group, 2014.

Smith, Adam. *The Wealth of Nations.* Introduction by Robert Reich. Edited by Edwin Cannan. New York: Modern Library, 2000.

Sun Tzu. *The Art of War.* Introduction and Notes by Dallas Galvin. Translation by Lionel Giles. New York: Barnes and Noble Books, 2003.

Tegmark, Max. *Life 3.0: Being Human in the Age of Artificial Intelligence.* New York: Alfred A. Knopf, 2017.

Thoreau, Henry David. *Civil Disobedience.* Bedford: Applewood Books, 1849 (Original publication year).

U.S. Constitution: Declaration of Independence, Bill of Rights, & Amendments. Wounded Warrior Publications, 2014. ❧

ABOUT THE AUTHOR

Mark J. Hartwig has a law degree (Lewis and Clark/1995) and a BA in International Relations (Hawaii Pacific University/1989), both earned as an adult. He acquired his GED in 1987. Hartwig practiced law through 2018, representing domestic and international clients, and has undertaken a variety of small real estate development projects. Hartwig held a master mariner's license and worked in the commercial maritime industry prior to attending law school. He has also worked as an oil spill response coordinator, investigator, forest fire fighter, ranch hand and in construction and has volunteered as a search and rescue crew member. Mark J. Hartwig divides his time between Livingston, Montana, Sonoita, Arizona and various locales in Mexico. ∞